Unbound

Unbound

Transgender Men and the
Remaking of Identity

Arlene Stein

PANTHEON BOOKS
New York

All rights reserved. Published in the United States by Pantheon Books,
a division of Penguin Random House LLC, New York, and distributed
in Canada by Random House of Canada, a division of Penguin Random
House Canada Limited, Toronto.

Pantheon Books and colophon are registered trademarks of
Penguin Random House LLC.

Library of Congress Cataloging-in-Publication Data
Name: Stein, Arlene, author.
Title: Unbound : transgender men and the remaking of identity /
    Arlene Stein.
Description: New York : Pantheon Books, 2018.
    Includes bibliographical references and index.
Identifiers: LCCN 2017046998. ISBN 9781524747459
    (hardcover : alk. paper). ISBN 9781101972502 (ebook).
Subjects: LCSH: Transgender people—Identity. Female-to-male
    transsexuals. Gender nonconformity.
Classification: LCC HQ77.9 .S74 2018. DDC 306.76/8—dc23.
    LC record available at lccn.loc.gov/2017046998

www.pantheonbooks.com

Jacket photographs by Wynne Neilly
Jacket design by Jenny Carrow
Book design by Cassandra Pappas

Printed in the United States of America
First Edition

9   8   7   6   5   4   3   2   1

For Ben, Lucas, Nadia, and Parker,
and in memory of Bishop

The cultural face of transgender has shifted from a middle-aged man in a dress trying to be a real woman to hot young female-to-male folks who are defining their male gender as they go along.

KATE BORNSTEIN, 2011

If the modern "problem of identity" was how to construct an identity and keep it solid and stable, the postmodern "problem of identity" is primarily how to avoid fixation and keep the options open.

ZYGMUNT BAUMAN, 1998

All the young dudes carry the news.

DAVID BOWIE, 1972

Contents

Unbound

Introduction

en sits in the waiting room of a plastic surgery clinic at a strip mall in South Florida. It is eight in the morning, and he barely slept the night before. Drawn by word of mouth and the power of the Internet, he has driven 1,500 miles to see a surgeon who will masculinize his chest. Ever since the surgery was scheduled six months ago, he's been counting the days until he can look in the mirror and see a flat chest. Now it's nearly here, and his excitement is palpable. A high-energy twenty-nine-year-old who spent ten years as a photographer in the extreme water sports industry and as a political organizer before deciding to return to college, Ben calls himself "a super-late bloomer."

Bess, as he was then known, short for Elizabeth, befriended a couple of transgender men while working on a campaign for marriage equality in Maine, where he lived. He felt a sudden frisson of recognition, which led him to wonder whether his lifelong feelings of estrangement from his body and his femaleness meant he was transgender. "So I think I'm having a gender crisis," he told his good friend Allison. "Dude, OMG, that makes perfect sense," she replied. "You've always hated your boobs."

During the next year, Ben underwent a process of soul-searching that led him to undergo a gender transition. He asked his friends and family to call him Ben while he went on testosterone, investigated the possibility of surgically modifying his body, and posted the following on a crowdfunding website:

Hello there! My name is Ben Shepherd. I'm a trans man (meaning I was born female-bodied but identify as a man) and I am working to raise the funds necessary for me to have reconstructive chest surgery. This is important to me because it is the one area of my life that causes severe anxiety and often bouts of deep depression. I am currently a large chested person which means it's very difficult for myself and others to view me as the man I feel I am. I can rarely fit into men's dress shirts, even when wearing a binder. In order to wear dress shirts and other clothing that I feel more comfortable in I need to wear a binder which flattens my chest, but it also restricts my breathing and can be incredibly painful to wear. Even as painful as it is to wear, it is often more comfortable than going without it. Often, I'll wear my binder for over twelve hours out of necessity, the recommended max time for wearing a binder is at most 6–8 hours.

The good news, there is a remedy for this dysphoria. There are surgeons all across the country that perform the kind of chest reconstruction that I am looking to have done. I am saving to go to Dr. G. in South Florida as he is one of the best in the country at one of the most affordable price points. Dr. G. has an estimated cost of roughly $7,000 with all the hospital and surgical fees included. Once the surgery is complete I have to return to Dr. G.'s office a week later to have him remove the dressings and drains. During that week post op I will be heavily medicated and won't be able to lift my arms so I will need someone to care for me during this time. This means

that in addition to the $7,000 for the surgery I need to raise
$1,500 to cover the travel for myself and one other person for
one week from Maine to Dr. G.'s office in South Florida. Once
my top surgery is complete I will feel like my whole self and
my transition will feel complete. That means the total I need
to raise is $8,500. I'll start by making the $8,500 the goal on
this site and as I personally add money to my savings account
for top surgery I'll decrease the total goal to accurately reflect
what's left to raise.

My goal is to raise these funds by April 5, 2015, so that I can
have my surgery on May 11, 2015 (Dr. G. requires full payment
4 weeks before the surgery date).

Every little bit helps, thank you so much for your kindness
and generosity,

Ben

Over the course of ten months, eighty-six people—friends,
family members, fellow activists, former schoolmates, and even a
few people Ben had never met—contributed an average of $35 to
help finance the surgery, and Ben put the remaining $4,000 on
his credit card. Bob and Gail, his parents, agreed to drive from
Maine to Florida with Ben, and used points they had accumulated
through a Disney Vacation Club timeshare to book a hotel for the
weeklong stay. Gail is a fifty-five-year-old middle school principal;
Bob is a meteorologist with the National Weather Service.

On the eve of the drive south, Ben recorded a video of himself in a baseball cap, with a wispy mustache, and announced their
departure with a big grin: "On the road!!! Headed south for the big
surgery!!! Thank you all SOOO much for all your love and support. I can't thank you all enough. I really am one of the luckiest
humans on the planet!!" He and his parents narrated the Bye-Bye

Tatas Trip, as Ben affectionately dubbed it, for friends and family. Ben and his dad tag-teamed, driving through the night without stopping to complete the twenty-three-hour journey. Along the way, there are posts from the Waffle House in Stephens City, Virginia, and a Dunkin' Donuts in Hardeeville, South Carolina. When they arrived in Vero Beach, Florida, Ben mugged for the camera, offering a big thumbs-up.

The drive down from Maine was taxing, but the emotional journey was far more arduous, as it is for most who undergo gender transitions. When I meet them in the doctor's office, Bob and Gail are sleep deprived. While Gail has come to terms with her child's choice, Bob seems more ambivalent about the whole thing. As Gail recalls, Ben told his parents he wanted to "look the way he feels." He's never been girly, and often went to great, often unsuccessful lengths to perform femininity. Five years earlier "she told us she was dating someone named Joe," Bob tells me "She didn't tell us what sex Joe was, but I figured it out. Joe was Jo. His high school friends said, 'Finally!' They could sense it."[1]

Gail didn't quite get it, but thought, "Okay, no big deal. We've had gay relatives. My parents have gay nieces and nephews—it's not a major thing. We have plenty of friends that are gays. I told Ben: Enjoy your life. Glad you're happy." Coming out as gay "was no big deal," Bob agreed. "It's a lifestyle choice. But this is huge." When Ben declared he was transgender, "that was a lot harder to comprehend," Gail told me. "Gender is more fundamental. It affects everyone around us. It has been an education, that's for sure."

In November 2013 Bess started going by Ben, and a few months later he announced that he would begin to inject testosterone. Bob and Gail saw it as yet another sign of their child's impetuousness. Ben was passionate about whatever he was into at the time, whether it was surfing, photography, or political campaign work. Would this be just another fleeting interest? They battled over his decision to transition. "No, you don't need to go and start it in thirty days," Bob told him. "You've got your whole life ahead of you. Just stop everything and seriously think about what you're doing here." He thought it was just another of his child's frequent whims. "I was thinking, 'Oh God, here we go again,'" said Bob. "Bess was always a person who embraced different ideas, did totally different things. It was familiar in lots of ways, but also way extreme. I mean, this is out there." He said to Ben: "This is serious. You're talking about sex change and everything else. You need to seriously calm down and think about this." Bob and Gail were concerned that although their child had loads of friends, there was a kind of darkness at his core. He regularly slept until noon and had trouble keeping his room, and his life, in order. He seemed aimless, as though he was always searching for something but didn't know quite what it was.

When Ben came out on Facebook, a few of Bob and Gail's friends found out. Ben apologized for not preparing them first. "It was difficult telling people," says Bob, "but we managed to do it. It's the larger circles that are really hard. I've lost friends over this," he tells me. "People talk, say she's a freak. They don't say it to his face, but I hear secondhand."

As Bob inadvertently switches Ben's pronouns midsentence, he ponders how to tell the people he works with about Ben. Meteorologists are not, as a rule, the most socially enlightened folks, Bob says. A few weeks before Ben's top surgery, an aspiring weather forecaster who happened to be a transgender woman visited Bob's workplace to shadow staffers, and people said some really rude things about her afterward. Bob isn't typically one to make waves, but the experience hit home, making him uncomfortable. "I kept my mouth shut. These are supposedly educated people," he said, expressing his displeasure.

Gail has fared better at her workplace. She sent an e-mail to staff at her small school north of Portland: "I am taking next week off to take my transgender son to have surgery," she announced, though she concealed that information from the school district. While she wanted those she works with to know, she preferred that those "outside the building" be kept in the dark. She sent the e-mail on Friday at the end of the day, when everyone had already left for the weekend, Gail told me. "And they were fine with that. They didn't really say anything."

Coming to terms with Ben's decision to transition wasn't easy for his parents. They listened to their child's pleading and watched a bunch of educational videos together. And they did a lot of talking and crying. Eventually, Bob and Gail came around, along with nearly all of their friends and family. But they still sometimes slip and call Ben by his former name, Bess. They worry, too, about what to do with all of the framed photographs that adorn the walls of their home in the outskirts of Portland, of the child who had been assigned female at birth.

"I will miss Bess," says Gail, "but I have to support Ben in his new life."

Until recently, people who were assigned female at birth but who grew up feeling that their bodies did not adequately reflect their gendered selves had little choice but to live with their smooth skin and protruding chests. They did not have access to medical technologies with which to alter their bodies, or the cultural affirmation for doing so. Today, however, thousands of Americans, and travelers to this country, are finding their way to surgical offices like the one Ben visited in South Florida, asserting their right to craft masculine bodies. I wanted to better understand what brings them there and how, collectively, transmasculine people are challenging popular understandings of gender.

––––––

In current parlance, I am "cisgender," which means I do not identify as transgender. (The prefix "trans" is Latin for "on the other side," and "cis" in Latin means "on the same side.") That is, I experience my assigned sex and gender as congruent, at least to the degree that it has not become a major challenge in my life. When I was a kid growing up, I remember thinking that it would be cool to be a boy. Since I am now middle-aged, I can remember a time when girls were compelled to wear dresses to school, abortion was illegal, and team sports were something that boys, and not girls, could participate in. Boys got to play with electric trains, which I lusted after but my parents refused to give me—they were "boys' toys." Men didn't have to go through the pain of childbirth, and they fronted the best rock-and-roll bands. Why wouldn't one dream of being a man?

For me, identifying as a feminist and a lesbian enables me to express my femaleness in ways that seem true enough. But over the years I learned that there are others who feel that they were assigned a gender at birth that seems inauthentic and wrong—so much so that many seek out body modifications to bring their bodies into alignment with their selves. A number of years ago, I noticed a young man working in my campus bookstore who seemed vaguely familiar to me. I stared at him for several moments out of the corner of my eye, racking my brain to figure out how I knew him, while trying my best not to attract his attention. Suddenly, I realized that he had once been a student of mine, and that I knew him as female, but now he had peach fuzz on his face, a deep voice, and was all but indistinguishable from the other young men who worked alongside him selling camera equipment. But I was so ill-equipped to figure out how to respond that I pretended not to recognize him, and he did the same.

And then in February 2013, Kate, an artist friend of mine, accompanied a close friend of hers who was undergoing top surgery—chest masculinization—in Florida. "You would not believe the numbers of people there," she told me, describing the long line of individuals, mainly in their twenties, who were waiting in the surgeon's office. South Florida was once known for a Spring Break scene that drew legions of college students eager for hot fun in the sun—a scene immortalized by the 1960 comedy *Where the Boys Are*. Today it is also where the "bois"—young, female-assigned people, who identify as masculine, some of whom undergo gender transitions—go to masculinize their chests.

The scene at the doctor's office surprised Kate. "There were people from everywhere you could imagine, and many of them were very young," she told me in her soft Texas drawl. "Some even brought their parents!" In a nearby gated community, a guesthouse had been established to accommodate the steady flow of patients who needed a place to stay while they recovered from surgery. My curiosity was piqued when, a few months later, I happened to hear about another friend whose nephew also underwent "top surgery" in South Florida, and then I saw a mention of the same doctor in a magazine. Why were so many people flocking to Florida to modify their chests? What were they seeking? What did they find? More broadly, what does it mean that more and more female-assigned individuals are choosing to masculinize their bodies today? What might it tell us about how our notions of gender are changing more generally?

Sociologists, or at least my breed of sociologist, try to get as close to a subject as they possibly can, immersing themselves in it. That's how I met Ben. I came across the crowdfunding website he had set up and I e-mailed him. He quickly agreed to let me tag along during his surgery week. So I booked my room and plane ticket and traveled down to Florida from my home in New Jersey to meet him—and, as it turned out, his parents too.

At Dr. Garramone's office, I also met the four others who were scheduled for surgery the same day as Ben. Three of them were good enough to agree to speak with me: Lucas DeMonte, a twenty-three-year-old health outreach worker from Gainesville, Florida; Parker Price, a twenty-four-year-old software sales manager from Austin, Texas; and Nadia Khoury, a twenty-eight-year-old employment counselor from St. Louis, Missouri. Lucas, Parker, and Nadia, along with Ben, are the subjects of this book. They have allowed me to interview them and their friends and family, and over the next year, they permitted me to follow them at regular intervals, spoke with me over the phone and Skype, and even welcomed me into their homes on occasion. As I got to know them over the course of the next year, I came to better understand the lives and choices of a younger generation of gender dissidents. You can learn a lot about people by listening to their stories.

––––––

The "dominant scientific tale" about sex differences, according to researcher Rebecca Jordan-Young, goes something like this: "Because of early exposure to different sex hormones, males and females have different brains," which in turn determines many of the differences we observe between men and women, such as men's greater propensity to be fiercely competitive, and women's more nurturing, relational character.[2] My generation of feminists pushed back against those views. Influenced by Simone de Beauvoir's claim that "one is not born, but rather becomes, a woman," we spent a lot of time refuting the view that biology is destiny. Society, not nature, creates many of the differences we observe between men and women, we declared.

If women are less competitive than men, it had less to do with how their brains are wired or their bodies are made and more to do with the fact that they are excluded from team sports growing up, channeled into nurturing occupations like nursing and teaching, and they are surrounded by advertising images that perpetuate certain ideals of womanhood. We feminists therefore set out to create opportunities for women to make different choices if they wished. "Who knows what women can be when they are finally free to become themselves?" asked Betty Friedan in 1963.[3] We encouraged women to embrace their more masculine sides, and men to become gentler and kinder.

Thanks to our efforts, twenty-first-century Americans are less likely to believe you need to be a boy in order to climb trees, play with model trains, compete in high school sports, or even be president. But despite the best hopes of many members of my generation, gender differences haven't faded away. Gender continues to be what sociologists call a "master status." It is a primary way we divide up society, and through which we distribute social benefits, material resources, and even love. It continues to influence what kinds of toys we give kids, the kinds of jobs we seek, and the expectations others have of us on the job, in our families, and in public—though perhaps less than in the past. For some people, gender differences can be a source of pleasure, too, as many of those who have spent a lot of time hanging out on baseball diamonds, or planning bridal showers, can tell you.

But even as we have made gender roles more expansive, encouraging our daughters to be strong and athletic and our sons to be expressive and nurturing, it seems that we shoehorned many people into categories that never really fit them. We assumed that the world comprises two groups: men and women. And we took for granted the belief that if you have a certain set of genitals and secondary sex characteristics, you have a particular gender identity too.

Doctors make a determination of a baby's sex, a *sex assignment,* based on what's visible—genitals. Yet so much about sexed bodies, such as chromosomes, hormones, and reproductive organs, is invisible. Using an infant's genitals as a way of determining sex is a pretty crude instrument, it turns out. Some babies have genitals that are ambiguous, and not clearly male or female—they are referred to as *intersex.* But even those bodies whose genitals are pretty unambiguous, and seem clearly female or male, may be far more complex than they seem on the surface. Our bodies do not divide as neatly into male and female as many people commonly believe.[4] Nor do our minds. As Magnus Hirschfeld, the pioneering early twentieth-century sexologist, argued, "the human is not a man *or* woman, but rather man *and* woman."[5]

But societies are organized quite differently, and they tend to divide the population into two different groups. Once assigned to one gender or the other, individuals are expected to abide by the rules. Be a man. Be a woman. Don't step out of line. A host of social institutions, such as marriage, public restrooms, sex-segregated sports teams, and prisons, reinforce this distinction, as do manufacturers of toys and clothing. Individuals who flout the rules, refusing to conform to one gender, risk being kicked out of their families, and they are likely to encounter job insecurity and higher rates of bullying and violence.

While most cultures divide men and women into two groups, as far back as we know there have been those who establish a specific social role for members of a "third" sex or gender. In the early

1700s, Western observers noted that many Native American tribes recognized gender-variant individuals and at times accorded such individuals, now called "two-spirit," honored roles. Different cultures have varied names to describe members of an intermediate sex: in India, there are hijras; in the Philippines, bâkla; in Thailand, kathoey; and in Brazil, travesti. In contemporary Japan, onnabes present themselves as men to heterosexually identified women who frequent Tokyo clubs. There are many, many other local examples of such gender variation.[6]

At different moments, and at different times, individuals have devised different strategies for grappling with their *gender variance*—the fact that they do not identify with the gender to which they have been "assigned." At times, such individuals seek to cross over and migrate to the "other" gender. In twentieth-century Europe and the United States, some female-assigned individuals used prosthetic devices, hormones, and sartorial style in order to live the gender of their choice, "passing" as men in all, or nearly all, aspects of their lives. Jazz musician Billy Tipton, who was born in 1914, recorded two albums and toured the West, eventually settling in Spokane, Washington, where he married and parented three sons. Two of his wives, according to biographer Diane Middlebrook, never realized that he had been assigned female at birth. Tipton claimed he had been in a serious car accident resulting in damaged genitals and broken ribs, and that it was necessary to bind his damaged chest and use a prosthetic device to engage in sexual intercourse.[7]

During the course of Tipton's life, medical sex reassignment became available to select individuals who wished to bring their bodies into closer alignment with their gendered selves. In 1930, Lili Elbe, born Einar Magnus Andreas Wegener, transitioned from male to female in Denmark (immortalized in the 2015 film *The*

Danish Girl), with the help of Magnus Hirschfeld and his associ-
ates at Berlin's Institute for Sexual Science, who performed the first
sex change surgeries until the Nazis destroyed the clinic in 1933.
The following decade, Michael Dillon became the first female-
assigned person to medically transition. Born in 1915 to an aristo-
cratic English family, after cross-dressing and identifying as male
at an early age, Dillon spoke with doctors about his belief that he
was a "man trapped in a woman's body," pleading with them to
take on his case. He argued that transsexual men are members of
an "intermediate" sex. Convincing doctors that he could gain relief
by transitioning, Dillon underwent a double mastectomy in 1942
and two years later, at age twenty-nine, changed his birth certificate to reflect his new male name. He enlisted a world-renowned
specialist in reconstructive plastic surgery to construct a phallus,
and eventually he became a medical doctor himself.[8]

In the 1950s, medical and psychological experts drew a distinction between *sex* and *gender* that helped establish a framework
for medical sex reassignments. Based on his work with intersex
individuals, John Money, a professor of pediatrics and psychology
at Johns Hopkins University, described sex, one's designation as
male or female, as rooted in biology and the body; gender, on the
other hand, is influenced by a host of social expectations about
masculinity and femininity, which encompasses roles and identities, he argued. The author of thousands of academic articles and at
least a dozen books (including *Venuses Penuses* and *The Breathless
Orgasm*), Money was a pathbreaking, controversial researcher who
helped shape popular understandings of sex and gender during the
twentieth century.

By opening up the possibility that biology does not wholly
determine gender, he and others came to acknowledge that some
individuals cannot or do not wish to conform to their gender

assignment; their gender identity does not "match" their sexed body. They believed that the mind was less malleable than the body, and that bodies could—and should—be refashioned to align with an individual's gender identity. Harry Benjamin, an endocrinologist and sexologist, devised a spectrum of gender variance that placed transvestites (who liked to cross-dress) on one end, and transsexuals (whom he believed required sex reassignment, including hormonal therapy and surgery, to live successfully) on the other. He helped to establish the first gender clinic at Johns Hopkins University in 1966, which offered select individuals the possibility of modifying their bodies.

During its first two years of operation, three thousand people applied and only about thirty people were accepted for surgery—nearly all had been assigned male at birth and were transitioning to become female. To be eligible for surgeries, individuals were required to attest to the fact that their transgender identity was early and enduring—that they had "known" that they were transsexual since they were young children, and that they felt they were "trapped in the wrong body." But since no insurance plans covered body modifications, individuals had to be able to finance them themselves—as well as take time off from work, have a means of traveling to a clinic, and be able to leave their families, and their jobs, to do so. They were also required to live as "normal" heterosexuals after they transitioned, hiding their past from others.[9]

And thus a new medical apparatus for reorganizing the relationship between sex and gender for certain select individuals, who were willing to subject themselves to stringent rules for "changing sex," was established.

Today's transgender individuals owe their existence partly to this legacy: they are coming of age at a time when aligning one's body and gender identity is possible—because we have the medical technology to do so, and the cultural frameworks that can support the decision to transition. Younger transgender-identified individuals share the belief that transgender is a medical issue, but they also push up against that view. Armed with newer understandings of gender variance, they are challenging the assumption that the world is divided into two, and only two, sexes.

In the 1960s, when it first became possible to undergo a "sex change" in the United States, the phenomenon of transsexuality was associated mainly with individuals who were assigned male at birth, then known as MTF (male-to-female). Harry Benjamin had declared that there was one female-to-male for every eight male-to-female trans people.[10] Jamison Green, a transgender male activist who grew up in California in the 1960s and '70s, recalled, "I had no idea that others like me existed."[11] Even as late as the 1980s, when she was training to be a sex therapist and couples counselor, Margaret Nichols, who founded a counseling center in New Jersey that specializes in LGBT issues, was informed that female-to-male transgender people "barely existed."

If transgender men have been vastly outnumbered by their male-to-female counterparts, it is partly due to the fact that they have, until recently, been excluded from access to medical technologies. The case of Pauli Murray, an activist and lawyer who played pivotal roles in the civil rights and women's movements, is instructive in this regard. Murray grew up in segregated North Carolina. She became the first African American to earn a Juris Doctor degree from Yale, participated in the formation of the National Organization for Women, and was a friend and associate of Eleanor Roosevelt. Murray's legal work was foundational in challenging racial segregation in the landmark *Brown v. Board of*

Education case. Throughout her life, Murray struggled with her gender identity and believed she was male. She was unsuccessful in persuading doctors to prescribe testosterone; the doctors told her she was delusional.

"Anything you can do to help me will be gratefully appreciated," she wrote to one doctor, "because my life is somewhat unbearable in its present phase, and though a person of ability, this aspect continually blocks my efforts to do the things of which I am capable."[12] (I use female pronouns to refer to her because those are the pronouns she herself used.) Would Murray identify as transgender today? It is likely, though we cannot know for certain. What we do know is that during her lifetime (she died in 1985) transgender men were mostly invisible, lacking a subculture or social movement of their own. Openly identifying as transgender, or undergoing hormone replacement therapy, let alone top surgery, was practically impossible for people like Murray. Murray resisted gender norms, dressing in pants and slicking her short hair back with pomade. While some of her peers found refuge in the butch-femme lesbian world of the 1950s and '60s, she longed for confirmation that she wasn't really a woman at all—and the possibility that medical technologies could be harnessed so that her body could be brought into alignment with her deep sense of maleness. But these procedures were nearly impossible for female-assigned individuals, particularly racial minorities, to access.

Today, over half a century later, those who were assigned female at birth constitute the fastest-growing population of transgender-identified people, and they are increasingly visible and vocal. There is growing parity among females and males who call themselves transgender, at least according to mental health professionals who work with the trans population.[13] Whereas once gender clinics limited access to body modifications to only a select few individuals, today a small but growing coterie of surgeons, endocrinologists, therapists, and others dedicate themselves to serving gender-variant patients. Body modifications are much more readily available to female-assigned individuals—to people who can afford the time and money, or who have access to insurance that covers such procedures.

In May 2014, Medicare lifted its ban on covering gender surgeries, and federal employees' insurance plans quickly followed suit. The Affordable Care Act prohibited discrimination against transgender surgery and led the way for a number of states to begin covering transition-related care. Other legal reforms followed. The Obama administration enacted rules that allowed individuals to change the gender listed on passports, and in May 2016, rules that directed all U.S. school districts to allow transgender students to use bathrooms consistent with their gender identity, rather than the gender they were assigned at birth—policies that led some to dub Obama the "Trans-Rights President."[14]

In addition to enjoying greater access to medical technology, and more legal rights, today's gender nonconformists also enjoy greater access than prior generations to language and concepts that make the idea of modifying their bodies more imaginable, including such terms as "trans," "non-binary," and even "transmasculine," and the introduction of questions such as "What are your pronouns?" They are busily fashioning new vocabularies to describe gender diversity, they are communicating with one another using innovative technologies, and they are modifying their bodies in varied ways. "Cultures emerge slowly, but sometimes a culture or subculture turns on a dime," Kate Bornstein, the trans activist and writer, tells me. "That's what's happened with transgender subculture—big changes in just one generation."

That sense of collective exuberance has since been tempered by the election of a president who ran on a platform that promised to turn the clock back, and several years after Bornstein uttered those words, the successes of the transgender movement now seem somewhat more precarious. Yet in some respects, the cat is already out of the bag. Younger people growing up today are less likely to believe that the world is divided into male and female, or that one's anatomy is fixed for all time. They are more likely to see gender as a matter of choice, rather than something that is given at birth. If my cohort pioneered the idea of sexual liberation, and the belief that one could live in accordance with one's desires, and come out as gay or lesbian, or even bisexual, for today's younger generation the issue of gender seems even more central.

This book focuses on the stories of four young adults who, though assigned female at birth, found themselves together in one surgeon's office where they had come to masculinize their chests, at a time when more and more individuals are questioning taken-for-granted understandings about gender. It was written for general readers who may have limited acquaintance with the transgender world and who wish to learn more about it, as well as for those who are more intimately familiar with transgender culture. *Unbound* is a group portrait of those who choose to remake their bodies and lives using the tools they have at their disposal. Ben, Lucas, Parker, and Nadia graciously offered their full cooperation and indeed encouraged me to write about them over the course of more than a year. While researching this book, I also spoke with more than fifty others—family members, friends, co-workers, medical and psychological experts, and transgender activists. What I learned is that even as they are shaped by prevailing conceptions of masculinity and femininity, a younger generation of transgender men are prying open many of our assumptions about what it means to be men and women.

———

A note on names and pronouns. Transgender people wish to be identified by names and pronouns of their choosing. I follow that convention in this book, honoring their self-definitions. If I have permission to do so, at times I use individuals' assigned (pre-transition) names for illustrative purposes or when quoting friends or family members. I use pronouns of choice retroactively, referring to trans men as male even before their transition, in order to convey a sense of continuity over time, if that is how they see themselves prior to their transition. A few individuals are referred to as "they," reflecting their non-binary gender preference, or the fact that I do not know their pronoun preferences. Finally, some people's names, and the names of the towns or cities where they live, have been changed to protect their privacy.

ONE

Pre-Op

[He] resents [his] female form, especially the bulging breasts, and frequently binds them with adhesive tape until a plastic surgeon can be found who would reduce the breasts to masculine proportions.
—Harry Benjamin, *The Transsexual Phenomenon,* 1966

Broward County, Florida, west of Fort Lauderdale, is the land of strip malls and subdivisions. Bordered by the Atlantic Ocean to the east and the Everglades to the west, it is low, flat, and wet. Beginning in the 1920s, developers began to clear out the swamps that dominated this part of the country, building sprawling housing developments comprising identical detached houses. The developments were named Serene Lakes, Sunny Estates, and Rolling Meadows, immortalizing the natural features that were bulldozed to make way for them. At an unassuming strip of low concrete buildings perched behind a Publix supermarket, a sign announces PLASTIC AND RECONSTRUCTIVE SURGERY. In Florida, the third largest cosmetic surgery market in the United States, after New York and Los Angeles, it barely registers. "If there were an official state hobby," humorist Dave Barry once quipped about Florida, "it would be plastic surgery."

Inside, the large, comfortable reception room is painted a stylish gray and lined with contemporary oil paintings and modern, well-appointed furniture. A wall behind the receptionists' station is lined with diplomas, including one from Nova Southeastern University College of Osteopathic Medicine in Fort Lauderdale. On this day in May, about a dozen people, primarily young masculine-appearing patients in their early twenties, and their caregivers, await Dr. Charles Garramone, an unassuming forty-something man of medium build dressed in a white coat, with his name embroidered on the front.

Dr. G., as he is called, periodically enters the reception area, glances at the day's patient files without looking up, and then disappears into a back room. It is a Monday, and five patients are here for their pre-op appointments, in preparation for surgery tomorrow. Ben is one of them. He is with his parents, Gail and Bob. After the long drive down from their home in Maine, they're all looking a bit shell-shocked.

Ben and I had spoken on the phone, but this is the first time we're meeting in person. I sit with the family as Ben completes a long, detailed informed consent form for FTM Top Surgery, or "bilateral female-to-male chest masculinization."

"I realize this must be stressful for you both," I tell Gail and Bob, trying to defuse some of the tension in the air, including my own. I am gate-crashing a private affair.

Breasts are central, visible signifiers of femininity in our culture, and it's little wonder that those who are estranged from their femaleness would seek to have them removed. Writing in Europe in the early 1930s, the psychoanalyst Melanie Klein declared that female breasts, rather than the penis, as Sigmund Freud contended, are the central marker of difference between men and women. Plus, "bottom surgery"—the construction of a phallus—is extremely costly and surgically risky, and the method is far from perfected, so most transgender men retain their female genitals (a popular transmale magazine is called *Original Plumbing*).

In order to qualify for top surgery at this office, patients must present a letter from a mental health professional diagnosing them as having gender "dysphoria"—the medical term for distress caused by gender nonconformity—and attesting to their mental stability and capacity to make a fully informed decision. They must certify that they are not overly depressed or anxious or so troubled as to be placed at harm through the surgery. While some trans people object to these requirements on the grounds that they are fully capable of making the decision to modify their bodies without jumping through such hoops—after all, breast augmentation candidates aren't required to pass through gatekeepers—the Standards of Care (SOC) for "best practices" are established by the World Professional Association for Transgender Health (WPATH). The WPATH, formerly the Harry Benjamin International Gender Dysphoria Association, which is composed of mental and physical healthcare providers, formed in the late 1970s to guide policy on transgender medical practices.

Ben had health insurance since he had decided to go back to school at the University of Southern Maine, but his plan considers top surgery "elective." The growing belief that top surgery is reconstructive and therefore medically necessary has convinced more and more health insurance companies to reimburse for it. (One primer for those interested in the surgery cautions: "Try using the words 'I am seeking treatment for gender dysphoria.' Don't just say, 'I want to know if you will cover a double mastectomy.'")[1] But since Ben's insurance was unwilling to cover top surgery, and because Dr. Garramone does not accept insurance, Ben paid for the surgery out of pocket, in four installments of $3000, $2000, $500, and $1,800. On the day of the pre-op appointment, he handed the receptionist the final check.

Ben is slated for a "double incision" with "free nipple grafts," the method that is best suited for those with larger breasts or sagging skin. He has double D breasts. The tissue will be removed, along with the nipples, which will be trimmed and then grafted onto his new chest. Like others who are here, Ben is well versed in the lingo of chest masculinization. The other primary method used is called the "keyhole," in which breast tissue is removed through an incision in the lower part of the nipple. It results in less scarring and tends to preserve sensation in the nipples, but it can be performed only on smaller breasts, so it's unsuitable for Ben. Plus, the keyhole method is not particularly effective in controlling the nipple position: once the breast tissue is removed, the nipple and areola sometimes assume a lower place on the chest, and excess breast skin below the nipple can cause "contour irregularities" of the lower chest. In other words, you can't just take out the breast tissue and let the skin hang down if you're large breasted. You must reshape the chest to give it a "normal" masculine look.

Dr. Garramone steers most patients toward the double incision method, in which long horizontal incisions are made on the lower part of the chest, because it promises the "most aesthetically pleasing 'biological male' outcome," he says. Some patients undergo additional surgery for contouring, or liposuctioning areas around the abdomen, hips, and posterior, which costs thousands of dollars extra, and which Dr. Garramone calls "mansculpting." Ben opts out of these procedures. He admits that he's overweight, but he believes that he "can get rid of that extra flab by exercising."

Ben and Gail are ushered into a consult room to discuss tomorrow's procedure, and other patients arrive with their caregivers. In the waiting room on that Monday, I met a firefighter from suburban Sacramento, a nurse from Boise, and a retired schoolteacher from rural Tennessee, all of whom were accompanying children and grandchildren who had undergone surgery the previous week. On Wednesday, the scene is pretty much the same. Tuesdays and Thursdays are surgery days, and the office is closed Fridays. Patients show up, write their checks, prep for surgery, and follow the plan of care during their recovery week. It is all highly choreographed.

In addition to meeting Ben and his parents, I'm here to make contact with the others who are undergoing surgery the same day as Ben, who are having their pre-op appointments too. I hope to get them to participate in my project. I want to get to know some younger people who are undergoing body modifications, and hear their stories. My goal is to interview them while they're in Florida, and then regularly over the course of the next year, to try to better understand what motivated them to masculinize their chests, how they understand themselves in relation to gender, and what it means to them to be transmasculine. I began this project with a lot of curiosity, but with little expertise. Even though I had taught sexuality and gender studies for years, and had published books on gay and lesbian identities and on Christian conservative opposition to homosexuality, among other topics, I knew little about the transgender world. I found myself stumbling over terminology, and even at times inadvertently using improper pronouns. But I was eager to learn. One of the first things I learned, from Ben and his family, is that being transgender is never simply an individual matter. The second thing I learned, from talking with the others having surgery the same day as Ben, is that there is no one way of being transgender.

———

"Growing up, Bess had all those posters of guys in her bedroom," Bob tells me quietly as we sit together in the surgeon's waiting room, "but then she came out as lesbian. Now she's saying she is really a male. I can usually be a pretty good judge of people, but that caught me way off," he said in a lowered voice. "The first time I heard about it, it was like, that can't be. That doesn't even make sense. I don't know if something suddenly changed in her, or whether it was always there."

Scanning Ben's history, and the crushes Ben had on guys, Bob wonders: Was it all a lie? "I don't know if something changed during that period of all that swirling through colleges or getting involved with campaigns. Maybe that opened her eyes. I don't know. But it was a shocker to me at the time. Something turned. I still believe that something changed somewhere." Bob believed his daughter was never "that way." Ben began identifying as transgender when he got involved with the marriage equality campaign in Maine, in early 2012, and started associating with transgender people. Something changed then, according to Bob, who is wearing shorts and a Hawaiian print short-sleeved shirt. "It's because you're doing all of these campaigns that involve gender that you're around it so much you're not seeing clearly and you're getting sucked into it," he told Ben. "You were never that way. Is it because of that?" In Bob's view, Ben was highly impressionable and was led astray. Bob and Ben were arguing, in effect, over Ben's claim that he was "really" transgender. It's a common experience, according to trans people. Since the experience of claiming a transgender identity is so internal, so subjective, and transgender experiences are still relatively invisible in our culture, even those closest to trans people often just don't "get it."

As much as we say we want to allow our kids to be "who they are," parents expect their children to be extensions of themselves and to share their values, more or less. But what if the child is different from his or her parents in ways that they don't understand or are threatened by? "Children of color are in general born to parents of color," and "most people who speak Greek raise their children to speak Greek, too, even if they inflect it differently or speak another language much of the time," writes Andrew Solomon in *Far from the Tree*.[2] Ethnicity, skin pigmentation, language, and religion—what Solomon calls "vertical" identities—are typically passed down from parents to children. But some identities, such as being gay, or transgender, or even being deaf, are with few exceptions not passed from one generation to the next. Parents must come to terms with children that seem very different from them. Difficulties are often compounded by the fact that our society stigmatizes some of these differences.

For the past twenty-plus years, the Shepherd family consisted of a mother, father, a son, Chris, and a daughter, Bess (whom I will refer to as Ben). For Bob and Gail, there was a nice symmetry to it. Even though Ben was never a conventional girl, to his parents, he was still their daughter. Today, as Ben remodels his chest, he's also recasting his family structure. As we sit together in Dr. G.'s waiting room, Bob grapples with how to bring a son into a family that once consisted of a son and a daughter. "We've got pictures of her—I mean him—everywhere in our house," he says. "There are pictures of her as a kid, as a teenager, as a young woman, of the whole family together. What do we do with those pictures? Get rid of them? That's what we struggle with. How do you address that?" Having heard of at least one intrepid mother who decided to send out a birth announcement for her new son who transitioned when he was in his twenties, I offer Bob the following encouragement: "It sounds like you need some new pictures to go with the old ones." He looks at me quizzically and offers a hesitant nod. Ben and Gail return to the waiting room after meeting with the doctor, and the nurse instructs Ben on how to prepare for the next morning's surgery: eat a healthy and balanced dinner, refrain from eating or drinking after midnight, get as much sleep as possible—and shave his chest and armpits.

Afterward, Bob, Gail, and Ben invite me to join them for lunch at an Outback Steakhouse across the street, to debrief about the coming days. The doctor was "efficient and businesslike," Gail tells Bob. Dr. Garramone didn't ask why Ben is seeking the procedure, what brought him to his office, or why he wants to undergo a gender transition. "It was all nuts and bolts: what to expect during the surgery," she says. As we speak, David Bowie wafts out of the speakers, as if on cue.

Turn and face the strange.
Don't tell them to grow up and out of it. . . .
Changes are taking the pace I'm going through.

Gail asked the doctor about scarring, and he told her to hold off and "wait until the bandages are removed." He would discuss it at next week's appointment. Ben is a large person with imposing breasts, which poses a bit of a surgical challenge, Dr. G. told them. "The incision is going to come up to my armpit," Ben says matter-of-factly, "and way down there," pointing to below his chest. "So he's gonna cut your whole chest off?" Bob asks. "Yeah." Ben proceeds to describe in elaborate detail the plan for his new nipples. "The nipples will be reduced in size and will be positioned to follow the contour of my muscle." Ben will have a scar, the doctor says, extending from underneath the existing breast fold to the outside of the chest. The nipple and areola will be removed, resized, and grafted onto the chest—the lower outer portion of the pectoralis major muscle—in order to give it, in the doctor's words, a "convincing" male appearance.

After surgery, Ben will take it easy for a few days, but the bandages will stay on for a full week. No activity, no raising his arms, no driving. And no swimming until he heals. "There's lots of bacteria swimming around in the sea," the doctor tells him. This will be a challenge for Ben, a kinetically high-energy person who seems to have trouble sitting still for long periods, and whose passion is water sports—especially surfing and wakeboarding. "I've got to stay out of the water for the WHOLE SUMMER?" But it is, he reassures himself, for a good cause. He is excited about the surgery. It has taken him a very long time to get here—"thirty years," he says.

Bob, though, is still not completely comfortable with the idea. His kid has always been pretty impulsive, always "coming into the house and declaring that she's got a new idea," says Bob. "First she wanted to be an action sports photographer, and then she didn't. First she was gay, and now she's not." This time, Bob wanted to put his foot down. "Seriously think this one through," he urged Ben in the months before the surgery. "You can't change your mind. There's no turning back."[3] The irreversibility of the procedure scared Bob. He asked his child: "You sure you want to go through with it? You're going to have a tough life ahead of you if you're not sure and you want to change back or something."

As they prepare for surgery, Bob continues to try to dissuade Ben from going through with it. As Ben sits beside us, Bob tells me: "Yesterday I said to her—I mean him—any second thoughts?"

"That was super invalidating," Ben says. He told his father: "No second thoughts."

When a family member comes out as gay or trans as an adult,

other family members can at times feel deceived or dumbfounded. "What did we do wrong? How could we not know that this person was inside our child?" Gail found herself asking. She blames herself for not seeing the signs. Bob is afraid that Ben is making a decision he may later regret.

Throughout our conversation, Bob refers to Ben as "she," and then, stumbling, corrects himself and seems embarrassed by his gaffe: "It's going to take a while to get used to this—maybe over time, even years, it'll get easier." Gail refers to Ben as "he" more consistently. "It's been an education, for sure," she says. "I didn't know anyone who did this kind of thing. No one."

Later on the day of the pre-op appointment, the Shepherds plan to drive to the Everglades to look at alligators. "It's the last day I'll be able to do anything like that for a while," laments Ben. Afterward they'll travel north to their hotel and prepare for the days ahead. They need to buy baby wipes, because Ben won't be able to shower for a few days. "We need to get something for the itching after surgery," says Mom. "Oh, and I need to shave my chest and armpits tonight to prepare," says Ben. "And I didn't bring a razor, so I have to buy one," he tells his parents.

"I brought one. You can use mine," says Bob.

———

Parker, Lucas, and Nadia are three other patients who are also having surgery the same day as Ben. After we met in Dr. G's waiting room, I arranged to speak with Parker at the Fort Lauderdale apartment where he and his girlfriend, Darby, were spending the week. When I asked the twenty-four-year-old what brought him to Florida, and how he had found the surgeon, he told me that he had spent quite a long time looking up top surgery at bulletin boards on the site Reddit, which aggregates news online. He spotted a picture of the buff twenty-eight-year-old Aydian Dowling, a weight-training enthusiast and activist from Eugene, Oregon, who was a semifinalist in *Men's Health* magazine's 2015 "Ultimate Guy" contest, and who has emerged as a national transmale spokesperson: inspirational speaker, boy next door, sex symbol.

Dowling's well-defined abs and pecs compare favorably with those of any cisgender man. He has a pierced lip, a partially shaved head with a modified Mohawk, and a YouTube channel with more than thirty-five thousand subscribers where he posts videos about his life as a transgender educator/spokesperson. The videos show him working out, strolling around town in his undershirt and ripped body, meeting fans on college campuses, describing consumer purchases ("I bought this new green shirt at Target," he says in one. "Isn't it great?"), and addressing such topics as "Dating for Transmen"—all shot in reality-television style.

In a video posted on his YouTube channel, Dowling speaks of his life before transitioning, and how awkward and unattractive he felt as a self-conscious young butch—and he shows photos to prove it, marking the contrast to his current life as an entrepreneur, activist, and happily married man. He describes therapist Jennilee, whom he met online, as his "lovely wife." In the videos, which he shoots and edits himself, Dowling comes off as a knowledgeable, likeable educator for the transmale cause, confident and yet emotionally vulnerable, a hunky guy who spends lots of time lifting weights but who doesn't come off as too full of himself. He is an aspirational figure, to some at least.

Parker took one look at Dowling's sculpted chest, and after learning that he had gone to Dr. G., Parker decided: "Well, that's where I'm going," he says, in a deep, slow drawl. He worked out before he got here, so "that way I'll come out having pecs and stuff." Even though he has small breasts, he's been binding them. His girlfriend, Darby, a long-legged twenty-four-year-old with straight brown hair, is there to help care for him after surgery. They've been together ten months.

When they met, in May 2015, Darby was grappling with trying to understand what dating a trans man meant for her budding lesbian identity. Did it mean she is bisexual? The truth is, she says, "I just really like people." Darby thinks of herself as transitioning with Parker, in a way, she says. "It was just kind of like a whirlwind. It all just kind of happened." She says she's been opened to "a whole new world," and that "she's just going with the flow and trying to figure it all out."

A national sales executive at an Austin-based start-up, Parker works hard, until eight most nights, "cold-calling Hawaii and everyone else," he says, selling a software package for realtors. Younger colleagues view him with admiration, he says, though few know him as trans. He came out to one of his male co-workers who said: "Whoa, dude, I wouldn't even know. That takes so much balls." The company is a home and a family. "They let me be Parker. And Parker's a big personality," Parker says. He's grateful. "In my life, in the past a lot of people have told me no."

Dr. Garramone told Parker that he's got "lots of skin but not a lot of tissue," and recommended a "double incision" instead of key-hole surgery. Parker said the doctor told him his "nipples are hella low." A Texas surgeon he consulted for a second opinion agreed. For years, Parker told me, he had felt so uncomfortable in his body that he had walked around hunched over and therefore "couldn't breathe right." He often ends conversations early, he says, "so they don't notice something's weird about you." He wants to feel more comfortable in his own skin, and he looks forward to being "able to stretch out my arms and stand up straight and look people in the eye," he says.

Femininity, for Parker, meant being forced to wear clothes that didn't seem right, going to church, embracing domesticity, and being under the thumb of others—as his father controlled his mother, and his mother controlled him. "Growing up Catholic made me such a feminist!" he says. "Hello! They invented 'the Patriarchy'—literally!" For him, transitioning is a feminist act.

"Top surgery is so empowering because you get to take your image of who you are back. You're no longer controlled by others' image of you. You're the one who holds it, not them." Parker's body does not reflect how he feels "inside." But now he has the opportunity to create a different way of being in the world, one that feels truer, he says.

A similar motive brought twenty-three-year-old Lucas DeMonte, from Gainesville, Florida, to Dr. Garramone's office. Lucas is a health educator who identifies as a queer trans man. He's got a scruffy beard, a fairly high voice, ends a lot of statements with a rising intonation, says "like" a lot (as in "I was, like, ready" for top surgery), and comes off as kind and caring—good qualities for someone who works as an HIV prevention counselor doing condom distribution and safe-sex education, as well as some trans education. Lucas double-majored in psychology and Women's Studies, and his crowdfunding profile says he cares about animal welfare, children, civil rights and social action, and disaster and humanitarian relief, among other issues—in addition to transgender health. "In my spare time," he says, "I write and perform spoken word, pet cute fuzzy things, and smash the (cis)tem."

"I never felt like I was born in the wrong body," he says, referring to the dominant medical discourse, though he hated looking in the mirror and says he "felt extreme discomfort" with the body he had. Lucas has been binding his chest for two years using a compression sports bra, always a little too tight, usually followed by a

T-shirt and a man's shirt. He does so for safety, because he sometimes goes to rural Putnam County: "very small, really Southern
places," doing HIV education. "If they knew I was queer, let alone
trans, I would probably be killed, so I kind of have to keep all of
that very much on the 'down low' when I'm doing work out in the
community." But to his co-workers he is "very, very out." For Lucas,
undergoing top surgery is an assertion of what some feminists call
bodily autonomy. Pro-choice activists argue that the government
has no right to tell women what to do with their body; transgender
activists say that they have the right to change their body if they
please.

Lucas is at the surgeon's office with Oliver, a former boyfriend
who is also a bearded trans man; and Rachel, a bisexual Latina, his
"soul mate and sister." Lucas says he has "always known" he wanted
top surgery," even before he began injecting testosterone. A few
friends in Gainesville who had undergone surgery with Dr. Garramone became mentors to younger trans people in town like Lucas,
directing them to friendly therapists and doctors, and helping
them get letters for testosterone. Having crowdfunded the $7,000
he needed for top surgery, Lucas is giving away $500 to charity.

And then there is Nadia, a twenty-eight-year-old from St. Louis
who works as an employment coach at a nonprofit agency. The odd
girl out, she is having her chest masculinized, but not as part of a
gender transition. As a how-to book suggests, top surgery is "not
just for those transitioning from female to male" but also for others
on the gender spectrum, including "gender non-conforming, gender fluid, bi-gender, butch, and so on."[4] Nadia feels some camara-
derie with trans men undergoing top surgery and considers herself
"near the trans community, but not in it." She has short brown hair,
bushy eyebrows, and olive skin, and she is wearing large horn-

rimmed glasses, a men's shirt, and hip-hugging straight-leg jeans that look baggy on her slender frame.

When Nadia was twenty-one, her breasts suddenly grew to about a 32C. "They just went boom," she says, and she told me they felt outsized for her small frame. At certain points in her monthly cycle, when they bloomed even more, she couldn't even bring herself to get dressed. She felt more comfortable in an androgynous style, wore men's clothing, and hated the way her buxom bosom made her clothes fit. And she loathes having them touched. She identifies as female and has no interest in taking testosterone, but she sees her breasts as an impediment, a part of her body that does not reflect how she sees herself. Nadia's queer circle includes trans friends with whom she shares a deep sense of alienation from standard-issue notions of femaleness. She is here with her girlfriend, Flora, an art student whom she met on OkCupid four years ago; the two were drawn together by their mutual interest in art, politics, and graphic novels.

Nadia upends conventional notions of what women should look like and how they should be. She'll remain female, but she shares with the others here today the belief that their breasts don't fit and that by changing their bodies they can become more comfortable in their skin and more successful in their lives.

While some self-identified transgender men are happy to limit themselves to testosterone treatment, content that facial hair is sufficient for them to be recognized as male, most consider top surgery an essential part of the process of transitioning. When the University of Chicago sociologist Kristen Schilt interviewed fifty-four trans men between 2004 and 2008, she found that the vast majority had either undergone top surgery or were making plans to do so. A flat chest, they believed, was an "integral part of crafting social malenesss."[5]

Body types vary, influencing this process. Different people also respond to the medical interventions in different ways. If you're tall and take testosterone, you'll have a relatively easy time passing as male. If you're short and have big hips, it may be more difficult to do so—but interviews suggest that testosterone-induced changes, such as facial hair, deepened voice, and male pattern baldness can cover for a variety of "shortcomings," including small stature, and even pregnancy.[6] Many achieve considerable changes through hormone therapy, which encourages mustache and beard growth. "Facial hair covers all number of sins," writes a trans man on Reddit. Still, some transgender men who have particularly feminine features choose to undergo facial masculinization to produce a more square jaw line or prominent brow, and some even have pectoral or calf implants to masculinize their musculature. Few trans men undergo bottom (genital) surgery, however, which is very costly and has a high risk of complications.

Dominant notions of masculinity lead us to believe that a person is truly male if he has a penis. But "gender attribution"—how people see you in the world—often has little to do with what you have in your pants. For female-assigned individuals who wish to masculinize their appearance, hormone-induced differences are important—facial hair and voice pitch are primary signifiers of maleness. So is having a masculine chest—the central focus of surgical masculinization. It's not simply a matter of not having visible female breasts, though that surely helps others recognize you as male in everyday life. My interviews with transmasculine individuals suggest that even those with very small, barely noticeable breasts covet contoured, masculine-looking chests. For many trans men, chest surgery constitutes a central moment in the process of transition. Hormonal changes are gradual; chest surgery marks a clear "before" and "after."[7]

But a lot of what makes us male and female, according to gender scholar Suzanne Kessler, "is the gender that is performed, regardless of the configuration under the clothes."[8] In other words, you don't need a penis, or even a male chest, to be recognized as a man in public—though the latter may help, at times. So although I met Parker, Lucas, and Ben as they were engaged in physically modifying their bodies, transitioning from one gender to another is about much more than surgery, or hormones. It is about crafting a sense of gendered self, a process that entails dress, demeanor, and speech, as well as surgical and hormonal body modifications. The kinds of body modifications and the performances people enact have become more complex as the meanings of transgender have become more varied.

Transgender encompasses at least three basic identity projects, according to sociologist Rogers Brubaker: "the trans of migration," the "trans of between," and the "trans of beyond."[9] The trans of migration, which is the version that is most familiar to the lay public, is exemplified by spectacular gender crossings such as Caitlyn Jenner's, and by many others who are far less visible. It refers to those who fully transition, or cross over from one gender to another, male-to-female or female-to-male. But, during the last decade, we have also seen the rise of formations that transcend identity binaries. So in addition to those who "migrate" from one gender to another, there are growing numbers who embrace a critique of binary gender, claiming a space "between" male and female, or the belief that one's gender is fluid, and may shift over the course of one's life, or even in different contexts. Finally, some position themselves in ways that transcend categorization altogether, at times calling themselves "agender" or "postgender"—signifying their desire to define themselves without gender categories. The young people I met in Florida represent different versions of these transgender identity projects, and at times they combine different aspects of them.

Parker fits the classic profile of an FTM: he wants to operate in the world as male, keeping his transgender status private, disclosing it only to members of his family, his closest friends, and intimate partners. Ben wants others to see him as male, too, but it's important to him to be out as transgender to co-workers, as well as to friends and family. He wants people to know that he was assigned female at birth, and that he now identifies as a trans man. Lucas's identity is even more radically gender nonconforming; though he identifies as male, more or less, he wants to shake up the binaries that divide the world up into men and women, heterosexuals and homosexuals, and he sees being trans as an act of refusal. Nadia is a gender bender who wants to remain female.

Together, they are hardly an exhaustive portrait of individuals who seek out top surgery. For one thing, they're relatively affluent, or affluent enough to be able to come up with the $7,000 for the surgery, and at least another $1,000 for the week's travel and hotel expenses, with the help of friends or family. They see themselves as empowered consumers who have the right to access the services they desire, on their own terms. As members of the first generation of "digital natives," they can't imagine a time before the Internet—and it was through the Internet that most of them found their way to Dr. Garramone's office. As millennials facing an increasingly competitive job market, a diminished social safety net, and (depending on where they live) an increased cost of living, they've been compelled to be flexible—about the sorts of jobs they seek, the places they will live—and to adapt to a labor market where there are fewer and fewer guarantees.

It is more than simply a temporary economic downturn. Many experts contend that we are seeing a fundamental political shift: economic inequality is growing at a feverish pace, but government is less likely to intervene to alleviate it. Compared to their parents and grandparents, millennials have been "trained to hold sacred our individual right to compete," writes Malcolm Harris, the author of *Kids These Days: Human Capital and the Making of Millennials,* who is himself a member of the generation whose plight he describes.[10] While they tend to skew left politically, if recent polls are correct, millennials also value self-reliance—they have no other choice. Confronted with grim economic prospects, and declining faith in collective solutions, many of them have no choice but to fend for themselves.

Transgender members of this cohort may be especially likely to feel this way. Since they are more likely to experience job discrimination based on their gender status, and are far more likely to have been rejected by their families than most people, transgender people have even fewer resources to fall back on than the average person. Nearly one-third of trans people who responded to a recent survey (of more than twenty-seven thousand, surveyed) lived in poverty, double the percentage in the nation as a whole; one-fifth had become homeless largely because of their transgender status. Trans women of color are particularly vulnerable to economic exclusion and experience higher rates of violence.[11] But even relatively privileged transgender people, such as the ones I profile here, face considerable challenges, too, as we shall see.

The decision to modify one's gendered body is profound in so many ways, hardly fated, and rarely simple. Those who share a feeling of not fitting into their assigned gender do not necessarily come to the same conclusions or make the same choices. Some people are not as strongly driven by their sense of gender variance. Others have never heard the term "trans" and are unaware that it is even possible to modify their bodies to align them with their gendered selves. Still others cannot afford the cost or manage the risk to their current lives and relationships. At times the decision seems to turn on a dime. You take a job, where you meet someone who discloses to you that they had undergone a gender transition several years earlier. You are reading a book, or watching a television program, and come across a transgender character and ask yourself: Is that me?

TWO

Gender Trouble

To maintain gender divisions, we must control those bodies that are so unruly as to blur the borders.
          —Anne Fausto-Sterling, *Sexing the Body,* 2000

W e're the type of family that does everything together," Gail
tells me when I visit the Shepherds at their home in Brompton, Maine, a picture-perfect New England town outside of
Portland, a few months after we first met in Florida. I also interview
a group of Ben's close friends in order to get to know more about
his early life. A friend describes the Shepherds as a "cul-de-sac
family"—inwardly focused, comfortable, with traditional views.
"We were always together," agrees Bob. There were the annual boat
vacations, the trips to Disney World. "We never even went out to
eat without the kids." Not once.

Twenty years ago, the Shepherds moved from the down-to-
earth town of Buxton, Maine, to this community where many lawyers, politicians, and professional families live. Even though they
were well-educated professionals, the Shepherds were not nearly
as affluent as many people in town. Ben was barely ten when they
moved. Ben and his brother, Chris, who is four years younger, were
inseparable. Ben introduced Chris to video games, skateboarding,

and Rollerblading. If Ben became passionate about something, the whole family became passionate. When Ben proclaimed that he wanted to be a biologist, Bob and Gail took the kids to visit every aquarium in New England.

In fourth grade, Ben became best friends with Chrissy, who grew up on a farm a few blocks away. Chrissy was active in 4-H and enjoyed playing rough. A "real Mainer," not one of the snooty kids, Chrissy was drawn to Ben's uplifting personality, and the fact that he was "different from the other kids at school." Ben dressed differently. The Shepherds used to get hand-me-downs from Bob's cousins in Rhode Island, and Ben inherited a red letterman base-ball jacket. Ben loved that jacket and wore it constantly. Kids teased Ben and Chrissy for not having cool clothes. Because of Ben's large size, and the way he carried himself, he was frequently mistaken for a boy. Kids called him "killer whale," and they harassed Chrissy, who was physically mature for her age.

In middle school, Allison and Emily became part of Ben and Chrissy's pack of girls, and Ben's brother, Chris, always tagged along. He called the gang his "sisters" and looked up to all of them, especially Ben. A high-energy person like Ben was faced with an array of injunctions to "act like a girl." Things improved when he started playing field hockey and softball: sports became a refuge. Title IX had already been in effect for more than twenty years, expanding athletic opportunities for girls and women at educational institutions.

Gail had also been a tomboy when she was growing up in Vermont. She had worked construction with her dad and hiked all over New England with her male friends. "It was no big deal. I didn't think anything of it," Gail tells me. But that was in the 1970s, when hippie style blurred gender distinctions, and androgyny was all the rage. Twenty years later, gendered styles seemed to return with a vengeance. Teenage girls often wore their hair long, and even flaunted their cleavage. Ben was not one of them. While Gail supported Ben's tomboyishness, she nudged him to be a bit more feminine, twisting his arm to get him to wear a skirt for his First Communion. Ben fought her but often gave in.

Then puberty hit, and Ben grew a large, prominent chest. Ben's chest was always there, "in your face, and she always hated it," says Chrissy. Sometimes it was embarrassing, but mostly Ben would just laugh it off. Chrissy was also an early-maturing girl, so she knew how it felt. "We were the easy targets," she says. "We developed first. We endured a lot." Ben was always popular, but others saw him as a bit of an oddball because of his failure to be a girly girl. He didn't care at first, channeling those energies into sports.

Eventually, when team sports proved to be too competitive, board sports—surfing and skateboarding—became Ben's passion. As soon as he got a driver's license, he'd go down to the skateboard shop to talk to the guys who worked there about surfing and skateboarding. It was the dawn of Tony Hawk, a pioneer of modern vertical skateboarding. When Ben got into skateboarding, his friends did too. When he learned to surf, he announced to everyone, "All right, you can rent a surfboard. Come out with me. You're going surfing with me," and friends became surfers too. When he was fourteen, Ben discovered wakeboarding—water skiing with a board.

Gail, always the accommodating mother, asked at the time: "What does that entail?" Ben asked his mother to drive them to Massachusetts, where he heard there were good spots for wakeboarding. "Sure, I'll drive you," Gail said. Bob had taught Ben and Chris how to drive boats, and Ben would bring friends on the boat to go wakeboarding, and then surfing. Ben liked that wakeboarding was a fringe sport. It felt good; it felt right. It was "about self-expression, art in motion." He wrote a letter to Shaun Murray, one of the best wakeboarders in the country, one of his heroes, and told him he wanted to meet him, and eventually he did.

On the surface, Ben seemed supremely confident and comfortable in his own skin, but his close friends knew that he hated his body and particularly hated wearing bras, despite his very large chest. "Oh my gosh, why do we have to do this?" he would ask them. He wore hoodies and refused to shave his legs. A couple of times, Gail insisted on taking Ben for manicures and pedicures. Ben did it for his mom, but he never relished those excursions. Despite his Goodtime Charley exterior, Ben felt disconnected, even from his closest friends, and lived with a sense of unreality, a sense that his world seemed different from theirs. Those feelings became more acute in high school.

When his friends started to put on makeup and dress up to go out to dances, "Ben would cringe. She hated it," Allison tells me, using a female pronoun to refer to her friend, and then correcting herself. "We would say, 'Let us do your makeup and let us dress you up,' and he would say, 'I have no idea what to wear. I don't know what I'm doing.'" Ben tried to take it in stride, and sometimes he made jokes about how clueless he was, but he was never comfortable playing the role of girl. He was far more comfortable rolling out of bed and pulling on cargo shorts.

Ben had what seemed like a typical girl's room, decorated with posters of buff, scantily clad stars like Usher, along with movie stars and sports figures; he had a particular thing for Harrison Ford and John F. Kennedy. Yet his friends never saw him as a typical girl. While they daydreamed about falling in love and having kids one day, for Ben, the thought of going through childbirth was unappealing, even disgusting. "I would never want to go through that—it sounds like hell," he told his good friend Allison, who recalls that Ben always wanted to walk around topless and was jealous of guys' freedom to do that. "You don't typically hear girls talk like that," says Allison, who considered Ben "kinda no frills." Allison recalled that Ben had "such a big personality that you didn't think of gender so much in relation to him." He was such a singular character, so exuberant.

Ben tried to date guys a couple of times, but it was always awkward. Sometimes, when he went out with girlfriends, they would get really drunk and would make out with guys. Ben was attracted to guys, but when he had the chance to be with a man, "It was like gross, no. I just don't actually want that," he tells me. While Ben's friends were beginning to experiment sexually, he never went all the way. He felt lonely and wanted to be with someone.

Ben went to the prom with a guy he met snowboarding at Shawnee Peak, after initiating a conversation with him on the ski lift. "Ben was so awkward at the prom!" recalled Chrissy. The senior prom picture shows him in a flowing two-piece black dress with a scooped neckline. His shoulders are hunched over, and his smile is forced. It was the third time Ben had ever worn a dress. "It was horrible for Ben! It wasn't him at all," said Chrissy, "but it made Gail and Bob very happy."

As he grew older, Ben had a difficult time becoming the kind of girl others expected him to be. Deep down, he wondered whether he was "really" a boy. Sometimes he prayed to God to make him one. "When gender-ambiguous young people are constantly challenged about their gender identity, the chain of mis-recognitions can actually produce a new recognition," writes gender theorist Jack Halberstam. "To be constantly mistaken for a boy, for many tomboys, can contribute to the production of a masculine identity."[1] The fact that others saw Ben as a boy, or as boyish, contributed to the sense that he really *was* a boy. He never told anyone about this internal conversation.

The years from twelve to sixteen were a roller-coaster ride, according to Gail. "Some days you were like, 'Okay, what mood is Ben in today?' All that roller-coaster stuff seemed pretty normal for teenagers." Yet there was an additional layer of pain for Ben, a feeling of being out of step with peers, a feeling that he mainly kept hidden. Secretly, he thought he was crazy. His moods got worse, and the cold, dark Maine winters didn't help. He slept a lot, and his room was always trashed. "She would basically just leave stuff all over the place, just trash the place over a period of a day and just walk away," Bob recalls, stumbling on pronouns again. Ben was clearly depressed.

At fourteen, Ben tried to commit suicide by stabbing himself with a pair of scissors. When Chris unexpectedly walked into the room, Ben quickly put them aside. At the time, Ben says, "I felt like something was wrong with me, but I had no idea what." Bob and Gail took their kid to different counselors. Some read Ben's difficulty "settling down" as a sign of attention deficit disorder. It was true that he had a hard time with follow-through and suffered tremendous mood swings. Ben tried medications but didn't like how they made him feel: jittery, nervous, depressed. One counselor thought he had a problem with his father. Although the two had certainly clashed while Ben was growing up, sitting in that therapist's office, they looked at each other and thought, "This lady's nuts. We're out of here." They never went back. "Those years were some of the hardest ever," Ben recalls, "but during that time I could not have told you why."

"To maintain gender divisions, we must control those bodies that are so unruly as to blur the borders."[2] This quote, from a feminist biologist, speaks of the ways our society regulates individuals, punishing those whose bodies fail to conform to conventional standards of what men and women should look like. Anne Fausto-Sterling's research focuses on intersex individuals, whose bodies mix male and female parts, such as a girl who is born with an unusually large clitoris, or a boy whose scrotum is divided so that it has formed more like labia. But people like Ben, whose external physical bodies fit conventional standards of gender, more or less, but who use their bodies in ways that flout gender norms, are also punished. The boyish girl who loves rough-and-tumble sports. The boy who refuses to be competitive with other boys.

Gender is never merely an individual matter, or simply a product of our biological makeup. It is also a cultural accomplishment, which "involves interactions between small groups of people," writes Fausto-Sterling. In other words, in playgrounds, at schools, in our families, at work, we become boys and girls, and men and women—but not entirely as we please. Classmates, teachers, parents, and friends unwittingly shape gender differences into "essential" male and female natures. This is how a boy acts. This is how a girl acts. Gender is also a system of social classification. At the time of this writing, identifying as either male or female on legal paperwork is still compulsory across North America—with the exception of Oregon and Washington, D.C.

Failing to respect gender categories has consequences: teachers and parents nudge and reprimand you, kids call you names and sometimes even slap you around and isolate you. You're declared a freak. While Ben had an unusually supportive group of family and friends, they still policed the boundaries of acceptable gender, reining in his nonconformity, often unwittingly. Those on the outer edges of his circle did so much more blatantly, even at times bullying him.

By the time Ben graduated from high school, he had spent years trying to conform, rebel against gender norms, and find a place to belong. It was a subtle disaffection, a search for a place where he could be himself. He flitted from school to school. Fiercely devoted to family and friends, he frequently placed their needs before his own. He seemed to have difficulty figuring out what he wanted. Clearly very bright, but never a good student, Ben had trouble focusing and easily lost interest in his studies. Yet he was always challenging himself, searching for the thing that would make him happy, looking for his calling, and trying to make a difference. His is the story of what happens when a female-assigned individual fails to respect the rules of gender. While not necessarily representative of the transgender male experience as a whole, Ben's story illustrates the ways gender norms, and specifically the belief in the gender binary, structure the early course of our lives, stigmatizing those who fail to conform.

————

Ben spent most of his twenties drifting. He enrolled at the University of Maine at Farmington, in the foothills of the mountains in western Maine. He didn't go to any classes and got kicked out after a semester. He then studied digital communications for two semesters at Lynn University in Boca Raton, but quickly tired of that. Bob and Gail were footing the bill, and Ben got Bs even though he rarely went to classes. At the time, he was getting more deeply involved in wakeboard sports and the wakeboard industry. He felt he was wasting his time at a party school. He also missed his friends in Maine.

Ben, Chrissy, and Allison continued to go on "ladies night out" romps and weekends away, where they did girly things like go to a nail salon. "We'd walk around in our swimsuits and go down to the hotel lobby. We'd get our hair done and have a spa day," recalls Chrissy.

After finishing photography school at the end of 2007, Ben moved to Central Florida with Meg, whom he had met and become close friends with while working at a photography shop in downtown Portland a few months earlier. Meg and Ben had decided to start a photography business together. Meg would run the consumer side of the business—weddings, portraits—and Ben would do action sports photography in Orlando, where the wakeboarding industry was based. While they were living together neither ever brought anyone home. Meg stayed over at boyfriends' houses at times.

Meg was the first person Ben ever heard talk openly about being attracted to women. "That rocked my world," said Ben. Though Meg identified as straight, she openly admired female bodies. "I couldn't even do that," Ben said. "I remember we would have shoots at our house, and female athletes would come over, and I always had to make super clear that I was into dudes." Meanwhile, Ben was falling in love with Meg. When Meg rebuffed Ben, it was a bit awkward afterward, but they worked it out. Ben was a rare kind of friend, Meg tells me. "He would give you the shirt off his back."

They shared a mutual love of water sports and photography, and Ben put his heart and soul into the wakeboarding industry. But being female photographers in a male-dominated industry wasn't easy. Once, Ben and Meg had trouble getting paid and had to go without hot water for two weeks. "We weren't taken seriously," says Meg. Ben was also acutely aware of the fact that homophobia was rife in the industry, and "gay" was a commonly used slur, even if he did not yet identify as gay. He missed Maine. "Sometimes sunshine can be overrated," he posted on Facebook. "I kind of want to get a dog and a piano. Is that random or what?"

In November 2009 Ben moved back to Maine, beginning a new period of soul-searching. "Every major change I go through I always question my decision: Am I doing the right thing? Am I giving up too easily? Am I giving up at all? Did I fail? Did I succeed? What's next? I suppose we all do this. I guess that's what makes us all so connected, that on some level, you understand and can connect."

Before they left Florida, Meg told Ben, "You should really try dating a woman." When he was ten or eleven, Ben recalled seeing a program on TV, the news magazine *20/20*, about being gay, and thought to himself: "Boy, it would suck to be gay." In retrospect, he recognizes he was deeply homophobic and imagined being gay was "the worst thing I could've been." When Ben was a teenager he once even went around telling everyone that Chris, his brother and close friend, was gay (he was not)—perhaps as a way of deflecting attention from his own attractions. The truth was that Ben didn't know anybody who was actually gay, or at least anyone who was out and proud about it. In high school, Ben told me, "there was one person who was openly gay, and he got so much shit." Ben recalled hearing a family member talk about "shipping away the gays." Up until that point, he hadn't "seen or heard a single positive thing" associated with being gay.

But with Meg's encouragement, upon moving back to Maine, Ben began to explore his same-sex desires and started dating online. There he met Jo. It was his first sexual relationship. He never explicitly told his family or friends, or came out to them; he just introduced them to the girlfriend. "I thought I had finally figured out what was 'missing' for me, that odd feeling of never quite feeling whole but not knowing why," Ben recalled. Jo joined the Shepherds' annual trip to Disney World, and in December 2009, Ben posted: "My face hurts from all the excessive smiling

I've been doing. I can't help myself. Life is good. ☺ And it's getting even BETTER! Which is the crazy part, who knew it could? Yay for happiness!"

Sometimes it seemed that Ben and Jo were playing out butch-femme roles. If they went camping, Ben built the fire and protected Jo, but often Jo seemed to be the more masculine one in the relationship, according to Ben. You don't need roles to make a relationship between two women work, of course. In the postfeminist era, butch-femme roles are at times played out with a knowing wink; yet gender differences do persist among many female couples. In November 2011, Ben reported that he "spent the day with my lady hiking," and talked about proposing marriage, but Ben's family and friends never really warmed up to Jo. Eventually the relationship frayed.

When they broke up the following month, Ben was, he says, "a hot mess." He rented a house at his favorite beach, Higgins, near Portland, and stayed there on his own for a month. He said it took him six months to understand that "Jo had not been good for me." Since then he's had a lot of crushes. He gets obsessed with one person for a few months and then moves on to the next person. He tends to pick the "wrong people," according to Allison: people he works with, or friends. Ben's friends encouraged him to "get back on the horse, and find somebody that you don't know!" But Ben wondered whether he really was cut out for a serious relationship with someone.

Even when he was in a relationship with Jo, says Ben, the word "lesbian" never rolled off his tongue. It implied that he was female, and he never felt like a woman. He called himself "gay." And even though he knew he was attracted to women, he never had what some gay people describe as a kind of coming-out epiphany, a sense of "coming home," of finally finding himself. Even while he and Jo were together, they never felt like they were part of a queer community. There were gay characters on television and a lively queer scene in Portland, but for Ben, who was hooked into family and friends in Brompton, it hardly existed.

"Speak the truth, even if your voice shakes," Ben posted on Facebook, along with a series of New Year's resolutions:

Start working toward bachelor's in leadership and organizing

Spend a week or more on the West Coast

Lose another 30–40 pounds

Work up to be able to do 100 consecutive squats

Run a 5k in less than 25 min

Get health insurance

Start wearing contacts

Do a 3-day backpacking trip

Do 100 consecutive push-ups

Learn how to read sheet music/play guitar

Learn how to play the harmonica

Camp on a beach

Try one new recipe a week

Hike Mt Katahdin

See DMB in concert

Attend a Wellstone seminar

Journal at least once a week and keep a "campaign journal"

Read a book a month

Pay off credit card debt

Create plan to complete BS degree in 3 years

List making was a way to account, aspire, and plan for the future, to engage in a kind of existential seeking, and to hold many of those questions at bay. Meanwhile, Ben's brother, Chris, was preparing to marry his fiancée. "Bra shopping for the dress fitting for Chris and Elise's big day was a success!" Ben reported on Facebook, next to a photograph that pictured him in an emerald-green bridesmaid's dress with a halter top. Elise had to tutor him in the art of wearing high heels without falling flat on one's face. Still, he wore the dress and heels to please his brother and parents.

During a family trip later that summer to Celebration, Florida, Ben posted a quote from Walt Disney: "We keep moving forward, opening up new doors and doing new things, because we're curious and curiosity keeps leading us down new paths." For Ben, that path led, in the spring of 2012, to volunteering for the Maine marriage equality campaign. His world began to open up. Once he became involved with a community of activists, many of whom identified as queer, who saw themselves outside of heterosexual norms, Ben became more empowered to acknowledge his queerness publicly. On Facebook he posted an eighth-grade picture of himself, short hair parted in the middle, wearing a boy's shirt and bangs off to the sides, and the question: "Remind me again how I didn't know I was gay?" Little did he know that his coming out would eventually lead him to claim a transgender identity.

————

The strategy of coming out, of disclosing one's same-sex desires as a way of disrupting the "heterosexual assumption"—the belief that everyone is straight unless proven otherwise—had succeeded in lessening the stigma of being gay for many Americans. By 2012, thanks to the fervent efforts of legal advocates and activists, same-sex relationships were increasingly recognized in the law. On the edges of that movement, some activists were challenging gays and lesbians to celebrate gender variance, and asking questions like: Does the gender binary—the belief that the world is divided into men and women—do justice to the way many people really experience their lives? Should those who cross over, and "change their sex," have a place in the gay and lesbian movement?[3]

For decades, open transsexuals existed outside of gay and lesbian subcultures. This division was imposed, in part, by mid-twentieth-century gender transition medical protocols that required those seeking out sex reassignment surgery to affirm that they were not homosexual and promise that after their bodies were aligned with their minds, they would live "normal" heterosexual lives. Gender variance has certainly long been an element of gay and lesbian subcultures, and many of the movement's most visible activists, such as the leaders of the 1969 Stonewall Rebellion, were butch lesbians, "sissy" men of all races, and trans women like activists Marsha Johnson and Sylvia Rivera. Yet in search of respectability and cultural power, the gay and lesbian movement often disavowed gender variance, emphasizing the manly men and femme women in their ranks. In 1993, when transgender people tried to openly join the March on Washington they were rebuffed by the organizing committee. "As gays and lesbians have found their pride," sociologist Aaron Devor noted, "many have retreated in shame from the transgendered and transsexual people who had always been among them."[4]

But in subsequent years, transgender people organized to demand a place at the table—adding a "T" to "LGB"—and to gain access to hormones, surgery, and more say over how psychologists, psychiatrists, endocrinologists, and surgeons treated them. Male-to-female trans people showed up at feminist-inspired women's music festivals, which were designated as "woman only," defying those who sought to turn them away on the grounds that they were not "really" women at all. In 1997, the National Gay and Lesbian

Task Force amended its mission statement to include transgender people. In 2000, three transgender speakers were included at the Millennium March for Equality in Washington, D.C. In April 2000, an article in the *Boston Globe* declared, "Issue of Transgender Rights Divides Many Gay Activists." But the following year, in March 2001, the Human Rights Campaign, which is perhaps America's largest gay and lesbian organization, amended its mission statement to include trans people. Female-assigned individuals began to demand access to medical technologies to modify their bodies, and in 2001 they established Gender Odyssey, an annual Seattle conference for those on the "trans masculine spectrum." A burgeoning trans movement created a new vocabulary to guide gender-questioning individuals ("misgendering," "cisgender"), and promoted technologies—such as plastic prosthetic devices for peeing in public bathrooms, and chest binders, among others.

By the time Ben began to work on Maine's marriage equality campaign, trans people had become much more visible. At campaign headquarters at the start of every training session, staffers and volunteers would go around the room and introduce themselves, specifying their "preferred pronouns." *Preferred pronouns? Was a pronoun something you could choose?* That had never occurred to Ben before. He replied: "she, her, hers." But the question lit a fire. *Hey, wait a minute,* Ben thought to himself: *Those are not my preferred pronouns. Those are the pronouns that have been assigned to me.* And he began to meet trans-identified people.

Holy shit. This is a thing?! I could be a dude in THIS lifetime?!

Meeting trans guys on the marriage equality campaign blew Ben's mind. He had never heard about hormones or top surgery, or the possibility of growing up with a particular gender assignment and then opting for another. But as he became involved in organizing, he became increasingly aware of the transgender movement that was rapidly gaining traction. He heard the term "gender dysphoria" for the first time. That marked a turning point.

Ben began a process of questioning and scanning his biography for clues from his past. On the playground, kids would ask him if he was a boy or a girl. Ben recalled, "I never knew how to answer that. Sometimes I'd say, 'Well, technically I'm a girl.'"

Ben remembered that as a teenager he once joked that he felt like a "gay man trapped in a woman's body." When he had his first physical, the doctor told him he had a male hair pattern and naturally high testosterone. But Ben had to bury the sense that he was masculine. It wasn't normal. He thought about the ways his body had been a problem since puberty—first because of the large breasts, and later because he naturally had what some considered to be excessive body hair on his face, chest, and legs, and had been diagnosed with polycystic ovarian syndrome—which meant that he had more androgens than the typical girl.[5] The combination of a large chest and a profusion of facial hair led to embarrassing mockery. By the time Ben was in his late twenties, the transgender movement presented a possible solution: he could affirm a sense of maleness.

When I suggested to him that had he been twenty years older, he might have gravitated to the lesbian world, Ben countered: "Lesbianism never felt like a good fit. I had a lot of internalized misogyny. I hated anything remotely feminine and/or anything that would admit my association or connection to womanhood." He reflected, "I was exposed to butch subcultures long before I ever came out as trans, and had I found what I was looking for in those spaces I don't believe I would have felt it necessary to come out as trans. My transition felt like an undeniable truth. Like the grass is green. No matter how hard I tried to look at it as yellow, brown, or any other color, I know it's green. And thus have to act accordingly. As soon as I learned about pronouns I knew innately this was my path and it was never a matter of 'if' for me."

Transgender people (and the psychologists and physicians who work with them) often take issue with the idea that being transgender is chosen at all. One does not *choose* to be transgender; one *is* transgender. To assert otherwise, some say, is to open the door to conversion therapy, and the claim that people can be "made normal." And, in fact, similar arguments have been made about homosexuality: one doesn't choose to be gay or lesbian; one is "born that way."[6] But while our bodies and our desires are powerful influences, they alone do not make us who we are. Because humans are meaning-making creatures, identifying as transgender, or as gay or lesbian, or even as Jewish or Italian, is a sociological process, and as such it is in flux. In the early twentieth century, scientific and other experts observed variations among individuals with respect to gender and gave a name to such variations ("transsexual"). With time, activists partially challenged these medical definitions with another name ("transgender"), and by doing so they shifted the population who would identify with such labels, making the barriers to entry much lower. Though people often experience their gender variance as an aspect of themselves they have little choice over, they exercise personal agency when they name themselves transgender, and when (and if) they undergo body modifications on the basis of those identifications. So it's about a lot more than biology.

In our culture, the label "transgender" has, for the past couple of decades, offered a space for gender nonconformists and gender crossers to come together and affirm a sense of difference. In 2016, researchers estimated that about 1.4 million American adults identify as *transgender,* signifying those who move away from their assigned gender, at times by surgically or hormonally modifying their bodies.[7] This constitutes about .6 percent of the population—doubling a prior estimate. The actual number of transgender people is probably even higher than that and is bound to grow even further. "Due to growing visibility and medical access," writes columnist Diana Goetsch, "millions of trans people are manifesting what in previous times remained buried."[8] As actress Laverne Cox recently told *Time* magazine, "We are in a place now where more and more trans people want to come forward and say 'This is who I am.' More of us are living visibly and pursuing our dreams visibly, so people can say, 'Oh yeah, I know someone who is trans.'"[9]

As he came to think of himself as transgender, Ben thought about his suicide attempt at fourteen, and the way every homophobic and transphobic "joke" he heard as a kid had been "seared into my mind the way a burn scars your skin" and had nearly destroyed him. He thought about his bedroom growing up, and the fact that it was covered with posters of beefy half-naked guys. Was he attracted to them, or did he just want to *be* them? Whenever he kissed guys, he felt like he was kissing his brother. "It didn't feel right," he told me. But then kissing girls didn't always feel all that right either—not while he was still trying to be female.

He put the pieces of his puzzle together. *Oh, so is this why I've felt out of step with those around me.* Ben acknowledged his long-term depression. He also learned that there was a way out. It was possible to transition, and to begin to present himself as a man. He no longer thought he was crazy. For the first time, he realized, "it's okay" to feel the way he felt.

This is me. I'm a male who was brought up as a female. My gender identity is at odds with my assigned sex. As Ben and others described this process to me, discovering the transgender category and identifying with it helped them to make sense of so much in their lives that had previously been confusing. The realization also presents options. One can do little about it, living as the sex one was assigned at birth to the best of one's ability. Another option is to choose to transition socially but not physically—that is, to change one's pronouns and name without modifying one's body. A third option is to change one's pronouns, adopt a new name, and undergo some body modification, such as masculinizing one's chest but not taking hormone supplements, living "in between." A fourth is to transition "completely," changing one's name and pronouns, and undergoing chest masculinization as well as injecting testosterone, and to try to fully assimilate into the gendered world and live in a "stealth" fashion, out of the glare of others. Finally, one can transition and live openly as a trans man.

These identity options are not necessarily mutually exclusive, and at different points in their lives, as we shall see, individuals may embrace different strategies. Furthermore, different contexts, particularly work environments, may demand different modes of self-presentation. If you're working in the corporate world, for example, you may have little choice but to go stealth—if you can. If you're an artist, or if you live in a particularly progressive town, living openly as a trans man is more possible.

Ben wasn't sure what his life would look like. But as soon as he knew that transitioning was possible, he knew he would do it. It terrified him, and he did a lot of careful thinking about it. And yet he had a "gut feel" that he should—it seemed like the logical end of having acknowledged his trans-ness. *Oh shit. I see the road I'm going to have to go down at some point,* he thought, *but I'm going to ignore it for now.* He couldn't bear to do it to his parents—they were too important. So Ben kept this desire to himself.

THREE

One Life to Live

There was a knowing that resided in my bones, in the stretch of my legs and arch of my back, in the stones lying against my skin, a knowing that whispered, "not girl, not boy."

—Eli Clare, *Exile and Pride,* 1999

I n June of 2013, after spending the prior year as a staffer on marriage equality campaigns in Maine and Rhode Island, where he developed a reputation as a hard-nosed, highly effective organizer, Ben prepared to move to Oregon to work on his next campaign. His close friend Meg decided to join him on the cross-country drive; they would make an adventure of it. Gail baked a cake that said HAPPY OREGON TRAIL, and Gail, Bob, and Chris dressed up in rainbow flags for the send-off. What they didn't know was that Ben had begun to share with close friends the fact that he was questioning his gender identity, weighing options he had never even known he had until recently.

A few weeks before, while on a walk in the woods in Maine with his good friend Allison, Ben admitted to her that he had "never felt like a woman, ever" and that he was thinking of transitioning, but he worried about losing his family. He wasn't sure it was worth it.

It didn't really come as a surprise to some of his friends. "My brain and my heart already knew that she was he," says his friend Chrissy. "Growing up, I knew he had more testosterone in his body; he was hairy." Of course many cisgender women are hairy—and the widespread belief that they shouldn't be fuels a multibillion-dollar industry of depilatories and laser surgery. Today, nearly half of young women between the ages of eighteen and twenty-four shave their pubic hair.[1] Being hairy isn't necessarily a sign that one isn't a "real" woman, but some of Ben's friends began to interpret it as such, and Ben did too.

Ben and Meg extensively documented their cross-country trip, assembling a montage of photographs that they posted on social media, showing them hamming it up along the way. Shortly after they arrived in Oregon, Ben began his new job as a canvas director for marriage equality, and Molly, with whom Ben had worked in Maine and Rhode Island, arrived to help launch the canvas program in Oregon. On a long weekend off, they decided to visit Crater Lake together. On the ride back to Portland from Eugene, they discussed Ben's belief that he might be transgender.

Molly asked him: "Do you want just to try it out? Do you want me to call you Ben?" Ben hesitated and eventually agreed. When they got back to the field office in Portland, he spoke with Ryan, his boss and roommate. "All right, would you like me to call you Ben too?" Ryan asked him. "Yes," said Ben. "Would you like to be Bess at work and Ben at home?" Ben said yes. They were launching the campaign and getting to know each other. Earlier, using handwritten flashcards, Molly had tutored Ben on using gender-neutral pronouns:

Gender goes by they/them/theirs.
[They] walked the dog.

Is that dog [theirs]?
No, that dog belongs to Molly.
Molly told [them] [they] could play with the dog.

Ben had learned about non-binary pronouns while working on an earlier campaign, but he "kept messing them up," he recalled. After a week of using the name Bess at work and Ben at home, and going by "they" and "them," and other gender-neutral pronouns, Ben decided: "Fuck it, I'm just going to do it." He told the team he wanted to go by Ben. After introducing himself to his team as Bess, he told them, "Actually, guys, just kidding, I'm going to go by Ben. Bear with me." And "they were super great about it." A couple of the canvassers who had been hired on the campaign revealed to Ben that they, too, were trans.

Ben's depression, his weight, and his ADHD had hounded him throughout his life. He began to think about the ways his general unhappiness with his assigned gender seemed to permeate everything he did, and to wonder whether changing his gender could alleviate his unhappiness and help him feel better about himself. He learned about dysphoria; the question of whether or not he was "really" transgender was never in dispute.

"My world expanded, and I came to understand that there are other possibilities out there," he told me. "I couldn't help but ask myself: Is this who I truly am? Am I doing an injustice if I don't explore this other avenue? Over time, the more I thought about it, it didn't feel like a choice. Once I knew it was possible, it would have been a choice not to do it." Listening to his inner voice and building a network of friends who would love and accept him unconditionally gave him the strength to come out as trans. "I always thought I'd come back as a man in my next life," he told me. He realized he "could do it now."

He also began to learn that there were therapists who could help him figure out how to transition, though he was somewhat leery of them, having had an unpleasant experience with a therapist when his parents sent him to someone to try to address his depression. She had little understanding of the role that gender variance played in his life. At the time, Ben was not fully aware of it, either, even if he seemed to intuitively grasp that his emotional challenges had something to do with his inability to conform to the gender expectations of those around him. But if Ben saw a therapist now, even one who was supportive of transgender people, did it mean he was sick?

———

Transgender is an identity that was initially founded upon a psychiatric diagnosis. Transsexuals, as they were once called, were thought to be "born into the wrong body"—their sex and their gender were at odds with each other—and they could be "cured" by undergoing "sex reassignment," changing their sexed bodies to conform to their sense of gendered self. The diagnosis rested upon a distinction between the inner (mind) and the outer (body) that suggested, in one observer's words, that "the body is the site of error/conflict, while the mind is the site of deep abiding truth."[2] In order to gain access to transition technologies, potential patients were required to accept a diagnosis that declared their gender disordered, wrong, out of place. They were also required to convincingly demonstrate to clinicians that "they are and have always been the gender they claim to be (inside)."[3] The goal of such interventions was to align the body and the mind, enabling the individual to become "normal"—and approximate as closely as possible the "typical" man or woman.

A debate has raged among social scientists: Are some medical conditions simply assigned to those who deviate from social norms? Benjamin Rush, known as the "father of American psychiatry," believed that African slaves in the colonial United States suffered from "negritude"—the "disorder" of being black. Perhaps the medicalization of gender variance is similarly problematic, representing an effort on the part of professionals to "medicalize" benign human differences, transform them into conditions that are treatable, and in doing so minimize the messy diversity of human experience.

A diagnosis is a curious thing. Identifying with a medical category requires one to consider the calculus of risks and rewards. The complexity of an individual's life is placed under the microscope and reduced to a label that signifies, in effect, that you are damaged. Yet having a diagnosis can be comforting, too, and can be an entry point to gaining access to medical interventions such as body modifications. To have a name for something that once existed only as a feeling suggests that there are others who share your sense of difference: you are not alone. "The diagnosis is a form of language that helps us to communicate something specific," says Jack Pula, a New York psychiatrist who works with many gender-questioning patients.

By the time Ben came into contact with transgender people, the stigma attached to identifying as gender-variant had lessened to some extent. Medical labels were changing, moving away from the notion that being transgender is a "disorder." The fourth edition of the big book of psychiatric disorders, the *Diagnostic and Statistical Manual of Mental Disorders* (1994), popularly called the *DSM*, which is used by clinicians, researchers, psychiatric drug regulation agencies, health insurance companies, pharmaceutical companies, the legal system, and policy makers, included the diagnosis of Gender Identity Disorder. (The *DSM*, writes psychotherapist

Gary Greenberg, "is a collection of short stories about our psychological distress, an anthology of suffering." It's our "book of woes."[4] But some transgender advocates objected to the use of the term "disorder," contending that "their gender is quite ordered, just not in conventional ways."[5] They fought to soften that language, and successfully pushed for the adoption, in the fifth edition of the *DSM* (published in 2013), of the term *"gender dysphoria."*

As defined by WPATH, dysphoria is the "discomfort or distress that is caused by a discrepancy between a person's gender identity and that person's sex assigned at birth (and the associated gender role and/or primary and secondary sex characteristics)."[6] Simply put, the term denotes the ways gender nonconformity causes psychological suffering: when you look at yourself in the mirror naked and experience anguish when you see ample breasts when you'd rather not have them at all, or when people call you "ma'am" but you don't feel like a female at all and are therefore troubled by it, or when you feel uncomfortable about using the women's bathroom.

The notion of dysphoria has become central to the ways trans people tell their stories, make sense of their lives, and gain access to medical technology to modify their bodies. Older notions of "gender identity disorder" saw gender nonconformity as inherently problematic, but the newer diagnosis of dysphoria acknowledges that gender nonconformity does not necessarily cause distress. Still, such definitions see transgender as a medical condition, for which a remedy (surgery and hormones) is available only if certain criteria are satisfied.

Over the years I have known many masculine women for whom gender-bending is a badge of pride, who have had little interest in gender crossing or living full-time as men. One of them was Nancy, a boyish girl who grew up to be a masculine woman, someone I lived with for more than twenty years. Tall and big-boned,

Nancy cut her hair short and wouldn't wear a stitch of women's clothing if she could help it. She lived for baseball season and was very close to her dad, Joe, a businessman and lifelong Red Sox fan. Throughout her life, Nancy was regularly mistaken for a man by gas station attendants, at airports, and by people who didn't know any better—once by an older gentleman who ran a furniture store in suburban New Jersey who engaged her in a lengthy "man-to-man" conversation about the best way to stain bookshelves—never realizing that the person he thought was a he was really a she.

Nancy was even "sirred" when she was eight months pregnant with our son. Mostly, Nancy laughed at these incidents, but when she was hounded out of bathrooms by fearful women or mistaken for a man by waiters in restaurants when she was out with her parents—who felt such mistakes were embarrassing—it was more than awkward. She took to wearing long, dangly earrings (we called this "gender control") to try to minimize such incidents. That worked—usually. Nancy never thought of herself as a man. Nor would she have described herself as dysphoric, even though her masculinity might have been uncomfortable at times. Some would say that's because she's not transgender. As she saw it, her distress was caused by society's restrictive gender norms.

Most kids whose gender expression is atypical—feminine boys, masculine girls—grow up to be gay, Margaret Nichols, a New Jersey–based sex therapist, tells me (although some suggest that this is less true for girls, who are permitted a greater range of gender expression than are boys). In contrast, individuals whose physical changes at puberty "trigger a reaction of self-hatred" often take on a transgender identity, in Nichols's experience. Puberty is the time when those feelings typically emerge, according to Nichols, who has long served the LGBTQ population and is well known for her work with transgender youth. Nichols, who is in her late sixties, is Jersey born and bred, with the accent and toughness to prove it. (A popular bumper sticker reads NEW JERSEY: ONLY THE STRONG SURVIVE.) In the 1970s, Nichols challenged her fellow sexologists to take seriously the psychological needs of lesbian and gay clients, who were once written off as mentally ill. Today, she's doing the same for her transgender clients, who make up a growing proportion of those who walk into her office.

Nichols's clients often speak of being betrayed by their maturing bodies and having body parts—breasts, hips—that seem not "really" to belong to them, a feeling that can trigger anxiety and depression. *I hate my body, I hate my body, I hate my body.* "They get suicidal when they get their period, the body dysmorphia is so intense," Nichols tells me. Transgender individuals, says the therapist, experience feelings of estrangement or disgust related to genitals and secondary sex characteristics, such as breasts, and these feelings often result in shame, *I am not worthy of love and respect.* "Imagine, when you look down, your body is the opposite sex from who you know yourself to be," writes activist Jamison Green, and "what it would feel like to live with that discrepancy?"[7]

Nichols and Green are among those who believe that there are clear boundaries separating those who experience gender dysphoria and those who don't. It may be common for masculine women (or conversely, feminine men) to experience social disapproval for their refusal to abide by appearance norms, they say, but transgender individuals' distress seems to have an additional, invisible component, even if that person is a manly man or femme fatale who conforms to outward gender norms. Think of Caitlyn Jenner before her transition. *I am not recognized as the gender I feel myself to be.* Some individuals are preoccupied by the persistent sense that other people are not seeing them for who they feel they are because they lack certain physical markers. Many experience the feeling of having a perceived defect or defects in their appearance, which seems to the outside eye as imperceptible or nothing more than a normal physical variation. If someone thinks of oneself as male, and the rest of the world identifies them as female, painful feelings of not being seen by others in the same way that one sees oneself, or of not really existing at all, can arise.

But others suggest that distress is not an inevitable feature of gender variance. If you grow up in a supportive family, or if you live in a particularly liberal place, it may not be a very big deal to be a girl who strongly identifies as male. Moreover, while many individuals whose gender nonconformity causes stress take on a transgender identity and begin to transition, not all do. Many transgender individuals are not particularly troubled—they're simply longing for an alternative. "I see lots of people who don't have gender dysphoria," psychologist Katherine Rachlin tells me. "They're not so unhappy in the gender they were assigned. But they're so much happier in their affirmed gender." Today there are hundreds of therapists who work with LGBTIA clients (the abbreviation including intersex and agender), but only a handful of people nationally have a great deal of experience with people who are undergoing gender transitions. Rachlin, who has long hair, a pleasant face, and a way of speaking that exudes calm and empathy, is one of them. When I interview her in her Manhattan office, she is wearing a flowing skirt that falls nearly to her ankles.

In the 1980s, a friend got Rachlin involved with an information network and support group that gathered female-to-male cross-dressers, transsexuals, and their partners together with doctors and other medical and psychological experts. They met in Rachlin's apartment on the Upper East Side of Manhattan. Since then, transgender clients have come to constitute the core of her practice. Rachlin is not convinced the true "test" of being transgender is whether one hates one's sexed body and feels oneself "trapped in the wrong body." In its broadest sense, she says, "dysphoria means unhappiness—the opposite of euphoria." Rather than define trans people in relation to distress, Rachlin likes to say that many are "pulled by gender euphoria," or by the desire to be happy.

That may well be true. Still, psychiatrist Jack Pula thinks that "it's important to talk about the distress" as well. A lot of his patients express "such severe distraction and distress about their body that they want to kill themselves," he tells me. We shouldn't whitewash that experience. "I think there's an expectation, in some circles, that transgender people are just so healthy. There's nothing wrong with us. Don't tell us about what's wrong with us. But that move is detrimental to our long-range health." In order to grant access to surgery and health insurance reimbursements, doctors seek to document the severity of the patient's dysphoria, and its persistence over time.

As Ben told me, he had wanted to be a boy for as long as he could remember, and "he prayed to God to make him a boy all the time." He had never been a conventional female; his gender nonconformity made him stand out in ways that were not always comfortable in his suburban town. Being a tomboy may have been cute when he was younger, but as he grew older, his gender non-conformity became a problem. It caused him distress. By submitting to the logic of medicalization, he believes he can minimize that distress.

While few of the transgender men I interviewed or observed online spoke about being trapped in the "wrong body" or having a disorder, most seemed comfortable using the term "dysphoria," which describes a set of feelings, a sense of unhappiness, as much as it does a medical condition. *I am dysphoric about my breasts. I feel dysphoric today.* This language expresses a sense of estrangement as well as solidarity with others who suffer because of their gender nonconformity. Ben invoked the term "dysphoria" when he sent out a mass e-mail asking his friends and family for help and when he crowdsourced funds for top surgery. But privately, with friends and family, he avoids that language. "I had to say 'dysphoria' in order to convince others to support my top surgery," he told me later.[8] "I don't really use that term otherwise. It's too 'sciencey.'" Ben sees being transgender as a natural gender variation, and an identity. "I was super excited about discovering the idea of dysphoria," he recalled. "It made me believe in God more because I remember thinking, 'Well, he tried to answer my prayers of becoming a boy.'" Ben's account of the origins of his transgender identity blends biology, spirituality, and psychology: God made him that way. He accepts certain aspects of the discourse of illness, perhaps to legitimize for his family and for medical professionals his desire to transition.

Social scientists tell us that illness labels provide insight into the culture that creates them. Some individuals would rather starve themselves than be fat because we live in a culture of thinness, where we—particularly women—associate being thin with being beautiful—and healthy.[9] Gender dysphoria might be seen as a medical term for a cultural problem: our inability, as a culture, to tolerate gender variance, and celebrate it. Transgender has more legitimacy, writes sociologist Rogers Brubaker, if it can be narrated as a "tragic mismatch between an authentic personal identity, located in the deepest recesses of the self, and an identity mistakenly assigned at birth—a mismatch overcome through an odyssey of self-awakening and self-transformation, culminating in the public validation of one's true self. These stories are framed as stories of individual alienation and redemption, not of systematic injustice."[10]

One could argue that you shouldn't have to prove you have a medical condition in order to modify your body. People make major decisions about their lives—they reshape their noses, undergo grueling exercise regimens, and join demanding religious communities—all the time without having to justify their decisions to others. Most adults are capable of making their own decisions regarding their bodies. We have a right, we increasingly believe, to be happy. But although such ideas are beginning to influence the world of transgender care, in order for patients to gain access to surgery and hormones they must still use the language of suffering, pathology, and cure.

———

"Most people don't have a tangible sense of where gender is or what it feels like because there's something about the way it functions for them that is what we would call 'normal,'" Katherine Rachlin tells me. "But if there was something so out of alignment that you were forced to pay attention to it, I think that would be different. You start to feel it because it's so out of sync with everybody else." Rachlin uses the example of her own struggle with weight. "It's my understanding that some people don't have to watch their weight," she says. "I've had to struggle with it all my life. It's very hard for me to understand what it would feel like not to have to do that. I think you experience something differently if you have an issue with it."

Those of us who do not have the experience of feeling at odds with our assigned gender and who do not know what it means to live with a body that just "isn't me" have a hard time picturing what it must feel like for those who have that experience. I listened to an interview with a writer, a woman in her seventies, who spoke about never really feeling that her name fit. Renata was the name her

German-Jewish parents had given her on the eve of World War II, when she was born, after they had settled in the United States and made a family there. Renata carried this rather European name throughout her life and had always felt that it was not really "her." She should've been a Jane, she said. Or even a Max, which, had she been a boy, she would have been. Her name, she said, "never really felt like me." And yet she never changed it. She didn't talk about why, but perhaps it didn't seem that pressing: she could go on as she was. Perhaps she didn't want to upset her parents, and by the time they died, it was too late. Perhaps she felt that changing her name would be making a statement that she wasn't prepared to make, and the costs she would have to pay—curiosity, disdain, from friends and family—would outweigh any benefits she would derive from changing it.

A person's name is a crucial element of their biography. It comes to shape them and identify them to others—which is why transgender people are so adamant about being addressed by the names (and pronouns) they choose. Many, if not most, grow up feeling that in addition to their names, or their faces, their sexed bodies are disconnected from the person they really feel themselves to be. They're anguished when others refer to them as Ginny instead of James, or Helen instead of Henry, and they have a sense of unease and disappointment when they look in the mirror, when they get up, when they shower, and when they leave their homes. Some liken it to a horrible, never-ending toothache.

Some may object to my attempt to compare gender identity to other aspects of selfhood, such as one's name, or one's weight, on the grounds that changing one's name, or even one's nose or one's weight, is relatively simple, while altering one's gender assignment is very difficult. True enough. In our culture, gender is a more fundamental marker of personhood. It is a primary way our society is organized. And since it is rooted partly in the body, one's gender tends to feel much more visceral than one's name. Still, the analogy isn't so far-fetched. Collectively we create norms, or rules for living, and subject others to abide by them. Most of us come to view ourselves as others see us, more or less—the early-twentieth-century social psychologist Charles Horton Cooley called it "the looking glass self."[11] And many people, perhaps many more than we can know, spend their lives feeling that their names, or bodies, or genders never seem to fit very well.

By transitioning, transgender individuals hope others will recognize them in relation to the gender that feels "right" to them, and that they will be able to use the bathrooms, be addressed by the name, and use the pronouns that they associate with their true gender identity. *This is my true self. I have a right to express it and be recognized by others as that person.* Most transgender people I met describe their gender identity as something that comes from within, as something they have possessed from an early age, over which they have little choice, an inner essence of which they are the sole, legitimate interpreter. Ben and other transgender people tend to believe that in order to be authentic, they must acknowledge what they feel inside: what is bedrock, unchanging.

But even that which is believed to be "natural" is predicated on social beliefs that are in flux. For example, the concept of transgender would not be possible without the idea of two sexes, but prior to the eighteenth century in much of Europe, according to historian Thomas Laqueur, such a concept did not exist. Women were not seen as the opposite of men. Nor did people generally believe that the body determines gender differences. It was only with the switch to a two-sex model, which coincided with the growing power of medical experts, that differences that had before been attributed to gender came to be seen in relation to sex and to biology. Women and men came to be seen as having radically different organs, functions, and feelings. In other words, categories we think of as being basic to who we are as human beings, such as sex and gender, turn out to be historically shifting.[12]

The notion that we have the right to express an authentic self is relatively new, too, and rooted in modern ideas of individualism and self-fulfillment. A belief in individual self-determination powered the development of universal human rights and inspired social movements from antislavery to socialism and feminism. It has shaped much contemporary psychological thinking, and the belief that individuals should seek to express their deepest selves, and that personal growth depends on conquering emotional blocks and tensions—and repression, in general—that prevent us from being "who we really are."

When they tilled the fields, worked as carpenters, and labored in factories, our ancestors did so to support themselves and their families, and to fit into the local economy of which they were a part. Work was not necessarily a source of fulfillment, or an expression of authentic selfhood. Much the same could be said of intimate relationships and family life. Marriage was a means to an end, a structure in which to produce and raise children, thereby ensuring generational continuity. Few people married for love, organized their lives to ensure their sexual fulfillment, or divorced because they felt inadequately fulfilled. Our long-ago ancestors expected their lives to be pretty much the same as the lives of those who came before them.

With industrialization, productive relations shifted from the home to specialized factories, and the "modern" nuclear family came to replace the extended family. As families were stripped of most of their economic functions, they were increasingly focused on the socialization of children and the provision of intimacy. Today we think of families, at least ideally, as the place where we can "truly be who we are."[13] Authenticity, the belief that we have the right to be who we wish to be, is a pervasive cultural ideal. We change careers, get our tummies tucked, and divorce our spouses, often in search of fulfillment. "We want to work for an authentic boss, marry authentic partners, and even vote for an authentic president," writes psychologist and management professor Adam Grant.[14] We wish to be seen by others for how we feel inside, and we believe we have the right to be who we want to be.

The language of authenticity was already familiar to Ben, whose Facebook posts often spoke of personal change and growth, letting go of old assumptions, moving ahead, and reinventing himself and claiming what is essential and true. He became convinced that he had a right to be the kind of person he had always wished to be and felt himself to be—a guy.

———

In Oregon, he started going by Ben, but he was still Bess to family and friends in Maine. He began to bind his breasts, flattening them so that they were less visible. At that point he knew he was transitioning, but he wanted to ease his parents and friends into the idea gradually. His parents and brother knew something was up. In June 2013, Ben called his brother, Chris, from Oregon. Chris and his wife, Elise, knew from Facebook that Ben had changed his name, but "we didn't really know what transitioning meant," Chris later told me. Ben described the process to them, explaining that the surgery would probably occur a year down the line. Ben had taken a campaign job in New Jersey. Gail was coming out to visit, and she and Ben would drive back east together. Ben wanted his mother to know before she arrived, but he couldn't bear to tell her himself, so he asked Chris to break the news to their mother.

Chris dutifully showed up at the Shepherds' house, a few blocks from where he and Elise lived, and told his parents: "Listen, Bess doesn't know how to tell you this, but she's been talking to Elise and me. She wants to go by the name Ben." They had a difficult time understanding it. "It was confusing. Really confusing," Chris recalled. "He told me that his whole childhood growing up, 'it never felt it was me,'" he told his parents. It was a difficult conversation, to say the least. "It was confusing. It was really confusing," Chris told me, when we met in a Starbucks in a Portland suburb. He changes the pronouns he uses to refer to his sibling. "It hurt because Bess was my best friend," he says, looking anguished. "I had all these memories with her. Those memories meant something to me, and now you're trying to discard them and say that wasn't me?"

Because we tend to think of sex and gender as congruent with each other, in binary terms, and as fixed, when someone discloses that they don't feel female, even though they have been living as such, more or less, for more than twenty years, it can come as quite a shock, and even be seen as a massive betrayal. *We've lived together as brother and sister, and you're telling me that the person I roughhoused with, told my secrets to, and looked up to is not the person I thought you were?* Accusations of deception often follow. If sex is invariant and is defined by one's genitals, as we tend to imagine, how could Bess not be a girl? That's why transgender people contend with the stereotype that they are "evil deceivers" or "make-believers," writes philosopher Talia Mae Bettcher.[15] Because many people believe that genitals determine one's sex, and that sex is invariant and unchanging, those who identify with a gender that is different from the one to which they are assigned based on their genitals are often seen as concealing the "truth" about their sex. Similar questions can arise when someone comes out as gay or lesbian, though the consequences are not quite as great, the revelations not quite as threatening—at least for most of us, these days.

By the time Gail arrived in Oregon in August 2013, she knew. When she arrived, Ben was packed and ready to go. Ben posed with a flower in his hair before they took off. They drove for hours, through the vast, barren eastern part of the state, and they were well into Idaho before Ben asked: "So, did Chris talk to you?" Gail said yes. Gail recalls the ride: "We would talk a little, and I would cry a lot, then Ben would drive. Then we'd swap." They did this for four straight days until they made it back to Maine.

During the trip, Gail asked Ben a lot of tough questions: Where did his desire to change sex come from? Where will it lead? What parts of your body do you want to change? Do you want a penis? Do you want your breasts gone? Can you remove your breasts and just be a lesbian? Who's going to love you if you're like that? The thought of a man without a penis was incomprehensible. "Those are questions a mom can ask," Gail tells me. "They're not questions that Bob would've wanted to sit and listen to." By the time they arrived in Maine, Gail knew a lot more than she had known, and she began to understand the kind of support Ben would need for the journey ahead. When she gave Bob the abridged version of things, he was skeptical: "Bess," he said, "you need to take more time and think about this. Have you really thought it through?"

There was a lot of crying at home. It was in many ways like experiencing a death in the family, Gail and Chris agreed: "Bess was gone." Gail worried for her child too. She had read about the high rates of suicide among transgender men. She told Ben, "You have to understand that suicide cannot be a way out for anyone, for any reason. If you ever have those thoughts, we need to get you all the support you need for this. I don't care what you are. You're my baby. You're always going to be my baby." As she relates this story to me, Gail's eyes tear up. "He promised me he would."

Ben returned to Maine to attend his brother's roaring twenties murder-mystery party, dressed up in his dad's double-breasted suit and wearing a fake mustache. His posts on Facebook were increasingly preoccupied with transgender issues. In August 2013, California Governor Jerry Brown signed a bill that would allow transgender students to use the restroom of their choice, the same month that military whistleblower Bradley Manning declared she was transgender and would be going by the name Chelsea.

In November 2013, Ben came out formally on Facebook.

I want to invite you all on a journey with me. This may seem random to some, shocking to others, and perhaps long overdue for those who know me well. I want you all to know that I am a trans man. What this means, I'm female bodied but I identify as a man. I'm still me, the person you all know and love, in fact I now feel like a truer version of myself as I've come to accept and understand this piece of who I am and who I've always been. While this journey is going to be a long difficult road I would appreciate your support and I understand if you can't support me at this time. What I do ask is that you respect me and use "he/him/his or they/them/theirs" for pronouns and refer to me as Ben or Be. I know this is a journey for everyone in my life and I welcome any questions or concerns you may have. I feel truly blessed to have so many incredible and supportive people in my life. Thank you all for standing by me, it's an honor and a privilege to know you all.

Ben, who didn't really know what to expect, was relieved that the response was almost entirely positive: 172 friends liked the post, calling him brave, and thanking him for sharing his journey.

"Be, you've always been the coolest, most authentic dude I know, and nothing has or will change, except your heart, as you've grown to love more and more, both others and yourself. I love, accept, and am so so proud of you. *Hugs!* With love and respect for you, I stand by your side, Ben," wrote Chris, one of Ben's closest friends, who was once his date for the prom.

The boyfriend of a former co-worker wrote: "Also I want to commend you and point out that it takes a lot to post something like this on Facebook. I remember being there for you asking 'how do you know?' questions. I'm so proud of you for making this journey. You have come a long way in finding yourself, being true to yourself, and loving yourself for who you are."

"Beners—you've always been a boy to me," wrote another friend. "You are amazing, talented, hilarious & hard working. I support you 110%."

Aunt Tammy, Gail's younger sister: "Hi Be, Ben, Thank you for inviting us on your journey. . . . I am SOOOO Proud of you! Your invitation to join you on your journey was bold, daring to put yourself out there. This is YOUR journey—YOUR invitation. . . . For some it will be shocking, for others it will be easy, for others it will be an adjustment." Ben had posted his announcement on Facebook before speaking with members of his extended family. His aunt Tammy tried to play the role of mediator: "I love you and will be there for you! I will accept you in whatever you do," she posted, addressing Ben.

To others, she wrote: "Everyone please also remember—for some of you this is easy—for the most invested people in your life 'B' it is a huge change. . . . Everyone do whatever you can do to be supportive in this adjustment, not only for Ben." Ben's grandparents on Gail's side were willing to affirm his new identity—to a point: "Bess, I will support you, and love you forever, but you will always be Bess to me, I will not call you by any other name, I hope you understand my situation, Love Mimi and Poppy."

Gail was even more resistant, posting: "You did not love and nurture Elizabeth A. Shepherd for 28 years," she wrote. "So don't judge those of us who have. I am mourning the death of my daughter. The person I went for pedicures with and fun girl shopping trips. Now you think I should flip a switch in my mind and say cool. You're someone new. Sorry but I am not there yet. Be I will always love you but I am not there yet. From a mother's broken heart." Gail had plans for weddings and dresses. "I had to give up those dreams. Other people don't really understand that. But Ben needs to be who he is," Gail told me, in retrospect.

Bob found the whole exchange painful and remained silent. As he saw it, he was trying to get Ben to slow down and really consider the decision to transition, while everyone on Facebook was cheering him on, saying, "This is great, this is cool." Bob felt they were doing Ben an injustice by interfering. "This is my daughter's life and future. It's not something you do on a whim." Bob quietly worried about Ben, telling him that he was going to have a "tougher life than normal." He cautioned him: "You will always have to be careful where you go, where you're accepted. You're always going to watch your back. You're going to have problems. You're going to have issues getting on airplanes with your current ID. It's going to impact your life. Things that you want to do are not always going to be easy anymore, as they are for a normal person." As we speak, he catches himself and corrects himself, qualifying his reference to "a normal person," adding: "it's just because society says they are normal."

Ben's brother, Chris, feeling hurt, was also silent on Facebook. Privately, he wondered whether Ben could just be Ben without undergoing surgery, he tells me. He wanted to tell his sibling: "Can't you just stay as Ben but in the form that I've always known you as?"

"Thank you so much for all the support everyone," Ben posted on Facebook.

> I just want to say my family has been absolutely incredible with this transition. Mom, when you introduced me as Ben at Goddard I almost cried. I know that this is a process and a journey for everyone and I can't even begin to express how incredibly fortunate I feel to have my family and friends. I know that the support I have is rare to find in this world and I am forever grateful every day. Mimi, mom, Aunt Pat, and everyone else, know that I totally understand where you are at and I fully support you in this journey. I understand that this does have an effect on the lives around me and I know it's not easy. It's taken me 28 years to get here!
>
> From when I was 5 throwing a fit about wanting to be superMAN not super woman, to not knowing how to respond to kids on the playground when they asked if I was a boy or a girl, to burying it deep and trying sooo hard to be "normal" through my teens and early 20s it's been a journey for sure. I don't expect anyone to get there overnight. Again, it took me 28 years to accept myself and I'm still working on it. Thank you all sooo much for your unwavering support and unconditional love. I know that no aspect of my life has been easy on my family and they have cheered me on every step of the way. I wouldn't have had all the incredible experiences and opportunities that I have been fortunate to have if not for the

unyielding support of friends and family such as all of you.
I am truly blessed. Thank you, thank you, thank you.

In the meantime, Ben continued to post information about transgender activism: a project called "I AM: Trans People Speak," and about the annual Transgender Day of Remembrance. He also shared an article from the *Bangor Daily News*: "Teen Describes Growing Up as a Girl, Graduating High School as a Boy in Maine." And then a week later, writing from Freeport, Maine:

OMG IT'S SNOWING!!!!! This is A W E S O M E !!!!!!!!!!!

FOUR

Transitioning

Does the body rule the mind
Or does the mind rule the body?
I don't know.
　　　　—The Smiths, "Still Ill," 1984

Political organizing can be physically and emotionally grueling, and Ben was struggling with burnout. He was falling into a deep depression. After putting off the decision to medically transition, he finally decided it was time in August of 2013. He decided to move back in with his parents because, he says, "They need to be part of and bear witness to that process," and he needed to save money. Over the next two years, he thought, he would transition and finish his undergraduate degree.

That fall, Ben consulted an endocrinologist at the Maine Medical Center who is well known among the trans community in Portland, and asked him: "What do I need to start hormones? Do I need a letter from a therapist?" Dr. Spratt informed him of the potential risks posed by testosterone, including high blood pressure, and something called polycythemia, which is an elevated red blood cell count, and told him that the latest recommendations for transitioning did not require him to present a letter from a psychologist in order for a doctor to prescribe hormones. He verified that Ben did not have any pre-existing conditions that might be exacerbated by testosterone, such as breast or ovarian cancer, or heart disease, and advised him to think about whether he wanted to begin testosterone. "Whenever you want to do it, just let me know," the doctor said. Ben didn't anticipate it was going to be this easy. He thought to himself: "Let's just throw on the brakes here. I'm not quite ready yet."

A month after his first appointment with the endocrinologist, after considerable soul-searching, Ben made a second appointment. "All right, let's do this," he told the doctor. At the end of January 2014, as he prepared to begin hormone replacement therapy, he announced on Facebook:

> Me I will always be. I might look a little different or sound a little different in the future, but let's be real, who doesn't? We all change and grow and that is an awesome thing. I'm not dying, or going away. I am here to stay and I will always be the me that you all know and love. I just get to be a more authentic me, and isn't that truly the best?
>
> Bess, besscalator, besserism, bessey, bestopher, Elizabeth, Betty, Ben, Beny, Benerator, pooper scooper, and all the other silly fun names I have been called; I collect them all and hold them all with me dearly. I'm not erasing my history, I'm embracing it.
>
> I will always want to cook with Mom and go to the water with Dad. I will still love my family and my friends and will continue to be forever grateful for the incredible people in my life. I will always regard the people in my life as the best gift I could ever have and my number one asset. I love you all. I'm not erasing the past, I'm cherishing it. This is just the next

chapter in my book. The part where the caterpillar turns into the butterfly.

I know change is hard, but fear not. Celebrate with me! This is a great thing!! Cheers to the future!

P.S. I know some close friends and fam still prefer to call me Bess and that is A-OK!

His old friend Allison posts: "Awww. Made me cry. Whatever I call you, I'll always be proud to call you my best friend," to which Ben replied: "Awww, you're gonna make me cry!!"

"You are one of the most amazing people I know," writes his friend Viviana, "and you don't need to change a thing about yourself. Evolve, yes, we all do but your core will always remain as beautiful as it has ever been." And Blake: "I was blessed to know the you you are and the you you will be. You blessed me!"

Visiting the endocrinologist cost Ben $250. He saw the doctor initially to begin the testosterone treatment. After a month, the doctor did follow-up blood work. Ben went again three months later, and six months after that. After that, the visits would be annual. The testosterone costs Ben $80 every other month. Since the health insurance plans he had access to through the Affordable Care Act cost upwards of $250 per month, Ben calculated that he was better off paying for the hormones himself, out of pocket. More than half of transgender people who sought coverage for transition-related surgery in the past year were denied, and 25 percent of those who sought coverage for hormones in the past year were denied, according to a recent survey.[1]

Ben began testosterone on February 21, 2014, a few days after his twenty-ninth birthday, which he thinks of as the day of his rebirth. He continues to administer 25 milliliters subcutaneously, once a week, via a small needle that he sticks under the skin of his gut (rather than in the thigh, which is more typical). His injection ritual: first he opens the alcohol swab and wipes the top of the testosterone cypionate bottle, and uses the other side of the same swab to clean a spot two inches to the right or left of his belly button. Then he attaches a 22-gauge needle to the syringe, punctures the top of the bottle, and then flips it upside down to draw from it. He fills the entire syringe and then presses the plunger until it reaches .25. Finally, he swaps out the 22-gauge needle for the 25-gauge needle and injects into the clean site, filling the syringe slowly. Sometimes there's some bleeding, but the injection doesn't hurt. Injecting the hormone into fatty tissue rather than directly into the bloodstream ensures a slow, steady release and means there are fewer testosterone spikes—or sudden upsurges in the hormone. After a couple of months, Ben offered an update on Facebook:

> Crackling voice: check; Acne: check; Hungry always: check; Exhausted always: check. Yup. I've hit puberty 2.0. Let's hope this round is a lil more graceful than the first one!

The testosterone caused Ben's voice to drop, gave him facial hair, and stopped his period. It also caused acne and increased his libido. On Facebook, Ben described the odd, sometimes thrilling experience of feeling like an adolescent boy grappling with his budding manhood.

> I have started squeaking obnoxiously! I went out surfing Friday night and caught one of my best rides ever and went to yell in excitement and all that came out was some shrill squeaks. It was a humbling moment, haha!

Going on testosterone "helped his family and friends to see him in a different way," he told me. "It was amazing when Ben decided to take the T," recalls Chrissy. Ben called a month after going on cross-sex hormone therapy and spoke to Matt, her husband. "Guess what? I have the same amount of testosterone as you!" he told him. As Chrissy recalled, "Ben doesn't hold back. That's why we love him." Sometimes Ben's ADHD-ishness kicked in and he forgot to take his shots, but it didn't seem to matter all that much. He was transitioning.

Friends offered advice. "Having gone through male puberty once, my advice, stay active and get lots of exercise," says one. Transmale friends also weigh in: "Exercising kept me calm in my puberty 2.0, if that helps." Another advised: "Give it another week or so and you'll be hornier than a mofo!! I suggest putting that energy into working out. A LOT LOL."

"I think I understand what's happening," posted Neil, who attached a video from the Disney song "I'll Make a Man Out of You" from Disney's *Mulan*:

> *Tranquil as a forest but on fire within*
> *Once you find your center, you are sure to win*
> *You're a spineless, pale, pathetic lot*
> *And you haven't got a clue*
> *Somehow I'll make a man out of you.*

Transitioning is more than a simple matter of ingesting hormones and watching a series of biological changes wash over one's body. It is also about developing knowledge: about the meaning of gender, the process of transitioning, and about what happens afterward. That knowledge is easier and easier to obtain these days, via transgender health conferences, websites, and transgender-affirmative mental health professionals, as I found out once I started looking around.

That summer, as he watched his body change, Ben attended a transgender health conference in Philadelphia, and he later posted a video that declared that "there's no such thing as a sex change." The notion that someone "changes sex" is outmoded and "misrepresents the depth and breadth of gender variance," it explained.[2] The belief that one begins a transition as one sex and ends up as an entirely different sex has fallen out of favor. Today we are more likely to think of transitioning as confirming a gender that is constant and unchanging, that aligns the body with that identity.

Life went on as usual, more or less, for Ben. Ben, Gail, and Bob saw *Mary Poppins*. Ben signed up for classes at the university, which he paid for himself, enrolling in Introduction to Criminology, Introduction to Microeconomics, Economics of Social Change, and Introduction to Political Science. "Soo stoked! Wicked pumped!!" he reported, and during his second semester he made the dean's list for the first time, receiving a full scholarship. Even Mimi and Poppy, Gail's parents, had begun to refer to him as Ben, much to his surprise. He was transitioning.

———

There's a recognized script for those wishing to transition from female to male. It goes something like this: you accept the diagnosis of gender dysphoria, consult an endocrinologist to get a prescription for testosterone, start confiding in your family and friends, and then change your name and pronouns. While testosterone's effects are kicking in and before physical changes become evident, you tell more distant friends and relatives. About a year into the process of transition, you arrange to have your chest masculinized.

Medical and psychological experts and transgender activists collaborated to devise the script, which is known as the Standards of Care (SOC). Since 1979, WPATH, the leading international organization promoting evidence-based clinical treatment, education, research, and advocacy for transgender people, has issued the SOC, a document that sets forth best practices for health professionals caring for transgender people; insurance companies use it to decide whether to cover different procedures. The seventh, most recent version came out in 2011.[3]

But many individuals reject the notion of dysphoria, and they may choose to customize the SOC's suggested transition script, altering it to suit their needs. "I know lots of people who come to identify as trans, then get top surgery, thinking that will be enough. Later, it is not enough and they start hormones. Some use testosterone but never undergo surgery. Others have their chest masculinized but don't go on hormones," sociologist Raine Dozier tells me. Ben, for example, decided to transition socially, changing his name and pronouns, before undergoing any medical treatment, a practice that is especially common among college students. The standards offer a template, a way of regularizing the process of transition for both medical providers and patients. They assert: This is how things should be done. But they are not a mandate.

At times, psychiatrists and transgender people have waged pitched battles against one another, with trans people pushing for access to surgery and hormones, and shrinks acting as gatekeepers, limiting access. Psychiatrists needed to certify that patients were transsexual before they could grant them access to hormones and surgery, which led patients to tell canned stories in order to try to convince therapists to write the letter that would qualify them for hormones. *Yes, I always knew I was a boy trapped in a girl's body. From an early age I wanted to be a boy.* Since medical experts decreed that gender comes in two flavors, male and female, and that it is fixed at birth, they are called upon to document cases where that is not so, and advise patients how to go about "correcting" bodies that fail to conform to that norm.

While the general model of transitioning has not changed appreciably during the past sixty or so years since it was first designed by Harry Benjamin, what has changed is the role that transgender people have come to play in the process. The seventh version of the Standards of Care moved toward an "informed consent" model, which makes hormones available without a therapist's letter. Transgender people were given the ability to act as empowered consumers. Over the past two decades, psychiatrists have ceded power to clinical psychologists and social workers, who tend to be less attached to the idea that transgender people are somehow pathological, and who are also more likely to be better acquainted with transgender activists.

"We're at the point now where psychiatry is no longer the gatekeeper it used to be," says Jack Pula, a forty-four-year-old psychiatrist. After living as a masculine woman in a long-term relationship with another woman, Pula transitioned a few years ago. In his practice, which is located across from New York's Central Park, he works mainly with people who are trying to figure out whether transitioning is right for them. If the acrimonious relationship between psychiatry and transgender people is mellowing, it is partly due to the fact that people like Pula, who were once outsiders, are becoming insiders. He is certainly not alone. Jamison Green, a longtime transmale activist who wrote an important early book on FTM, *Becoming a Visible Male*, is now the chair of WPATH. A host of trans-affirming therapists (including Katherine Rachlin and Arlene Istar Lev, whom I interviewed for this book) are members of the committee that oversaw revisions for the latest edition of the Standards of Care.

In evaluating someone seeking body modifications, a mental health professional tries to determine whether the patient's wish for surgery has been stable and consistent over time, how intense and enduring that wish is, and how well the patient makes decisions in other areas of their life. They are doing a kind of discerning on behalf of the patient in order to best advise them. All of this adds up to, says therapist Rachlin, "Do they know what they're getting into?" Some therapists act as gatekeepers, actively seeking to minimize patients' access to body modifications. Others are "cheerleaders" who will write letters for anyone who comes through their door. Somewhere in between are people like Rachlin, who will write a letter if the patient is exploring their options in an informed manner and at a reasonable pace. "Most people have done their homework and are well-informed and well-prepared," she says.

When writing a letter, "you're putting your own license on the line for someone. It really is an investment," she tells me. "But if a person has wanted it for a long time, and they're capable of making their own medical decisions"—which usually means that they're not suffering from severe mental health issues beyond depression or anxiety—then "I wouldn't stand in their way," she says. Sometimes she'll encourage people to hold off for a while—until they go through a divorce or until final exams are over, or if they're going through a major life trauma. They may go on a low dose of hormones to see how it makes them feel, and then decide that transitioning isn't right for them.

Rachlin works with her clients to figure out how to best address their gender dysphoria. She helps decipher the complicated, painful feelings that patients bring with them into her office. Most people who see him, says Pula, who is a psychoanalyst, "feel bad enough" but they don't necessarily know why. Some call it gender dysphoria, but others speak of anxiety. Often they arrive with multiple problems, such as depression or eating disorders. Pula tries to help people tease out what might be going on with them. "What does it mean to you that you are transmasculine, and that you feel you're more a man than a woman? Or do you feel you're a butch? I want them to consolidate enough of an identity that they can actually move in the world and live and exist and feel good about that."

Though data suggest that relatively few people who transition regret their decision to do so, some body modifications are reversible. If you cease taking testosterone, you will start menstruating again. If you decide that top surgery was a mistake, you can have implants, if you can afford to do so. But some of testosterone's effects are permanent. Even after one ceases to take it, many of its effects linger: testosterone can permanently deepen one's voice, increase facial and body hair, create male pattern baldness. It may make becoming pregnant more difficult.[4] A supportive therapist will help a patient think through the transition process and educate them about various technologies, and their possible long-term consequences, without trying to influence their decisions.

"I'm really neutral on whether people have surgery or not, or transition or not," Rachlin says. "I'm more focused on process than on outcome." A therapist who has experience with gender issues will try to figure out more precisely how their patients see themselves. Do they identify as the gender "opposite" to the one they were assigned, or somewhere in between, along the spectrum of gender? While many female-assigned individuals who identify as male will choose to seek out hormones and surgery, lots of people choose to have top surgery and not hormones, or hormones and not top surgery. As medical gatekeepers have less sway and the availability of technologies for transitioning are increasingly market-driven, consumers have more power to choose which, if any, body modifications they want.

"A huge amount of treatment [in therapy] focuses on the question 'How is this going to work in my life?'" says Margaret Nichols, the psychologist. When patients come in with multiple issues, such as alcoholism or mental illness, things can get tricky. Nichols told me that she worked with an adult who was an active alcoholic, and she told the patient that the patient must go six months without a hospitalization before she would be willing to write a letter certifying that the patient was ready for surgery.

Different questions come to the fore depending on a patient's age. "Many adults have been sitting on this for years," says Nichols. "You rarely get a thirty-year-old who says, 'I think I might be transgender. I just thought about it six months ago.' Usually it's been going on for years and years and years." Even if some individuals seem as though they've decided overnight to do something so seemingly radical and transformative, they've often been sitting on the decision for quite some time. "Some transgender men have the experience of hitting a certain point in their aging process, and saying, 'Well, I can't maintain this particular body and this particular way of life until late adulthood," Jack Pula tells me.

The average age of Rachlin's patients during the first two decades she worked with gender-questioning people was about thirty; today it is closer to twenty, and growing numbers are of college age. Other therapists and surgeons I spoke with have observed a similar trend: the median age of those who are consulting professionals about matters of gender variance is getting younger and younger. Diagnosing younger teenagers can be particularly challenging. In adolescence, a turbulent time for everyone, "You don't fit in anyplace, you feel vaguely like something is wrong with you, you're awkward," says Nichols. "I've seen some adolescents who sort of grabbed on [to transgender] and then backed off after therapy," before starting hormones. Nichols wants to encourage adolescents to keep their options open. "Don't decide immediately that you want a full transition. You might change your mind. You might feel comfortable presenting as male, for example, even if you don't do anything to change your appearance. They might say, 'I'm genderqueer and I want to look like a boy, but I don't have to modify my body.'"

Nichols also works with gender-nonconforming children, a population that has only recently begun to receive popular attention. Many people who identify as transgender, perhaps a quarter according to a recent survey, began to acknowledge their feelings of gender variance by the time they were ten.[5] There is now a pathway for many of these children to undergo transitions if they, and their parents, in collaboration with therapists, see fit.[6] Some experts prescribe hormone blockers at an early age to stave off puberty. Proponents of early intervention see gender identity as innate, and fixed by early childhood; they argue that the earlier one intervenes medically, by offering puberty blockers, the less anguish the gender-variant child will experience. Others believe that gender identity is fairly fluid, at least until adolescence; they tend to counsel a more conservative, less medicalized approach.

A consensus seems to be emerging that parents should support their children's desires to dress and act in ways that may seem unconventional in relation to gender, without imposing labels or interpretations of that behavior upon them. "Listen to your kids—they know what feels right and true to them," says Zil Garner Goldstein, program director at the Center for Transgender Medicine and Surgery at Mount Sinai Hospital in Manhattan, and Matthew

Oransky, who directs the Psychology Training Program in ado-lescent health there.[7] By the onset of puberty, around age ten, if physical changes seem to be causing a great deal of anguish, Gold-stein tells families to consider allowing their child to be treated with hormone-blocking agents, as a prelude to a possible gender transition.[8]

Beginning in the 1960s, declaring that "gay is good," activists set out to transform how we think about homosexuality, encouraging everyone who had ever felt homosexual desires to come out. The problem, they argued, wasn't with gay people themselves; it was with a society that stigmatized homosexuality. In 1973, homosexu-ality was removed from the mental disorders listed in the *DSM*. During the following decade, gay-affirmative therapists argued that rather than trying to "correct" gays and lesbians, we should help them live more effectively in society, while they learn to grapple with the psychological costs of homophobia and "minority stress." Same-sex desire was in effect de-pathologized, and transformed into a somewhat benign sexual variation. Will being transgender eventually follow the example of homosexuality and shed its status as pathology?

It seems probable that gender dysphoria will eventually cease to be a psychiatric or mental health diagnosis, and the phenomenon will be replaced by more affirmative notions of gender diversity. That doesn't necessarily imply that people will no longer seek out medical interventions—though it does suggest that gatekeepers may be less able to restrict access to such interventions. In some parts of the country, it's already relatively easy to gain access to hormones: you can go to Callen-Lorde Community Health Center, in Manhattan, which offers care for members of the LGBTQ popu-lation, for example. Eventually, some predict, therapists, endocri-nologists, and surgeons will work with trans people to help them live more happily in whatever bodies they choose to inhabit, free of judgment.

But for now, it's often difficult to access surgery without a letter from a mental health professional, which usually means spending some time discussing one's life with a trained psychologist. "I'd rather not be asked to write those letters," says Rachlin, who has worked with thousands of transgender patients in New York since the 1980s. She feels uncomfortable in the role of gatekeeper, and yet, she says, most of the time, "people do welcome an opportunity to sit and review their decision with a therapist." Therapists can help individuals weigh their own desires against the demands of family and the "outside world," and they can "offer assistance in the practical and emotional tasks entailed in transitioning," says activist Jamison Green. "It's a good idea to get engaged with communities so that you can hear a lot of stories and find your way through things." That is especially true for younger people. "But some people, especially if they're older, or who have strong networks of support, may not need such help," says Green.

In fact psychotherapy played a fairly negligible role in Ben's decision to transition, or in managing the logistics of the process. By the time he decided to transition, he was in his late twenties. He had felt burned by therapists in the past; he didn't believe they could help him, and he wasn't insured. Ben saw a therapist a few times, but as soon as he knew it was possible to transition, he knew he wanted to do so. He knew he wanted to "go all the way"—and modify his body so that others recognized him as male, by going on testosterone and undergoing top surgery. And he spent a great deal of time thinking, reading, talking with friends and workmates, and surfing the Web.

Sixteen-year-old Kye dreams of having a masculine chest one day. "A big chest is extremely dysphoric for a lot of transguys," he says. Though he has small breasts, wearing a bra "enhanced them and made them look bigger," so he started binding them, flattening them to minimize their appearance. Like Kye, many trans men hope one day to have top surgery, but in order to do so, typically they must wait at least until they are eighteen and gain access to sufficient funds. In the meantime, many bind, or flatten, their chests. In a five-minute YouTube video, Kye displays his flattened chest and instructs others on how to achieve a similar effect; more than 83,000 viewers have seen it. "I'm a real boy!" he proclaims in the video, which was shot on his computer in his bedroom, poised in front of a DINOSAUR XING poster, a series of hand-drawn animal cartoons, and the cover of a Broadway playbill.

Many trans men bind their breasts for months, even years, often as a prelude to undergoing "top" surgery. "Wearing sports bras is better than nothing," says Kye in a video post, but "binders are what trans men need to start passing as men"—that is, to be seen by others as male. Kye, who lives in Illinois, can't afford commercially made binders, such as undershirts that have two or three layers of spandex, so he wears a sports bra that is one size too tight. He puts the tighter one on first, then a looser one, and if his chest still protrudes, a light undershirt. He cautions viewers not to affix Ace elastic compression bandages across their chests with safety pins. "When wrapped too tightly," says Kye, "they can do damage." Even binders can tighten over time and restrict breathing, causing fluid buildup in the lungs, and broken ribs.

In his videos, Kye thinks out loud, figuring out ways of minimizing the social tension that occurs when gender presentation raises questions in public, and sharing what he's learned with others facing similar challenges. He's trying out a different body, helping others to do the same, and building an intimate community with other young trans men. These opportunities for public self-reflection are particularly important for those who live in the liminal space of their family homes. Being out in public can at times be difficult, if not dangerous. Trans men can be bullied at school, or assaulted on the street if they disclose their transgender status to others. By narrating their life stories and sharing information they are creating a networked public made up of young trans men, building emotional bonds with similar others.

Kye is among a growing number of young transgender males who are coming out of the shadows, at younger ages—and online. For increasing numbers of gender-variant people, the Internet has become a community, a scattered web of gender-questioning peers who are instantaneously connecting with one another, sharing knowledge, and forgoing the authority of experts at younger and younger ages. While looking for evidence of transgender men's lives online, I stumbled upon Kye's video, and an entire genre of YouTube video diaries that document the process of transition. I was struck by the lack of inhibition of their young narrators, who seemed more than willing to reveal the deepest recesses of their lives for an audience of strangers.

In YouTube videos, trans men document their decision to assume a male gender, disclose that decision to family and friends, and undergo surgical and nonsurgical body modifications. Over the course of three years, Kye has posted twenty videos on subjects ranging from "How Do You Know You're Trans?" to an interview with his girlfriend: "How to Date a Transman." People have viewed his YouTube channel, which has more than 1,000 subscribers, more than 145,000 times. His is one of thousands of video blogs, or vlogs, produced by young female-to-male individuals on the Internet. Today, those in their twenties and younger are likely to have first encountered the idea of transitioning online. Chest-binding techniques are a particularly popular topic of discussion. Searching for the terms "transgender men" and "chest binding" on YouTube yielded more than 4,000 videos.

In the first of more than forty videos documenting his transition, Connor introduces himself: "The name is Connor, and like many other people in the world I am transgender. I know there are a million videos that you can watch about trans stuff, but now you have another one. I am here to help and to entertain. DUUHH! A'ight, so love you, my friends. Enjoy the page." In a video titled "Moment of Major Dysphoria," his room is dark, illuminated only by the glow of the computer, and he discusses his estrangement from his natal body, others' inability to recognize him as the gender he truly feels himself to be, and his desire to transition. "I really need to get it done. It's hard to wait. I want to get on T. It gets better, I think. It just takes time." He is crying.

When he went to work the other day, everyone called him Connor, his chosen name; "that was really cool." A few people even "called me sir," he said, "but it doesn't fool me." He desperately wishes to be recognized by others for the gender he feels himself to be. "I want my parents to be okay with it, and I just want to get things done"—get access to chest surgery and hormones. "Looks like some of you are watching," Connor tells his unknown audience. "I hope everyone else who has this problem is hanging in there. . . . Don't give up. Hopefully you guys are rooting for me, and I will root for you, too. Peace and love, I'll talk to you guys soon."

He addresses his viewers, the "guys," with familiarity and affection, and describes "meeting buddies online," though they have never actually been in the physical presence of those they communicate with and probably never will be.

By producing and consuming YouTube vlogs, young trans men are creating a visual record of the transition process and creating what Internet researcher danah boyd calls "networked publics"—spaces that are structured by networked technologies for people to "gather, connect, and help construct society as we understand it."[9] They use vlogs and other social media to document the decisions to move away from their assigned gender, bind their breasts, change their pronouns, pass as male, and, often, undergo chest surgery—and to work out the emotional challenges such choices pose.

As a teenager in the 1970s, I made my way to the local public library, where I found a medical textbook that told me all about the lurid world of homosexuality. Those scary pictures of naked people looking plaintively at the camera, arrayed like mugshots, probably set my own coming-out process back at least a decade. Who would want to live such a sad, lonely life? College wasn't much better. In the late 1970s, none of my courses—I was a history major and took lots of anthropology and sociology—mentioned queerness. And I was too scared to search for "abnormal psychology." Eventually, I ended up in San Francisco and joined a support group, basically a coming-out group, found my way to lesbian bars, and all was well.

During those pre-Internet days, even though I knew that I was attracted to women, it took ages to admit it to myself, and even longer to act on it—until I found a subculture of my own. The fact that there was at least a five-year gap between that first realization and the time I eventually used the L-word to describe myself would be unthinkable today. The Internet has made it possible to articulate one's desires in the privacy of one's home, or childhood bedroom, and find others who share that interest practically instantly. Googling "I am a girl but feel like a boy" turns up more than eight million results.

To the outside observer, these young people seem extraordinarily willing to share the deepest aspects of their private lives—and even overshare, at times. When he first saw these videos on YouTube, sociologist Sal Johnston, a member of an earlier cohort of trans-gender men, worried that their publicness would invite voyeurism, disdain, and mockery, he tells me. "Why would you do that?" he wondered at the time. Online and offline lives blur into each other today. Millennials who openly narrate their experiences online, even experiences that are at odds with the vast majority of their peers, seem downright normal. Perhaps many of them assume that the sheer volume of information available online means that only like-minded others would be interested in viewing their videos, and that those who lack a direct investment in such concerns would have little interest in them.

While few barriers to public gawking actually exist, norms of mutual respect generally seem to operate on transgender vlog sites. "In networked publics, interactions are often public by default, private through effort," writes danah boyd. "What's at stake is not whether someone can listen in but whether one should."[10] Even though transgender vlogs tend to be open for all to see, the more than fifty videos that I looked at revealed only a half dozen instances of negative feedback. In each of these cases, a member of the community, or an ally, came to the defense of those who were attacked. When someone named Ethan posted a vlog of his flattened chest, discussing the virtues of a particular type of chest binder, and was taunted: "If your [sic] a dude why can't you show your chest?" another viewer responded in Ethan's defense: "If you think it is wrong and/or nasty, then why would you search for it to begin with? Ethan is not a woman, he's a man. . . . You deal with it."

Responding to one of Kye's videos, a viewer writes: "Ok so, I'm not FTM or MTF but my boyfriend is FTM and watching your videos has helped me. Thank you so much, and keep up the great Vlog." She adds: "P.S. You're great for starting these to help people. Not just to bitch or try to get famous. You're an amazing guy, and I appreciate you!" Another viewer writes: "You inspire me beyond belief. Maybe one day I can come out too."

A year after he began posting videos on YouTube, Kye underwent top surgery; his final video documents the effects of testosterone on his changing body. Today, Kye, an art student studying illustration, lives full-time as male and no longer posts videos online. But only a few years ago, his vlog was a lifeline, enabling him to publicly document his transition and help others to do the same.

In theory, individual vloggers can control their privacy settings, deciding which videos to share and which to keep private. But creating boundaries around online spaces is difficult. The greater the number of viewers, the less isolated vloggers feel, and the more information they are able to share. For those who participate in these networked publics, coming out online can be personally powerful.

In their everyday lives, transgender people must be acutely aware of how they appear to others, particularly when they use bathrooms and travel through public places. Transgender women are particularly vulnerable to what sociologists Laurel Westbrook and Kristen Schilt call "penis panics"—perceptions of sexual threat in gender-segregated spaces such as bathrooms. Trans women are particularly threatening, they write, because they present the "terror of penises where they 'should not' be." In contrast, transgender men are seen as a sexual threat mainly insofar as they are a "source of homosexual contamination to heterosexual cis women."

According to Westbrook and Schilt, trans men's "perceived lack of a natural penis renders them biologically female" and therefore "unable to be highly sexually threatening."[11]

Once they are perceived by others as men, transgender men report that they are subject to homophobic violence from cisgender men who perceive them as insufficiently masculine. Black trans men also report feeling vulnerable when in the presence of men in positions of institutional power, such as police, according to interviews with forty-nine transgender men in the Midwestern and Western United States conducted by sociologist Miriam Abelson.[12] Much of the violence directed against transgender men, in other words, is very similar in character to that which is directed against men in general. Men police other men, often in violent ways. "Moment to moment, day to day, you have to be careful," Sal Johnston tells me. "It's an exhausting way to live."

By openly narrating their lives on YouTube, young trans men are throwing off their internalized shame and making a claim for attention in a world where getting attention is key to creating a self. They have grown up with reality television and social media, in an age of publicity. Young people understand the search for attention as normal—and inseparable from our "brand culture," according to communication scholar Sarah Banet-Weiser. Brand relationships, she argues, have become cultural contexts for everyday living, individual identity, and personal relationships.[13]

FTM transition vlogs are a mash-up of coming-out stories, *Consumer Reports* product reviews, and reality television self-revelations. Short, personal, and informational, they are embedded in the commercial culture in which they have sprouted, appearing next to videos instructing viewers on "How to get a flat stomach in a week" or ads for Epson printers, exemplifying the freedoms as well as the constraints of self-creation with new media. Those who master the art of getting attention have some potential to earn money by directing traffic to ads and becoming "content management partners." Brandon has posted forty-three videos, has 177 subscribers, and has a YouTube channel of his own. "I have about four guys who are going to be doing videos," he says. "I'm still going to be doing videos here, and also on our channel. A thirteen-year-old is our youngest." He meets lots of his "buddies" online, he says, and plans "to get a couple more guys so that we can have a video every day."[14]

"The Internet changes everything," says Jamison Green, who organized FTM groups in San Francisco in the 1980s the old-fashioned way—face-to-face. The Internet breaks down barriers and enables people to communicate with others privately, but it also enables them to be seen if they wish. An increasing number of younger people, so-called "digital natives," are completely at home in social media. They have never known a time when it wasn't possible to access a deluge of information about what people are consuming, what they look like, what they're thinking. While peer groups have historically played an important role in exchanging information about the emotional, social, and medical aspects of transitioning, it was not until those who were questioning their gender seized upon the Internet, and social media, in the 1990s that the movement really took off. The Internet has enabled younger people to "break down barriers," Green (who is in his midsixties) acknowledges. "It's had a huge impact," opening up possibilities for people to stand apart from their families and communities.

Green wonders whether social media also "creates a sense of isolation for people" and enables questionable information to enter circulation far too easily. On the Internet, "you don't know if the advice you're getting is reasonable or not," he tells me. "It's very, very difficult to suss that out with the cold frame of the screen." He remembers how special, and at times electrifying, it has felt to sit across from someone you hardly know and utter a statement like "I think I am a man," and then spend the next hour with that person, and ten other people one barely knows, to process that information and use it to imagine alternative ways of being in the world. Face-to-face gatherings have their problems, Green acknowledges, and some transgender support groups exert pressure on individuals who are gender questioning to "go all the way"—and undergo a gender transition. Others send the message to certain individuals that "they are not masculine enough" or "trans enough."

Still, Green believes, there is no substitute for the physical presence of others, especially because many people are disowned by their families once they come out as transgender. Cross-generational bonds among transgender people, in which older people offer support and mutual aid to younger ones, are in particularly short supply, he says. Lower-income transgender communities of color are "better at raising their young and imparting their knowledge," says Green. In the 1960s and '70s, black drag queens and trans women developed their own rich subcultures, exemplified by the urban "ball scene," pageants featuring queer African American (and Latina) contestants—documented in the 1990 film *Paris Is Burning.* "In many transgender communities of color, elders socialize the young, and there is a sense of continuity from one generation to the next," says Green, describing the system of mutual self-help and community.[15]

These days, transgender visibility has brought greater family acceptance. When he first started performing top surgery in San Francisco in the 1970s, in one of the first private practices geared toward transgender men, Michael Brownstein recalls: "Most of my patients were totally isolated." Occasionally, they'd come in with a friend, or a couple of friends, but never with their parents or family members. "It was a very lonely experience for them." Today, in contrast, he says, "transitioning is much more widely accepted," and many patients bring their parents with them. Some, like Ben, even move back home in order to transition.

———

"Ben could have moved away," Gail Shepherd told me. "That's what most people do. They do it on their own. But he came home because he knew it was important for us to do it together." Gail and Bob were transitioning, too, in a way, watching their child's bodily changes and talking through the questions. What happens if you forget to take your testosterone? Is long-term hormone use dangerous? Will you get a penis one day? As Gail acknowledged, "It wasn't always easy."

When we spoke in the spring of 2015, Ben was living with his parents, luxuriating in his budding masculinity and trying to grow facial hair, but his in-betweenness had become a problem. "I've got a beard and tits, which is weird," he told me, and he never knew which bathrooms to use. "I don't want to scare women," he said. "But men's rooms terrify me." He had a locker in the women's locker room at the gym that he hadn't gone near in three months. Which bathroom should he use? Using the women's room no longer seemed like a possibility, but if he used the men's room, how would he avoid detection?

Even though he felt that he was, deep down, a man, he was pretty clueless about so many aspects of masculinity that others seemed to take for granted, like shaving. When Chris and Ben got together, Ben would try to get his younger brother to give him some pointers about shaving and using bathrooms. "It takes years to get good stubble," Chris told him. "When you walk into a men's room, you don't look other people in the eyes, and you don't talk to them." But he never really felt comfortable teaching Ben how to be a man—somehow it seemed too personal. Chris had always looked up to his sibling, who seemed to be comfortable in his own skin. Now Chris wondered whether he had ever really known Ben at all. Nonetheless, he wanted to be supportive, so when Ben would ask him which bathroom to use, Chris would say: "Just use the men's, just be confident and do it." Now Chris had to be the leader, the self-assured one—a role that he wasn't used to playing with his powerful sibling.

Those in-between days when Ben was using testosterone to masculinize his body but still had a large chest were difficult ones. But then again, Ben's chest had always gotten in the way—when he went surfing, when he played sports, especially—and close friends, including Chrissy, always knew that he "hated his chest" and "wanted surgery before he knew it was possible." It was the "one thing that was super clear," agrees Ben. As soon as he knew it was possible, he wanted to do it. "Just like the hair on my head's going to turn gray, I knew it was going to happen. The only question was when." As testosterone was rapidly masculinizing his body, he realized that his chest was an "even larger barrier" than he had ever thought it was, he told me, and that more than ever it "holds me back from doing things."

While the people who knew him intimately were coming to see him as more masculine, he was still perceived as a woman socially—strangers couldn't help but notice his large chest. So he began to peruse Tumblr and a number of websites looking for a top surgeon who would help him get rid of it, narrowing the choices to doctors in Cleveland and Florida. "Ninety percent of the reviews said Garramone is the best thing since sliced bread," Ben told me, and a couple of friends in the campaign world had also recommended Dr. Garramone highly, so after a phone consultation with the surgeon, Ben decided to make an appointment for top surgery in Florida in a few months' time. Having the surgery performed there was more expensive than going elsewhere, but he decided he would try to fund-raise the money. "There are a lot of things that I'm pretty frugal about," he told me, "but this is not one of them. I have to live with this body forever." He knew it was possible to revise less-than-perfect results, but he wanted to make sure "they get it right the first time."

He needed someone to write him a letter that would qualify him for surgery, a letter that would specify that he suffers from dysphoria, is not crazy, and that he understands all of the implications of surgery—including its permanence. So he found a therapist who would write one. (That therapist declined to speak to me.) The sessions cost $100 a pop. Ben saw the psychotherapist a few times, and in the end the doctor signed a "Letter of Recommendation for the FTM Top Surgery Procedure," which simply entailed checking boxes on Dr. Garramone's form, stating that Ben was at least eighteen years of age and that he had met the criteria for chest surgery, the "next step in the transition process." It also stated that the "patient has a persistent, well-documented gender dysphoria or breast dysphoria" and that he "has the capacity to make a fully informed decision and to consent for treatment with surgery."

Ben was ready for Florida.

FIVE

Designing Men

New technologies of the body . . . infiltrate and penetrate
daily life like never before. . . . Contemporary men live in
technotesto times.
                              —Paul B. Preciado, *Testo Junkie,* 2013

en is second in line for surgery scheduled for nine o'clock
in the morning. When I arrive at the low-slung outpatient
building across the street from a suburban medical center, he
is wearing a green hospital gown, booties, and a blue hair net—
"Not exactly a fetching outfit," he jokes. A nurse connects him
to an IV and shaves his chest, while an EKG monitors his heart.
Dr. G. draws two black circles on his chest where Ben's new nipples, resized and repositioned, will appear. Dr. Leibowitz, an affa-
ble anesthesiologist, checks Ben's blood pressure and other vitals
and asks whether he has eaten or drunk anything during the past
eight hours and about the significance of his tattoos.

Ben's tattoos commemorate political campaigns he's worked on:
geometric symbols on his right ankle symbolize the Maine marriage equality campaign. Below is the word "hope," Rhode Island's
state motto, which marks a successful campaign for same-sex marriage; and there's an outline of the Idaho map on his left thigh,

symbolizing winning a nondiscrimination campaign in Pocatello. Ever the organizer, Ben takes opportunities to educate others. He posts a picture of himself in his hospital garb with the caption "pre-op prep" on Facebook, and pulls up his gown to show off the thick black Magic Marker lines. "Above there and below this," he says gleefully, pointing to his breasts, "it's all going." I am struck by how easily he shows his breasts in the presence of his father. They are little more than impediments to overcome.

"I am so happy for Ben. He's waited so long for this," says Gail when I ask how she is feeling. Ben reassures her that he is in good hands with the surgeon, reminding her that he had the chance to go to a local doctor, but since that doctor had only limited experience performing the procedure, he had decided to "go for the best."

As Ben is prepped for surgery, Lucas lies in the next bed, separated by a curtain, with his friends Oliver and Rachel sitting nearby. "Are you related to the photographer Annie Leibowitz?" they ask the anesthesiologist, who laughs and replies, "No, she's Leibovitz, not Leibowitz."

Ben tries not to eavesdrop. "I'm excited, but I can't wait for this to be over," he says as the anesthesia begins to take effect.

Two hours later, after the procedure is done, the surgeon, dressed in scrubs with a bandana on his head, goes out to speak with Gail and Bob in the waiting room. "It went great," he tells them. "Couldn't have gone any better." About an hour later, Ben wakes up and is wheeled to the post-op room. He is dazed and confused, but he feels no pain, and though he's groggy, he soon manages to sit up. His breasts have been replaced by an Ace compression bandage that is wrapped over the chest dressings. Attached into the bandage are two drains that suck extra blood and fluids from his wounds through a tube, into a bulb, preventing the accumulation of fluid in the body. Thin tubing attached to the drains follows the incision line, exiting near the armpits.

That afternoon, Ben, Bob, and Gail drive back to their hotel, along with a new stash of pain meds, antibiotics, and something to help with nausea. Gail posts: "Ben Shepherd in recovery. He is looking good." Uncle Larry posts: "Get well Ben unk larry love ya," and aunt Patty chimes in: "Take it slow and heal quickly. Love." A family friend writes: "Yes, you are Ben! You have a great attitude so keep your sense of humor through the healing!"

———

A momentous day in the lives of Ben, Lucas, Parker, and Nadia is just another workday for forty-five-year-old Charles Garramone, who over the past ten years has performed thousands of top surgeries—more annually than anyone else in the world. He is one of the very few who devote their practice to it. During the past decade, thanks in part to growing demand and an increasingly global cosmetic surgery market, his practice has steadily grown. Satisfied customers call him an artist, post photographs of their new chests online for others to admire, and send him gifts: Canadian maple syrup, English beer, even pistachios from Iran. "The bottom line is that we get good results," Garramone says, accounting for his popularity, but doing good work is not enough, he tells me. "You also have to be a nice person and have a good office that gives patients good care and advice." All of that is true. But in the age of the Internet, with the rise of medical advertising and reality television shows like *Extreme Makeover,* one must also be a digital-age entrepreneur.

Before devoting himself to masculinizing chests, Garramone had a busy practice devoted mainly to making women more voluptuous. Breast augmentation is, along with liposuction, the most frequently performed cosmetic surgery in the United States. In 2015, American women spent more than a billion dollars to enhance the size of their breasts.[1] A dozen years ago, a patient walked into Garramone's office and asked him if he would perform a radical mastectomy, and Garramone agreed. It went so well that the following week ten people called to ask whether he would perform the surgery on them too.

Garramone made more money doing boob and nose jobs, he told me—$20,000 to $30,000 a pop—but once he began to work exclusively with trans men, he was able to create his own office and take greater control over his hours. Working with transmale patients may be less lucrative, but he likes them more, he says. "They smile. You've changed their lives. The guys are more grateful," he says. Once he fell into the specialty, he soon realized that there was a niche market. Only a few other physicians performed the procedure in the United States.

One of them was Michael Brownstein, who served the FTM community for more than four decades out of his San Francisco office, specializing in top surgery. Brownstein retired a few years ago. I called him at his home in Sedona, Arizona, where, well into his seventies, he still rides horses and motorcycles. When he first began working with trans patients, he was "a pariah in the surgical world," Brownstein tells me. People accused him of interfering with nature. "How can you treat those people?" they asked him. Writing a decade earlier, Harry Benjamin praised the "courageous and compassionate Danish physicians who, for the first time, dared to violate the taboo of a supposedly inviolate sex and gender concept," who heroically "considered their patient's interest before they thought of possible criticism by their colleagues."[2]

In the 1950s and '60s, Americans seeking gender-related surgery were limited to clinics at large research universities like Stanford and Johns Hopkins, which offered transgender surgery to select patients (almost exclusively those who were making the transition from male to female) who managed to pass a battery of exams, and who agreed to undergo full genital surgery and live full-time as a member of their chosen gender. Brownstein was an early solo practitioner who, beginning in the 1970s, specialized in one element of the transition process—top surgery—and catered to female-assigned individuals, who were vastly underserved. Patients arrived in his office, often alone, describing in hushed tones the ways in which they were oppressed by their bodies. "Most people considered them sick and twisted, and they believed that the surgeons who treated them were sick and twisted too," he tells me.

Brownstein was legendary for his skill and for his compassion for his patients, whom he placed at ease by sitting in a giant purple-and-yellow throne. Perhaps theatricality runs in the family: the surgeon is the uncle of Carrie Brownstein of the band Sleater-Kinney, which melded feminist sensibilities and punk music to broad acclaim, and who has since gone on to a successful acting career. In her memoir, the musician's surgeon uncle, a long-time Republican and NRA member, figures briefly in a portrait of the quirky family Thanksgivings.[3] "How could you be so caring and compassionate, and be a right wing Republican?" his attorney brother used to ask Michael Brownstein, he recalls. "I guess I'm a jack-of-all-trades." Over the years, Brownstein became known as the "top" top doctor in North America, performing about two hundred surgeries a year.

Garramone, who admires his elder colleague, proudly tells me that he does two to three times as many procedures: an average of ten or twelve surgeries per week, with one month off—or about 550 top surgeries annually. Ten years ago, the doctor invited a patient to post a video of his surgical "reveal"—the moment he removed the bandage from the patient's chest after surgery—on YouTube—showing his newly masculinized chest, scars and all, in the style of reality television. Ten thousand people viewed it, and the floodgates opened. "My phone started ringing off the hook, and I started getting patients from Europe and Japan," Garramone says. Patients arrive from all over the country, and around the world—mainly Europe and Australia, but also more recently from the Middle East, China, and other far-flung places. Most are in their twenties and thirties—patients must be at least eighteen, the age of medical consent for major medical procedures. During the past five years, patients in their forties, fifties, and even some in their sixties have sought out top surgery.

Because he does not accept insurance (though he will provide paperwork that enables some patients to get reimbursed for surgery) most patients pay out of their own pockets. That means they are somewhat more affluent, or better networked, than those who seek out other, less high-profile doctors. I met Jackie, from London, in the surgeon's waiting room, and they told me that they could have had top surgery paid for by the National Health Service, but they weren't impressed with the results their friends got ("the scars were very dodgy"). They decided to save to have the procedure done in the United States, having researched options online and located Garramone. Across Europe, gender surgery is paid for by the state, but getting approval for it can be difficult, and choosing your surgeon is next to impossible. Also a trip to Florida would be a dream vacation. By having the surgery done here, Jackie, a twenty-three-year-old with Afro-Caribbean roots, told me, they "killed two birds with one stone"—and also managed to elude the scrutiny of family. Many of the patients I met in Florida crowdsource to raise money for their surgery, organize benefit parties, or save for years.

Patients arrive here confident that they are placing themselves in the hands of a surgeon they can trust, who devotes himself exclusively to transmasculine individuals, a fact that minimizes uncomfortable encounters and questions (such as "You want a mastectomy and you don't have cancer?"). Garramone's staff, which includes his wife, who sits at the front desk, is prepped to use the correct pronouns—most of the time, at least. When patients strike up conversations with others in the waiting room, there is some measure of shared experience.

For someone whose patient base consists largely of millennials who are dispersed throughout the country and around the world, having an effective online presence is crucial.

When you Google "trans top surgery," Dr. Garramone's website is one of the first to appear. On message boards filled with lots of talk about the comparative advantages of this surgery over that, this surgeon over that one, he receives consistently good reviews. After making contact with his office, prospective patients send him a photo of their naked chest and set up a phone consultation to discuss whether surgery is appropriate for them. Some obtain second opinions.

Shopping around for a top surgeon used to entail attending transgender health conferences, where there were show-and-tell sessions. In the pre-Internet days, someone who had surgery with a particular doctor—say, Dr. Brownstein—would ascend a stage so those contemplating surgery could inspect the handiwork. People with different body types would announce: "This is how big I was before," tell everyone what procedure they had had done, and detail the cost. They might talk about any complications and what their general impressions of the doctors were. Today surgeons are more likely to post galleries of before and after pictures on social media along with patient-made videos. The Internet has upended traditional word-of-mouth referrals, spawning new informational resources, such as the websites TransBucket.com and topsurgery .net, for those contemplating gender surgery and shopping for a surgeon. Reality television has transformed plastic surgeons into celebrities and encouraged many of them to brand themselves. Patients who find their way to Garramone's office are looking for medical competence and empathy, and at times for star power.

A ten-minute montage of body transformations on Dr. Garramone's website ends with an interview with the doctor in which he says that "these dramatic results are dwarfed by the social liberation this surgery has given my patients." He has been a particularly savvy user of patient testimonials. In one patient-made video, "Top Surgery Reveal / 9 Months Testosterone," a sweet-faced twenty-something guy with an English accent who is wearing a baseball cap documents his surgery, set to "Modern Man," a bouncy song by the band Arcade Fire.

> So I wait my turn, I'm a modern man
> And the people behind me, they can't understand[4]

The patient reports bloating, constipation, a sore back, and kidney pain. His mother hopes the discomfort and the effort are worthwhile. "I'll be really happy to get all this off," he declares, as the doctor removes the bandages and snips off the drains. "You look awesome!" he tells him, instructing him to start showering tomorrow, cautioning him not to face the shower and to avoid heavy lifting for six weeks, and explaining to his mother how to change the dressings. At the end of the video, the smiling patient says: "I'm so glad I came out to Florida to do this. This is the first day of the rest of my life."

———

The actual technology for masculinizing chests hasn't changed much over the years. Top surgery is, in effect, a radical double mastectomy; it resembles the procedure breast cancer patients undergo. But rather than leaving a flat or concave chest, top surgery entails resizing the areolas and nipples, repositioning them so that they're symmetrical, and sculpting the remaining tissue into a more male-appearing chest, complete with pecs. "You have to match the patient's morphology," or body type, says Dr. Brownstein. In heavy patients, for example, "you want to leave enough tissue so that the chest matches the abdomen below it. You don't want it to protrude, or be too concave. The challenge is to achieve both contouring of the breast and symmetry, as well as realistic nipple grafts. A realistic chest is one that nobody pays much attention to," he told me.

If the surgical procedure hasn't really changed over time, the meanings attached to it have. Garramone initially saw himself conducting "sex reassignment surgery," he told me, but in recent years, as transgender people have come to enjoy greater access to medical interventions, and the term "sex reassignment" has fallen out of favor, replaced by "gender confirmation surgery," he has come to say that he "helps people with gender dysphoria." Gender is "such a fluid identity," he tells me. "People have very different understandings of who they are." Some of his patients, he tells me, identify as male. These are "textbook reassignment patients." Others identify as gender-variant. Still others identify as women. "They are looking for somewhat different outcomes. I had a different view earlier.

I thought, 'Oh, this person is transgender and they want to be a man.' But I learned more and more. It's confusing to many people. I don't even think about it now."

Garramone patented the term "FTM Surgery Procedure," eliciting some skepticism from his fellow surgeons, and even some transgender activists, who suggest that the name, and the procedure, had been around for decades before he started his practice. One can't patent surgical procedures—only their names. Top surgery—subcutaneous (or under the skin) mastectomy—is a "relatively simple operation which any good plastic surgeon can do," Dr. Sherman Leis tells me when we speak at a transgender health conference in Fort Lauderdale. "It's a bit more complicated than breast augmentation," says Leis, a professor of the plastic and reconstructive surgery training program at the Philadelphia College of Osteopathic Medicine, "but it's not rocket science."

These days, Leis, who is in his seventies, mainly does transgender surgery: "one or two facial surgeries a week, one or two breasts a week, either add them or remove them, and one or two bottom surgeries a week." More and more people, he says, are coming out of the closet about being transgender. "Every time there's a Caitlyn Jenner or Chaz Bono, more and more people realize, 'That's me. That's my life. They did it, and I can do it.'" Leis remembers Garramone, who was once his surgical resident, as a "nice guy, meticulous and detailed," though he expresses some negative judgment about Garramone's decision to make a career out of doing top surgery alone when he could be doing a range of different, more challenging procedures as well, including facial masculinization, phalloplasties, and vaginoplasties—much like himself.

Leis performed his first transgender surgery in 1977, after a Philadelphia psychiatrist referred a patient to him for "female-to-male genital reassignment." At the time, he knew little about that world, and he offered to try to find someone who would perform the surgery. "Forget it. I've already looked around," the patient told him. "There's nobody here that does that work locally, and I'm not going to Bulgaria or Thailand to do it." So Leis accepted the challenge: he did some research, asked around, and learned that the surgical concepts involved in transgender surgery—tissue transfer in the form of skin grafts and flaps, and reconstructing body parts—are the same ones he used in his plastic and reconstructive surgery practice—with "a little bit of urology and endocrinology thrown in." And he created a phalloplasty with penile implants and testicular implants. That surgery "turned out okay," he says.

He is proud of the fact that his patient, with whom he is still in touch, "has since gotten married and lived a very good life—in southern Florida, in fact—and has two girls, both of whom have graduated from college." Like most of the surgeons I spoke with, Leis has a view of the world that is hierarchical, orderly. *This is what it means to be normal. We all want to be normal. I can alter your body to make you more normal.*

Leis sees transgender as a medical condition rooted in the brain, and a matter of anatomy over which individuals have little control. About a dozen years ago, researchers at the University of Amsterdam, he tells me, found that the part of the brain called the bed nucleus, in the hypothalamus, is different in males and females, and that transgender females, though they are biological males, have a "female bed nucleus," and the converse for transgender males. It's the best explanation, he says, of the etiology, or origin of transgender, and it explains why even very young children feel at times that they've been assigned to the wrong sex, he believes. Research on a possible biological basis of gender variance remains inconclusive, according to experts.[5] Still, Leis is adamant. That many of his patients felt "different" early in childhood is evidence of transgender's biological roots, he believes.

"Why does a little biological girl insist to her mommy that she go to the boys' room and get her hair cut short or she'll cut her own hair short, and wear boys' clothes even if she's three to four years old? They have no control over how they feel." He goes on to say: "We can't change the brain yet. Maybe in the future they will. But now we can only change the body to coincide with the brain."

But what about those who don't really feel distress, or who don't believe that they're "trapped in the wrong body" at all, but who nonetheless identify as transgender? Or those who think of themselves as neither male or female? Leis admits there may be "no reason to change the body" other than to eliminate the dysphoria, the "unhappiness with that individual's image of themselves." But if we're going to change the body, he believes one should go all the way: move from female to male, or male to female. At times psychologists and transgender people challenge him, telling him that "there's a whole realm of variation in the spectrum of human gender and sexual identity" that he's not seeing, he says. While acknowledging that "we don't have to be plugged into just male or female," he holds tight to the notion that transgender is a disorder with a discrete, though not altogether known, cause, and that transgender people, as the old phrase went, are "born into the wrong bodies." Like Leis, most surgeons I met while researching this book describe transgender as a condition, a "birth defect" that can be corrected by a medical fix—sex reassignment, or gender confirmation surgery.

Psychotherapists, in contrast, speak of individuals' personal journeys, using the language of selfhood and identity. "When someone walks into your office, it's important to ask people how they identify at that moment. That is likely to change," says Marilyn Volker, a grandmotherly sexuality educator and therapist who works with transgender clients in Florida, "because gender is fluid, and identities change." At a workshop for social workers and other practitioners at a transgender medical symposium sponsored by Florida's Department of Health, Volker told the crowd, "Figure out how that person wishes to be addressed, and have the integrity, respect, compassion, and love to honor that person's body and their heart—not just their parts." Therapists like Volker, working alongside transgender activists, have come to exert more power over clinical definitions of transgender, in organizations such as WPATH. It's time to move beyond the disease model, they say.

Sherman Leis begs to differ. As he puts it, "The order between the brain and the body is not right. There's a discrepancy there." In his practice, Leis has treated "an enormous range of individuals, from blue-collar workers and laborers to every profession and job you can imagine, including college professors, doctors, lawyers, and dentists," he tells me. What they share is a sense of dis-ease, of not being normal, he says. It's therefore appropriate that in order to undergo surgery, they must have a letter from a mental health professional that attests to their gender dysphoria, he says. If there's talk among WPATH members of expanding the range of what is considered normal and making the patient's informed consent sufficient for them to undergo surgery, Leis is resistant: "Is there nothing that is abnormal? I'm told that there is just a great diversity of human beings and that I should refer to them not as normal or abnormal, but as typical or atypical."

In 2008, Thomas Beatie, a trans man who kept his internal reproductive organs, gave birth to the first of three children. When interviewed by Oprah, he said he had a reproductive right to bear a child independent of his male gender identity. "It's not a male or female desire to want to have a child—it's a human desire. . . . I'm a person, and I have the right to have my own biological child." Writing about Beatie, political scientist Paisley Currah notes, "Trans people's bodies can confound conventional expectations." While our "notions of sex are still governed by logics demanding coherence," some bodies "disrupt those expectations." Such calls for a more expansive understanding of gender can, at times, raise the hackles of surgeons who believe that they should be in the business of creating bodies that reflect, as much as possible, "natural" binary gender differences. In the past surgeons steered patients toward modifying their bodies to conform to dominant gender notions. Today, though such expectations have somewhat less sway, doctors are often reticent to depart from the binary gender model.[6]

The other week, Leis tells me, a patient came in to see him who wanted a more feminine face, but without transitioning completely. "He's somewhere on the gender spectrum, somewhere in the middle, halfway between here and there." Leis was willing to take on the job, he says, because it seemed pretty reasonable. He won't entertain more unconventional requests, however. "Can people have multiple genitalia or no genitalia? What if someone wants a penis on top of their head? Or a vagina in the back of their ear, or something in the middle of their neck? Where does it end?" This is a version of the slippery slope argument. As conservative anti-marriage equality activists once proclaimed: if we permit men to marry other men, and women to marry other women, soon people will want to marry their dogs. Personally, I know many dog owners who love their pets, but I've never met one who wanted to marry them. Similarly, while there are certainly growing numbers of individuals who have little interest in conforming to binary notions of gender, few, if any of them, are rushing to surgically embed penises on the tops of their heads.

Today, Leis is one of a handful of surgeons nationwide who perform all aspects of transgender surgery, including bottom surgeries, which are the most complex. When he started, he tells me, "there were about four of us." Now, he says, there are more than twenty surgeons who perform bottom surgery in the United States. In the past few decades, he has performed about sixty phalloplasties himself. Only a small percentage of trans men choose to have them. For one thing, they're notoriously difficult to pull off successfully. (As one surgeon quipped, "You can make a hole but you can't build a pole.")[7]

Dr. Harold Gillies, who performed the first phalloplasty on a man named Michael Dillon in the mid-1940s, invented the procedure to reconstruct the maimed genitals of World War I war veterans. More recently, the U.S. military announced that in order to address the needs of military personnel who have suffered genital wounds in Iraq or Afghanistan, it is developing penis transplants that will enable urinary function, sensation, and the ability to have sex—but not produce children.[8] Many younger transgender men, who often have a more expansive view of gender, believe that they don't need a phallus, and they can use prostheses to please their partners. As Ben Shepherd told me, he's "happy to carry his purple sparkly manhood along in a bag." Leis doesn't quite understand that view: "If one wants to be close to one gender or another, why wouldn't one want to have all the necessary equipment? It minimizes social problems."

Dr. Christopher Salgado, who runs a transgender clinic at the University of Miami Health System, would agree. At a transgender medical symposium held at a Fort Lauderdale hotel, Salgado tells audience members that some patients opt for bottom surgery because "they want to remove that final birth defect." Like Leis, Salgado seems to divide the world into two clearly distinct groups, male and female, and he sees anyone who departs from that model as deserving of a cure. According to him, to have a nonstandard body—that is, a body that lacks breasts but has female genitals—is a problem. It needs correction. There's little space in this model for those who feel that they're neither male nor female, or those who feel more comfortable embracing a more complex gender palate. Despite all the talk about "being who you want to be" and "embracing your authentic self," medical discourse continues to be a powerful definer of what is normal and natural—and it tends to separate the boys from the girls.

Tall and rugged-looking, forty-year-old Salgado works at one of only two university hospitals nationwide that offer all aspects of transgender health. He tells the audience at the healthcare conference that in order to create a convincing-looking penis, or neo-phallus, "You gotta take it from somewhere." Doctors take skin from the forearm, groin, interior thigh, or muscle on the back, but removing skin from the leg "looks like a shark bite, so I like to take it from the forearm." He shows a neo-scrotum fashioned from the labia major, and vivid images of fistulas—abnormalities that can occur when one tries to fashion a phallus to permit one to urinate from the base of the penis. Audience members cringe and gasp, turning away, so he offers some comic relief, in the form of a slide of tattooed phalluses. When transmale patients who have tattoos on their forearms undergo phalloplasties, transferring the skin from the forearm means that the tattoo transfers too. Salgado shows a picture of a newly constructed phallus emblazoned with the word "intellect" and another that reads "to thine own be true." He cracks a smile while explaining that his goal is to please his patients while managing unrealistic expectations.

Surgeons can make a phallus that looks pretty realistic, but it's not fully functional. Erections are impossible without implants, which have a tendency to shift position, cause infection, or extrude, becoming dislodged. Sherman Leis likens the effect to putting a pencil or a pen into a block of butter sitting on your dining room table: "if you push that pen or pencil it'll go right through the block of butter and come out the other end." To urinate standing up requires a urethral extension, a procedure that is fraught with complications. While warning against inflated expectations, Salgado shows a photo of one satisfied customer: a smiling trans man holding a pump. "He doesn't need to use a strap-on anymore," we learn. He's been married five years, and "his wife is so happy. She's able to look down there now. And he can now urinate in a urinal."

But in fact most trans men in search of bottom surgery have metoidioplasties, which are less expensive and less risky than phalloplasties. In a metoidioplasty, the testosterone-enlarged clitoris is taken from inside the hood, separated from the labia minora, or vaginal lips, and lowered to the approximate position of a penis. The result is a "micropenis" of about two inches, which isn't large enough to allow for penetration. "It certainly works for a lot of people," says Salgado. (And it's good enough for Buck Angel, the transmale porn star.) "Some patients come in and say 'I want an eight-inch penis,'" Salgado says. The largest penis, he says, is thirteen and a half inches when it's erect. He tries his best to give his patients what they want. But to those who want large testicles and a big scrotum, he cautions, "Mo dick, mo problems," including a greater risk of complications from surgery. "Size," he acknowledges, "is overrated anyway."

In the universe of transgender surgeons, Leis and Salgado hark back to a day when plastic surgery was performed mainly to restore physical capabilities to those injured in wars, or to minimize disfigurement due to diseases, accidents, or congenital deformities. (Early in his career Salgado was a major in the U.S.

Army and chief of plastic surgery at two army hospitals in Texas.) They speak of "righting wrongs," distinguishing between cosmetic surgery designed to make people more attractive (such as breast augmentations) and reconstructive work (such as breast reconstructions after mastectomies), which enables people to appear "normal." While the former are elective procedures, the latter are, they claim, medically essential. They view themselves as saving lives and addressing injuries of birth, if not of battle, and doing the virtuous work of bodily reconstruction, in contrast to the cosmetic surgeons who practice "aesthetic surgery," servicing middle-aged women who are trying to improve their appearance in order to keep their husbands.[9]

―――――

For the past twenty years, Dr. Russell Sassani has offered facelifts, breast enlargements and reductions, body contouring (liposuction and tummy tucks), and laser skin treatments out of his Fort Lauderdale office. He also performs facial feminization procedures on transgender women. When I heard that he had recently started doing FTM top surgeries in Dr. Garramone's backyard, I visited him in his office, which is furnished in white Italianate style, with faux marble floors and a Leonardo da Vinci knockoff painting. Brochures advertising an injectable implant that fills in wrinkles and folds inform me that "life is a journey" and that I shouldn't let my wrinkles tell my story, while an operatic version of "Maria" from *West Side Story* plays on the sound system.

I am a fish out of water here with my unvarnished middle-aged face, unshaven legs that peek out from under my khaki shorts, and upper arms that are beginning to sag—amid svelte receptionists with perfect skin, full lips, ample bosoms, and no discernible wrinkles. Mike, the hunky office manager, is the doctor's partner and co-parent of their young daughter. They are active in Fort Lauderdale's gay community, where they are among the founders of the local Pride Center, and are generous donors to transgender and other programs. Recently, Dr. Sassani was featured on the reality television show *I Am Jazz*, filmed in South Florida, which tells the story of the transgender teenage girl Jazz Jennings. Jazz and her mother, Jeanette, show up at the doctor's office for a consultation about how best to feminize Jazz's breasts, and while they're at it, Mom decides to address the age-related folds around her mouth, and the doctor injects her with a wrinkle filler. The episode, which began with a focus on Jazz, quickly morphs into a mother-daughter bonding session at the cosmetic surgeon's office.

Much has changed since the 1960s and '70s, when Black Is Beautiful advocates like Huey Newton, Kathleen Cleaver, and Angela Davis encouraged African Americans to stop straightening their hair and helped to popularize the Afro and when feminists initiated a national conversation about the ways women are oppressed by the "beauty system," compelled to adhere to body ideals that are not only impossible to meet but that also have to be met, paradoxically, "naturally," that is, without effort or artifice. They pointed out that beauty rituals—depilatories, electrolysis, hair straightening, painful tweezing—are performed in secret, and frequently with a sense of shame. Activists urged women to refuse to abide by the standards of the dominant culture: stop shaving one's legs and undergoing painful cosmetic surgery—accept one's body, warts and all, and love it.[10]

When we were younger, my friends and I followed that call. We rarely shaved and didn't spend time at Weight Watchers. We didn't fuss over our bodies. And we cheered each year when a contingent of large women who called themselves Fat Dykes proudly strutted their stuff in the annual Pride Parade, reclaiming their large bodies as badges of courage. My friends and I wore blue jeans and T-shirts, mainly, and sensible shoes, and though we may have wished to be taller or thinner or to have more perfect features, we didn't spend a lot of time laboring over our bodies or identifying with the shiny celebrities we saw on television. We certainly never thought of cosmetic surgery as a solution to our problems. And if we did, we would never have admitted it to one another, or even to ourselves. But then again, while we often felt oppressed by the gendered world, we did think of ourselves as women, more or less.

When I recount this history to Dr. Sassani, a fellow baby boomer who was certainly exposed to such ideas, he looks at me as though I live on another planet. "I don't view it that way," he responds good-naturedly. "People want to feel comfortable in their skin." That's true of both trans and cisgender people, he says. And thanks to the availability of surgery, "they can actually be who they want to be now." He relates his own story as a gay man who grew up in sub-urban New Jersey and who did not come out until relatively late in life. "Had I been a bit more open-minded and accepting of myself early on, I probably would not have made some of the choices that I made. I made so many choices in my life trying to make other people happy instead of trying to make myself happy. Yeah, I did the whole marriage thing, because I thought my parents and my preacher and everybody else wanted me to marry, and that was not the right choice for me." Coming out as gay, like having plastic surgery, can be an act of resistance, a claim to happiness despite the odds, he suggests.

Sassani has seen a lot of female bodies in his day: fat bodies, skinny bodies, women with large breasts who want smaller ones, small-breasted women who want larger ones, women with sagging breasts and drooping chins in search of perky breasts and sup-ple faces. A very youthful-looking fifty-five, the doctor says that patients often bring in pictures of what they want to look like—celebrities, or pictures out of *Playboy* or *Hustler*. He's gotten used to telling people that what they are looking for is unrealistic. The vast majority (92 percent) of plastic surgery patients in the United States are women, but more and more men are seeking out cosmetic procedures too.[11]

After working mainly with women, Sassani is now performing transmale surgery. When I asked the doctor how he knows what a male chest should look like, he smiles and tells me that he "looks at lots of guys with their shirts off"—patients, guys in the gay community. "Go to Wilton Drive [a section of Fort Lauderdale where many gay men live] on Halloween and guys are just wearing their thongs or whatever, and a cape. You get to learn what the normal male aesthetic is, and you try to emulate it as much as possible." For men, the current Western ideal is a mesomorphic (v-shaped) body with broad shoulders, a well-developed upper body with a flat stomach and narrow hips.

In South Florida, where warm weather and beautiful beaches mean that bodies are on constant display, the beauty system once reviled by feminists of my generation is alive and well—turbocharged by celebrity culture. Florida is the third largest plastic surgery market in the United States, after New York and Los Angeles. (The average plastic surgeon earns nearly double the income of a family practitioner, pediatrician, or internist, and considerably more than the average gynecologist or obstetrician.)[12] If having cosmetic surgery was once something people did in private, with more than a little bit of trepidation, these days "not having work done is the new shame," announces *Time* magazine.[13] That might be an overstatement, but undergoing cosmetic surgery has become more socially acceptable.

A consumer culture that treats the body as a vehicle for self-expression encourages growing numbers of people to view tummy tucks and liposuction as relatively easy ways to improve their appearance—easier, certainly, than maintaining a rigorous exercise regimen or modifying one's diet. In the United States, doctors performed more than 15 million cosmetic procedures in 2014, up 13 percent from 2011—more than twice as many as in 2000. "An industry that was once exclusively for rich Beverly Hills and Manhattan women," says *Time*, "has been thoroughly democratized." Having "work" done is no longer a dirty secret. "We now regularly celebrate doing something for ourselves as if it's a moral imperative."[14]

How did cosmetic surgery become normal? Surgeons got better at what they do, competition drove prices down, nonsurgical options such as Botox became more readily available, and reality shows demystified the process. Stories of spectacular physical transformation, such as *The Biggest Loser* and *The Swan*, are a staple of reality television. In *The Swan*, ordinary-looking contestants are assigned a team of experts—personal trainers, therapists, dentists, and cosmetic surgeons—over several months, culminating in the big "reveal" episode when their liposuctioned, sculpted, muscled bodies are unwrapped for all to see. Some observers say the rise of social media, which places everyone on display, may contribute to the homogenization of beauty. By posting selfies, people keep track of their lives, wrestle with how they appear to the rest of the world, and perform who they are—or would like to be—for others. But people have been undergoing body renovation projects for a long time.

Ethnic minorities began to seek out cosmetic surgery in the late 1800s in order to appear white, the historian Sander Gilman has documented. "Operations on ears and noses," he shows, "enabled individuals to 'pass' as 'normal,' that is, as neither Irish nor Jewish."

It was only later that other "aesthetic" operations began to "remove signs of aging or to transform the structure of the genitals."[15] I can certainly remember when the "nose job" was a rite of passage for many Jewish girls who wanted to resemble the WASPs they saw in Hollywood films and magazines. Today blepharoplasty, or double-eyelid surgery, which makes Asian eyes look more Western in appearance, is the third most popular cosmetic surgery procedure in the United States, and common across Asia. Many African Americans straighten their hair, and some, like rapper Lil' Kim, who was always told that she wasn't pretty enough, undergo surgery to try to make themselves look white.[16] "For all the gains that various women's movements have made possible," *Bitch* magazine editor Andi Zeisler writes, "rigidly prescribed, predominantly white standards" still prevail, and the expansion of consumer choice has made it possible to "bow to such standards in countless new ways."[17]

Despite all the talk of authenticity, about embracing the "real me," do we even know what "natural" bodies look like any longer? As more people demand the right to change their bodies for different reasons by ingesting steroids, spending hours at the gym toning their bodies, and having cosmetic surgery, the distinction between elective and essential surgeries, vanity and wellness, cosmetic and reconstructive surgery, has become exceedingly blurry. As if to make this point, in the early 1990s a Spanish social critic named Beatriz Preciado began to self-administer testosterone and keep track of the daily changes he witnessed, in a kind of "gender hacking" performance. Preciado, who eventually transitioned and became Paul, came to see his body modifications in relation to a world in which "new technologies of the body" (biotechnology, surgery, endocrinology, and genetic engineering) "infiltrate and penetrate daily life like never before." Transgender people aren't really "restoring" their bodies to their "true" gender, argues Preciado. Today all of our bodies are, in some sense, products of medical technology.[18]

"Of course it is true that plastic surgeries and sex reassignments are 'artificial,'" trans woman Julia Serano writes, "but then again so are the exercise bikes we work out on, the anti-wrinkle moisturizers we smear on our faces, the dyes we use to color our hair, the clothes we buy to complement our figures, and the TV shows, movies, magazines, and billboards that bombard us with 'ideal' images of gender, size, and beauty that set the standards that we try to live up to in the first place."[19]

———

One need not even be a licensed surgeon to perform basic cosmetic surgery these days; at least 90 percent of these procedures are performed in a physician's office or private clinic.[20] Ophthalmologists offer botox shots to women who want to minimize bags under their eyes; many dermatologists perform facelifts, eyelid corrections, or chemical peels. Even dental surgeons and oral surgeons are now doing facelifts. The rise of medical tourism—people fly to places such as Brazil or East Asia each year for cheaper tummy tucks, facelifts, breast augmentations, and other procedures—means that cosmetic surgery is an increasingly competitive field.[21] The globalization of plastic surgery and the rise of the Internet are major factors in this development.

"The Internet has transformed patients into consumers," Sherman Leis tells me, "though not necessarily well-informed consumers." He tells his residents: "If I want to limit my practice to rhinoplasties, all I have to do is market it. Charge a low price, get a good advertising person to make up some nice ads, get a website, tell everybody you specialize in noses and you're the only one in this area of the country or the world who does only noses, and you're the super specialist, and you'll get business. It's all in the marketing." Acknowledging there's an "enormous amount" of competition in cosmetic surgery right now, Leis predicts that more and more surgeons will begin to serve the transgender population, especially when "they understand that those of us who do this work are swamped with patients."

The Internet has been a boon to plastic surgeons like Garramone—whose reviews are, on the whole, laudatory. But negative reviews circulate at lightning-quick speed, too, and it's not hard to find complaints about "cookie-cutter" results and the doctor's lack of bedside manner. "He came across as very robotic and cold—not a warm and cuddly guy," says a twenty-something trans man who posted a review on YouTube that was viewed by more than eleven thousand people. "You've seen the YouTube videos— he says the same things to everyone."

"Before you even arrive at his office, you already know what he's going to say: 'Here's where your nipples are going to be. They're going to be on the lower border of the pectoralis.'" The reviewer cautions others not to "expect VIP treatment" or even to be treated "as an individual." The doctor just "does his thing"—collects his money, does his job, so that he can "get to the next person." His pre-op appointment, which lasted all of ten minutes, was "scripted," and the doctor was "stiff and robotic." He admits that he "didn't pay the doctor to be friendly," reminding others: "He's not a celebrity, just a guy doing his job making his money."

Today, as more and more surgeons are willing to treat transgender men, and more seek them out as patients, doctors will face growing competition. When I mentioned to Charles Garramone that I was interviewing a number of other surgeons for this book, including one in South Florida who had recently begun to serve the transgender male population, competing with him for a share of the top surgery market, he quickly touted his own superior skills. "Many new physicians are jumping on the bandwagon on top surgery because they see this surgery as a 'trend' and a new money-making revenue stream," warns Garramone, on his website. In one video, posted on the site, a young patient informs him that a friend has just had surgery with someone in the United Kingdom who is "supposed to be the best." Garramone responds: "That's not saying much!" Having seen lots of patients from the United Kingdom, he tells him, he's had "to fix lots of bad surgeries." Most new surgeons care little about their patients, he warns. "The result: horrifying, botched surgeries." Of the two thousand new patients he speaks with every year, Garramone says that 10 to 20 percent of them are seeking revisions of the procedures done by other, less experienced surgeons.[22]

However normal plastic surgery has become, modifying one's body as part of a gender transition is still a pretty radical act. Yet many more surgeons are getting into the game, performing top surgeries—often under the radar. The number will continue to increase in the future if transgender people continue to become more visible, and if insurance—and Medicaid—covers transgender procedures, as it has begun to do more frequently. As greater numbers of surgeons perform gendered body modifications like chest masculinization, results are likely to become more uneven. To avoid "bad results," Dr. Garramone's website advises patients to ask physicians several "simple and direct questions," including how many FTM procedures they perform per year, who trained them, and "why did you start performing FTM Top Surgery just recently, and why did you have no interest in FTM Top Surgery when you started your practice?" Finally, he asks, "If you believe in helping the Transgender patient population, then are you willing to do only Transgender-related procedures and dedicate your life to these patients?"

With the advent of shows such as *Botched,* which spotlights a cavalcade of plastic surgeries gone awry, such fears are never far away. In one episode, a fifty-three-year-old former Las Vegas dancer with mammoth breast implants that have collapsed and threaten to extrude, cutting off the blood supply and posing a lethal danger, exclaims: "I feel like a walking boob, and it is killing me inside because I know I am so much better than that." On the same episode, a twenty-five-year-old man with a deviated septum caused by a series of fistfights can't breathe through his nose after a surgery that went wrong: "This is the most deviated nose I've ever seen!" announces the surgeon.

We gasp at these monstrosities, hoping that medical competence will prevail, and that by the episode's end they will be made good by superior doctors, and, sure enough, the walking boob is transformed into a shapely middle-aged woman who comes back ecstatic about having the load taken off (we do not see the scars); the fellow with the crooked nose is now a handsome gentleman who promises the doctors he will stay out of fights in the future. Good doctors arrive to save the day, instilling fears of the surgical incompetence of others, and offering moral instruction about the importance of being a smart consumer.

While top surgeries can result in infections and grossly disfigured bodies, more common are minor surgical errors, such as when surgeons "over-resect," removing too much tissue, resulting in contour deformities such as "dog ears"—puckering at the end of a scar, frequently under the armpits after double incision—or chests that do not look completely flat, which contain uneven fatty tissue and skin. Insufficient retraction or trimming of the remaining skin can leave areas of sagging or puckering around the areola.

Sometimes tissues die and nipple grafts can be lost, requiring further surgery to remove the tissue, followed by additional surgery to tattoo a replacement "nipple" if desired. Dark-skinned patients are often particularly susceptible to keloids (thick, raised, fibrous scars), and some people don't heal as well as others. Dr. G. does revisions for free for his own patients. If it's someone else's mistake, he charges for the work.

Today, the days of strict regulation are over, and transgender surgery is now offered on the open market to those who can afford it or who have access to health insurance that will cover it. As transgender people become more visible and demand easier access to surgery, more surgeons have started performing chest masculinization—which means that top top surgeons like Dr. G. are going to have a harder time staying on top. But that doesn't seem to faze him. "Now, I'm not just the Top Surgeon for FTM Top Surgery in the World," he says. "I am now the 'Go To Guy' for Fixing Botched FTM Top Surgeries performed by other doctors."[23]

SIX

What Kind of Man Am I?

I turned into a man. . . . I saw myself between the dirty-white scrolls of the mirror and the results were indubi-table: I was a man. But what then is manhood?
—Joanna Russ, *The Female Man,* 1975

The steps entailed in modifying one's body with hormones and surgery are laid out in advance by medical and therapeutic professionals. But other, less tangible aspects of transitioning can be somewhat more difficult to figure out, such as: What kind of man will I become? And what makes a man a man? Transgender men are not simply retrieving the male that resides within; they're also creating themselves. When they decide to modify their bodies, they are changing the fleshy parts of themselves. Transitioning is an affirmative act, a way of taking control, exercising agency over one's life, but gender is actively shaped in myriad ways, as my interviews with Parker and Lucas, and my visit to a guesthouse in South Florida, showed me.

Parker Price has dirty-blond straight, stringy hair and a chiseled face. There's a lot of good-natured bluster about him—part hip-hop, part hippie, and lots of vanity. He resembles a younger, shorter Brad Pitt. Pitt also happens to be one of his favorite actors, particularly in the role of Tyler Durden in the 1999 film *Fight Club,* Chuck Palahniuk's story of men who engage in violence to combat the numbing effects of living in a consumer-oriented society. In the film, pain becomes a vehicle for self-realization. "I don't want to die without any scars!" proclaims Durden.

Parker's Instagram feed is filled with photos of him wearing sports jerseys and ripped jeans, holding joints, and drinking bottles of beer. He's a bad boy, a player. Thanks to testosterone and his chest binder, Parker is now "stealth" at work, which means he has made a choice not to disclose his transgender history to those he meets—he presents as male. While those who have known him for a while, including most of his colleagues, know full well that Parker used to go by the name Kate, new hires generally have no idea he is transitioning. Ultimately, Parker says, he'd like to be stealth in most aspects of his life. If someone asked him if he's transgender, he would tell them the truth, but he doesn't want to live in between. He wants to be known as a man. "I'm grateful that I have more of a strong male identity because that just works with my personality," he says, and he is determined to transition as completely as he can and become male in the eyes of the world—and to himself. In many respects, he seems to conform to the conventional notion of the "man trapped in a woman's body." As he sees it, his true gender lies beneath his exterior, waiting to be claimed.

But "men" are made, not born, argues Michael Kimmel, a professor of sociology at Stony Brook University. "Manhood is not a manifestation of an inner essence. . . . [It] does not bubble up to consciousness from our biological constitution; it is created in our culture."[1] In fact, people go to great lengths to perform masculinity. "From bodybuilders in the gym, to managers in the boardroom, to boys in the elementary school playground, a whole lot of people are working very hard to produce what they believe to be appropriate masculinities," writes Raewyn Connell, an Australian sociologist who is a leading theorist of gender, and who identifies as a transsexual woman.[2] The 1950s breadwinner ideal is long dead. Yet we still define masculinity in relation to bravado and control, competence, and the ability to dominate over other men and women. "Real men" don't show their emotions. Boys don't cry. They refuse to admit vulnerability or ask for directions. They exhibit mastery over women, and over men they perceive as less masculine.

Think about our image of the stereotypical popular guy in high school. He's an athlete, which means he's physically tough, and he's not afraid to dominate other guys. He values his female peers largely as sex objects and brags about his conquests. He calls boys who show weakness "faggots." This is the dominant masculine script, according to researchers in the field of "masculinity studies," which is informed, in part, by feminist ideals of gender equality.[3] Still, men "do" masculinity in different ways, at times resisting the script. Some openly flout the rules, rejecting the belief that "real men" are emotionally inaccessible. It's harder to successfully carry off the dominant gender script for those who are not white, or able-bodied, or physically imposing.

Although for many if not most cisgender men, becoming a man occurs without a great deal of reflection, transgender men must make a deliberate choice to be known in the world as men, and because of that, they are forced to consider what being a man means to them. In the process, they must also become acutely aware of the actual mechanics of performing gender: how to move one's body, groom, dress, and use one's voice, in relation to gender norms and expectations, to be seen by others as male. "I used to think masculinity meant fixing cars and being an electrician," says Antwon Fulu, a chef in Bedford Stuyvesant, Brooklyn, who identifies as a trans male. "I thought that being a cook was feminine." But now, he says, he thinks being masculine "is about how you carry yourself."[4] The meanings of masculinity, though culturally scripted, are also deeply personal. And there are different ways of living in the world as transgender men.

Of the transgender men I profile in this book, Parker's masculinity comes closest to the dominant ideal. He's white, muscular, and athletic. He's competitive in business and in pursuing women. He easily passes as male in public. We speak in Florida during his surgery week, and then three times during the next few months. As he constructs an understanding of what masculinity means, and what he would like it to mean, Parker reaches into his family history, his biography, and the culture around him. He draws upon his early childhood wishes and dreams, the influence of family and friends, nuggets from Hollywood films and popular culture, his girlfriends and significant others, and bits and pieces of trans, queer, and hip-hop culture.

———

Before Parker was Parker, he was Kate—Katherine Allison, to be precise—a navy brat who spent his early years in Virginia Beach, Virginia, and then Maryland, and Mississippi, until the family moved to Texas. Dad was a navy chief, and his mom was a home-maker. Kate was outgoing and loud, loved being the center of atten-tion, and was boyish. When he was three he told his mother he wished he had been born a boy. Kate hated wearing dresses, liked "looking all strong," and fought with his mother, a devout Catholic, who tried to get him to act more girly. His mother exerted pres-sure on him to wear dresses, particularly on Easter. "Oh, look at all the other daughters wearing their dresses; they look so pretty," his mom would say. "Why can't my daughter wear a dress too?" But since Kate had a "pretty loud mouth," he prevailed, and the family tolerated Kate's tomboyishness, more or less.

Parker says he remembers "constantly having to search to find strong female representation around me. It felt like a fight to be seen and valued." Masculinity, in contrast, signified freedom: riding ponies and playing rough as a kid, and being able to be brash, opinionated, and eventually a ladies' man. Parker never identified with his father's navy-officer masculinity, the straightlaced, stoic military man, he says. As he got older, Parker began to figure out his own relationship to categories of gender. He wasn't a male, at least in the conventional sense, so who was he?

Parker's early desire to be a boy resurfaced right before puberty was about to hit. He could "feel this tidal wave coming." His androgynous body was changing, developing breasts and curves. Sprouting hips was the worst part of it all, and he woke up each morning sad, depressed. He was attracted to girls—big-time. He "brought the gay" to high school in Corpus Christi, Texas, and was a role model to younger lesbians. And he busied himself trying to get with the girls. "Oh, who's he going to turn this year?" everyone joked. When he moved to Austin in August of 2008, after high school, Parker was "in the prime of [his] lesbian high." After having a "great high school career as a lesbian," he imagined that he would go to college and "meet lots of women, have lots of sex."

He began to fashion a sense of himself as a cool dude who never got riled up, a tough guy who knows the score, a ladies' man who can show his vulnerability. He was into preening and selfies, referring to himself as a "gurl" on social media, posting photos of himself surrounded by super femmes, and boasting about drinking and getting stoned. He worked out a lot, had well-defined arms and "a good stomach," and small breasts that weren't all that noticeable. But still, for Parker, "being a lesbian didn't seem to fit." He wasn't happy. Even when he was in a deep relationship, he didn't feel whole. "I wasn't coming to the table as myself." Though he could appreciate all of his "amazing qualities"—he was outgoing, smart, funny, caring, charismatic—when he looked in the mirror, he "didn't see his own soul," he told me. He saw someone "faking it."

At parties, even when he was having a great time, he tells me, "I'd go to the bathroom in the middle of the party, look in the mirror, and be disgusted with how I looked." When he came out of the bathroom, everyone would ask: "What's wrong? Your mood just changed." And he didn't know what to say. He couldn't explain it to others; he couldn't really explain it to himself either. He stuck up for women, loved his lesbian friends, and saw himself as a feminist. But he never felt like them. "I just saw myself as a heterosexual man, not like a lesbian," he says. Being a lesbian afforded him the possibility of being a different kind of woman, but eventually, he says, he came to believe that he was "not female" at all. His gender was different from the one he was assigned at birth.

At St. Edwards, a Catholic liberal arts university, in a course called "Basic Christian Questions," taught by Sister Angela, Parker first learned that there was such a thing as transgender. At the time, he associated being transgender exclusively with male-assigned individuals, and he had a strong adverse reaction to it: "It was not me." Six months later, a close college friend came out as trans. It rocked Parker's world. The friend stopped talking to him during that process. "We've been best friends as lesbians, and now you're telling me you're trans?" he recalls. "I was still in deep denial." But knowing someone who identified as transgender made it okay for him to come out too: "The difference between seeing something on TV and seeing it in front of you." He thought to himself: "Oh, shit, that's really me. I'm queer as fuck. All right, that's me."

In January 2013, Parker, still known as Kate, posted "Some people ask me if I think I'm trans. Nope" next to a photo of a young butch dressed in T-shirt, baggy pants, leather jacket, and the caption: "I love being a girl. I really do. I love my body. But I also love to dress as a boy. I don't usually feel very confident when I dress in feminine clothing. But when I dress more masculine, I feel so, so beautiful." In retrospect, Parker says, it was a lie designed to cover up the fact that he thought that "being trans was weird." He never actually loved his body at all. He felt an incredible void in his life. He says he started "messing with my body"—"overindulging" in sex, drugs, and alcohol because he was fearful about his future.

By this time he was working at a software start-up in Austin, Texas. His job made him feel powerful and competent. He worked long hours trying to prove himself to his bosses, and was respected and well liked. But despite Austin's liberal hipness, it was a pretty gender-conservative place, and mainly heterosexual. He was the only out lesbian, let alone butch lesbian, who worked at the software company.

About six months after he learned that there were transgender people and that one could change one's body to align it with one's gender, he began to identify with the label. That may seem like a short time to make such a momentous decision, but in the life of a twenty-year-old, it can feel like a long time, especially because he felt he'd been living a lie—he was "really" a guy. He searched online for a trans-friendly therapist, and after three sessions decided to work with her, and in the spring of 2014, after about five therapy sessions, he decided to transition. He always "kind of knew that [he was transgender] but didn't want to say that out loud." Going to therapy permitted him to admit it to himself: "Yeah, this is who you are." The therapist said, "Well, you're trans. You need to be comfortable saying 'trans.'"

A friend who had planned to transition ended up deciding not to go "all the way"—for lack of money, and because of the stigma. They decided that being "genderqueer" was good enough and stopped after top surgery. But for Parker the choice was clear—which isn't to say he didn't experience guilt. "In fact," he tells me, "I almost felt I was betraying my feminist roots and admitting that 'yes, being a woman is less desirable.' It felt like I was giving up the fight. I do not believe being a woman is less desirable as a whole, but for me personally, yes, it was."

Around this time, Parker also began to date Darby, also in her early twenties, who worked at a rival software start-up. Darby had considered herself heterosexual but decided she wanted to try to date women. She had known Parker for a couple of years, after they met at a party. Parker told Darby that he was planning to transition. "I was like, 'Cool, that's awesome, do it,'" says Darby, but at the time she didn't know very much about what it all meant. Parker asked her whether she could deal with it, and Darby responded that she thought she could, though secretly she wondered what it all meant, and what it would mean for her budding lesbian identity.

A few weeks later, Kate began to go by Parker and started injecting testosterone. It was July 2014. He immediately felt better, calmer, more in control. He loved the effects of testosterone on his body: the facial hair, deeper voice, wider face, and his veinier, thicker muscles. When I ask him if he experienced more libido too, Parker smiles and is uncharacteristically silent. Darby quickly chimes in, "Yes, for sure!" Testosterone made him feel everything "in a much more visceral way," he says. "Finally I was doing something in the right direction instead of being pulled backward by a zip cord in the wrong direction." He also began to bind his chest, which he found really uncomfortable, but that September Parker posted a photo of himself online. "So many changes already! Looking great," a friend responds, referring to him as "dude."

The following month, Parker came out to his employer, a software start-up that services the real estate industry, and the HR department promptly issued a memo to its staff under the subject line "Employee Transition." It read:

> Effective today, Kate, who is in the process of a gender transition, will exhibit some personal changes while at work. Below we have provided information that will be necessary for the gender transition.
>
> Kate will now be referred to as Parker at all times. We are requesting that all employees, including managers/supervisors and co-workers, use the appropriate pronouns "he" and "him" when making reference to Parker during all verbal and written communications. We expect all employees to continue to treat Parker with respect as outlined in our policies by not misusing the employee's name, incorrect pronouns or referring to former gender assignment.
>
> Parker will be using the restroom(s) appropriate to and reflective of his full-time gender presentation. This will be applicable to all company's facilities.
>
> We encourage you to maintain an environment of respect, understanding and support while Parker undergoes this process, and beyond.
>
> It is not required that you believe in or accept transgendering. Rather, Parker and every other employee is required to be treated with respect and dignity at all times.
>
> Parker, Human Resources, Department Managers, and the

Leadership Team, thank you in advance for your support and assistance.

Parker is proud of his employer, whose commitment to him makes him want to sell more, achieve more. But it's even more than that: for him, his colleagues are like family.

In 2011, a Court of Appeals in Atlanta ruled that firing someone based on gender nonconformity violates the Constitution's prohibition of sex discrimination. Several federal agencies have also updated their employee antidiscrimination policies to include transgender workers, defining "gender identity" as part of a person's sex; seventeen states and Washington, D.C., explicitly include gender identity as a protected category.[5] Texas, where Parker lives, is not one of them. Today, many transgender people openly transition and remain in their jobs, thanks to changing cultural attitudes and workplace guidelines that protect transgender employees.[6] Still, Parker says his goal is to "go stealth" in most aspects of his life, including his work life. Even though his closest workmates know his history, customers and vendors see him as a guy, not a trans man. While he likes it that way, he admits, "If you're in a loving environment, there's no need to be stealth."

Outside of his workplace, transitioning has been more complicated for Parker. At the start of his transition, Darby tells me, "We'd be out and people would be like 'Hello, ladies.' That happens sometimes now, like at the airport coming here. The lady said, 'Ma'am or sir, I don't know what you are.'" Darby: "And I was like, bitch." But Parker "usually passes really well now," says Darby. Restrooms continue to be a problem, however. Some transgender men carry reusable "stand to pee" (STP) devices, oblong pieces of plastic, about six inches long, which are shaped into a kind of funnel, and permit one to use a urinal discreetly. (The devices were first developed to enable cisgender women to urinate standing up while camping, traveling, at festivals, during long car journeys, and while at any kind of outdoor pursuit where the toilet facilities are absent or less than desirable.) One device, called "pStyle," instructs users to place it "so that the widest part is between your legs, centered under your urethra, and pressed firmly upward. Tilt the open end slightly down, relax, and pee. Bend the knees a little and pull the pStyle slowly forward with firm upward pressure to remove the remaining drops."

But easier said than done. Parker says he has always struggled to get the plastic funnels to work properly. "Am I supposed to carry this thing around in my pocket or pants? Gross." One day, at a bar in Austin, he was pretty drunk, and instead of using the STP he decided to "just sort of back my ass up and hover over the urinal." And then, "three dudes who worked there" walked in and assumed he was a gay man who was "attempting to take a shit in the urinal." They picked him up and carried him down the stairs, called him a faggot, and threw him out of the bar. Parker laughs as he tells the story, but it was a painful wake-up call, a reminder that presenting oneself as a man in this society often means enduring male violence.

The story of twenty-one-year-old Brandon Teena, who was murdered in the early hours of New Year's Day in 1994, is burnished into the collective memory of transgender men. A recent large-scale survey of transgender people reported that nearly half had been verbally harassed in the past year because they were transgender. Nearly one in ten was physically attacked. Restrooms are particularly contentious places: 12 percent reported being physically harassed when accessing a restroom. More than half of all respondents said they avoided using a public restroom in the past year because they were afraid of possible confrontations.

(Transgender women are more likely than trans men to become victims of violent attacks since their larger bodies mean they are less likely to be able to pass as cisgender women. That's particularly true of low-income trans women, who have less access to body modifications.[7])

In order for others to see him for the (heterosexual) man he understands himself to be, and to avoid difficult situations, such as the bathroom problem, and even violence, Parker feels he must repudiate the femaleness written on his body. He wants others to recognize him as male, and he sees top surgery as an important step in that process. His breasts weren't large and didn't give him away, but they made him self-conscious and uncomfortable in his own skin and caused him to be less present in relation to others in his romantic relationships, and at work. Everywhere, really. He has modified his body as well as he can on his own, he works out religiously, and he knows he looks good. But his chest posed a much bigger problem than his lack of a penis and seemed to contradict who he felt he was. There was, he says, a gap between his internal image of himself and the way he imagined that others saw him. Over time, he has grown closer to how he wants to look, he says. Top surgery is an important step in that process.

When I ask him what he would like his life to be like in five years, he replies, with a hint of irony: "Maybe in five years just get hella white-collar with it, investment properties. Basically just be financially secure enough. In nine years have some kids. Yeah, I want to be a white American male property owner. Really, it's a dream." Darby thinks he'll be a great dad one day. He's "such a good teacher," she says. "He can explain things very well, and I think that is a good trait in a dad. To be able to explain something to your kids and be very knowledgeable. Parker's just the epitome of a dad. That's how I see him."

Parker tells me he can picture himself in the future as an old man—"not as a little old granny." Of course women's aging bodies, their sagging thighs and withered cleavage, are a source of derision, even hatred, while men are often seen as more distinguished, more powerful, as they age. Is Parker buying into the misogyny that is pervasive in our culture? On Facebook Parker reposted "Straight White Male: The Lowest Difficulty Setting There Is," which offers a partial answer to that question. The post, written by a self-described "white guy who likes women," is a humorous analysis of how male privilege operates.

> Dudes. Imagine life here in the US—or indeed, pretty much anywhere in the Western world—is a massive role playing game, like World of Warcraft except appallingly mundane, where most quests involve the acquisition of money, cell phones and donuts, although not always at the same time. Let's call it The Real World. You have installed The Real World on your computer and are about to start playing, but first you go to the settings tab to bind your keys, fiddle with your defaults, and choose the difficulty setting for the game. Got it?
>
> Okay: In the role playing game known as The Real World, "Straight White Male" is the lowest difficulty setting there is.
>
> This means that the default behaviors for almost all the non-player characters in the game are easier on you than they would be otherwise. The default barriers for completions of quests are lower. Your leveling-up thresholds come more quickly. You automatically gain entry to some parts of the map that others have to work for. The game is easier to play, automatically, and when you need help, by default it's easier to get.
>
> All things being equal, and even when they are not, if the

computer—or life—assigns you the "Straight White Male" difficulty setting, then brother, you've caught a break.[8]

By transitioning, is Parker trying to access male privilege and grab on to the "'straight white male' difficulty setting"? What happened to the dream of challenging the rules of the game, and leveling the playing field, rather than just trying to win? In the current context of "neoliberalism," a term social analysts use to describe our laissez-faire age, collective responsibility is often transferred to individuals, leading us each to try to maximize our own self-interest. But such explanations tell only part of Parker's story.

I ask Parker: "What's the worst thing about getting old and becoming a 'little old granny'?" He responds: "If I grow old as a woman, I will never be seen by a lover for who I am. When you're having sex, and you look in their eyes and know that they're seeing you for who you are." His voice cracks. "As a granny, no one would have seen me." When it comes down to it, Parker simply wants the same things we all do: to be seen and understood by others, and to be desired, and even loved, for being who we are. He spoke of the fear of having a life that was unlived. The quest for male privilege, and securing material and other comforts, plays a role in his decision to transition, to be sure. But it's much more than that. Transitioning will, he hopes, enable him to put all the pieces of the puzzle together, so that he can see himself as a "whole person," and others can see that person too.

Yet Parker is also very much a product of his time. Like others of his generation, he has come of age when reality television shows celebrate the makeover of the body, and where entrepreneurship is touted as the solution to economic inequality. Rather than speak of collective solutions, we are more likely to celebrate the possibility of choice and strive to become empowered individuals. Rather than see men as the problem, today's "postfeminist" generation says: if you can't beat 'em, join 'em. So if life is like a video game, and it's possible to change your default setting and make winning easier, then why hold back? Who wouldn't opt for an easier life? While his search for male privilege was not Parker's main reason for transitioning, it was a side benefit, and no one out there was offering him any better choices.

Parker may well become a great dad, secure in his white-collar dream one day, walking around in Bermuda shorts and in some retirement community in Southern California, but for now, his fantasies call up *Fight Club*'s bad-boy protagonist. "Tyler Durden is the man!" Parker says. "Fucking Brad Pitt. He's such a cool dude. He never gets riled up. He doesn't talk much. He's good-looking. He's got all the answers, but he just doesn't give a fuck. That's how I see myself."

———

The day after I spoke with Parker and Darby, I visited New Beginnings Retreat, an 8,900-square-foot pink Spanish-style stucco house that accommodates people while they recover from FTM transgender surgery in the Fort Lauderdale area. Six to eight guests stay there for a week at a time. Leland Koble, who runs the house with his wife, Bonnie, calls his guests "the guys." For $124 to $144 a night, you get a room with two beds and a bathroom, access to a shared kitchen, transportation to all doctor appointments, and an instant community. "Guys are entitled to recover in privacy among each other," says Koble, who established the guesthouse in 2011 in a gated community. It was the first of its kind, and it is still the only accommodation in the United States (and probably the world) that caters exclusively to transmasculine and gender-nonconforming clients.

A map of the world hanging on a wall in the living room is covered with pins that mark guests' places of origin. Most states in the nation are represented, with a denser concentration on the two coasts, and especially in the South, Europe, Canada, and Australia. China, Japan, and even Mauritius are pinned too. The day I visited, four guys were sitting on voluptuously padded recliners watching *Breaking Bad* on a huge flat-screen television with their legs elevated and drains attached to their chests. A copy of *GQ* with a cover photo of Katy Perry showing lots of cleavage was strewn on the coffee table, and their caregivers were busy preparing lunch in the nearby communal kitchen.

At New Beginnings, Leland and Bonnie talk about forging a "brotherhood" among young transgender men in transition. The guesthouse offers individuals undergoing top surgery practical help during the recovery week, but it also offers social support and an opportunity to bond with other budding men—and their largely female caretakers—during this formative period.

Sally and her partner, Pete, who are both in their mid-twenties, have come from Topeka, Kansas. They were in a lesbian relationship until Pete decided to transition a few years ago. Billy, from small-town Tennessee, is here with his fiancée, mother, and grandmother. He declined to be interviewed. His mother, who is about forty, tells me that some people in her church "object to changing one's sex." They believe that "God made them this way," she says. "But if you had children who were Siamese twins, wouldn't you try to correct it?" Tristan, a blond former navy lieutenant from St. Petersburg, Florida, is here with his mother, Theresa, who is in her late sixties. He has two tattoos on his shoulder blades: one that says MOMMA'S BABY and the other that says DADDY'S GIRL.

There's a couple from Calgary, in Canada: Len just finished

college, and Linda works as a drug treatment counselor. Both are twenty-three, from Chinese immigrant backgrounds, and have been best friends since they were ten years old, and romantically involved with each other for the past year. They have never heard of k.d. lang, the butch country crooner with a powerful, velvety voice, who hails from their neck of the woods. Len saved for a year to be able to afford surgery, placing loose change and spare bills from tips he made as a restaurant server in a box every week. They're both from large Asian families who have not been accepting of their choices, yet they're living at home, waiting for the day when they can afford to move in together. And there is Jackie, from London, who is here with his best friend, Christian, a gay man.

They're all seeing Dr. Garramone, who doesn't accept insurance, and they've been able to come up with the funds for masculinization surgery although they are by no means affluent. They work as insurance adjusters, restaurant servers, and technicians. For the most part, they live in the regions they grew up in and want to stay there if they can, because they're hooked into their families, if they're lucky enough to have families that accept them, or they simply have no place else to go. Everyone I met had gone to great lengths to save for surgery, with little or no help from their families. It's all worth it, they believe. They're out as transgender to those closest to them, and they are careful about whom they share that information with. Some have managed to successfully integrate their gender transition into their work lives. Others are not so fortunate. Pete and Len were forced to take time off and retool themselves. Although it is now more possible for transgender men (like Parker) to openly disclose their intention to transition and still keep their jobs, that is not true across the board. (Fifteen percent of transgender people surveyed in 2015 reported that they were unemployed, at least three times the national average. Perhaps it is unsurprising that the unemployment rate was highest among transgender people of color.)[9]

New Beginnings is, like many of the individuals who stay here, one local activist tells me, "stealth in plain sight." It doesn't advertise its presence in the community, but the fact that it is here, nestled in a gated community comprising upper-middle-class families, is a bold act. In the past, individuals would show up in San Francisco or Philadelphia for surgery and "crash on each other's couches" and care for one another, says Ben Singer, a longtime activist for transgender health. The relative luxuriousness of New Beginnings, and indeed its very existence, is a sign of the growing clout of the transmasculine population. Still, several years ago, Leland and Bonnie were run out of town by an unsympathetic neighbor. They were forced to move the guesthouse a few miles away, to their present location, which proved costly and unsettling.

For Leland, New Beginnings, which in its five years of existence has accommodated more than six hundred individuals, is a business as well as a calling. "If you're doing it for the right reasons, and your motivations are right, money and stuff come to you," he says. "I don't have to think, 'I have to make X amount of dollars this year to survive!' You know what I'm saying? It just rolls for me, and it has always been that way. I've always been fortunate." The guesthouse is run as a nonprofit corporation. Guest fees cover the bulk of its operating expenses, and donors make up the difference. In addition to the guesthouse, New Beginnings offers a chest binder exchange program; a "big brother support system," placing former patients in touch with one another; a physician and therapist referral network; and a safe house for transgender people in "desperate need of housing and a place to start over."

Leland, who is in his mid-fifties, is stocky, has short-cropped hair, and projects authority. A thick gold chain loops around his neck, and he is wearing square silver-rimmed glasses, a Lacoste shirt, and baggy blue jeans. As we talk, phones ring, deliveries pile up, and guests mingle in the kitchen. "A couple of guys need to be picked up at the mall," he tells Bonnie. "Okay, sir," she replies. When they first got together twelve years ago, Bonnie asked whether she could call him "sir," to which he replied: "I like that. It's got a nice ring to it," and she has called him that ever since.

The idea of establishing a guesthouse for those who are altering their female bodies occurred to Leland as he was sitting in a waiting room waiting to consult with a plastic surgeon to have his own breasts removed. Leland grew up as a girl in small-town Iowa, population 1,000, in the 1960s and '70s. "I was not like all the other girls," he says. "I identified as a boy. When I turned twelve, developed breasts, and got my period, I knew it wasn't me. I always felt more comfortable as a boy than a girl."

While he was waiting to speak with the surgeon, someone from Italy and "someone from England, or something like that" were in the waiting room talking about the challenges of arranging transportation and hotels during their surgery week, Leland remembers. Then one day, as he recovered at home, it came to him. "I think I have a great idea," he said to Bonnie. "I want to start a guesthouse for people transitioning." So he went out and found a house to rent—a mansion, really—put a business plan together, and it worked. "I've always been the kind of person that attracts people in the sense that I'm a competent person. I have an idea, I set my mind to it, I do it. That's it."

For all his good-natured bluster, however, when it comes to how he sees himself in the gender landscape, Leland is more equivocal. "I'm not really a woman. But I'm not trans either," he says. He doesn't take testosterone to masculinize his voice or face because his cardiologist recommended against it—the doctor said it would increase his chance of having a heart attack, so he says, "I'm staying in the middle. I have a woman's body from here to here," he says, pointing from his waist to his toes. "There, I'm my mother." But when it comes to his chest on up, he says, "I'm my dad." "I don't know if I identify as trans." If he were younger, he probably would, he tells me. Instead, he just wants to help those who feel similarly estranged from their bodies. "It's not an easy place. I'm not in an easy place. People say Shit or get off the pot. Go one way or the other, and I'd be much better. I'm in a very confusing place for everyone. No one gets it. They're like, 'What? Are you a boy or a girl?' But I just identify as me."

————

A few of the people who are staying here have biceps covered in elaborate tattoos, which rival those of the most dedicated cisgender male bodybuilder. There is something both deeply subversive and at the same time traditional about this place, which is hidden amid the palm trees, and which offers comfort to those who are transgressing society's gender rules.

Marriage seems to be very important to many of those who come here. When you enter the house, the first thing you see is Leland and Bonnie's framed marriage certificate, lovingly placed next to an autographed photograph of Michael Jackson and one of his gloves. A number of the guys I met here are trying very hard to be, well, guys.

Even though he is clearly experiencing discomfort, I overhear one pumped-up guy talk about the surgery he had the day before: "Piece of cake," he brags, "though I'm glad I don't have to do it again!" he adds with a smile. The day after his bandages came off, Tristan, who had 38C breasts, proudly shows off the deep red lines that shoot across his chest as though they are battle scars. All the muscle flexing and displays of testosterone-fueled hair growth one finds here at times is for a good cause, says Leland: it builds brotherly ties. Particularly during the early part of the transition process, some trans men try to emulate the appearance, manners, and habits of hypermasculine cisgender men in order to prove to others (and to themselves) that they're men too. They live in Bro-town.

Those who come here to embrace their inner maleness are lovingly cared for by their wives, girlfriends, and mothers. A mother from Orlando, Florida, writes in the guestbook: "This week is epic in my son's life. He says it's like a dream. I say it's a magical reality long awaited. NBR have provided the perfect retreat for this dream come true. As a mom, I never worried thanks to you. Moms worry even when there's no surgery involved. My son, his fiancée, and I feel renewed here. You have taken the fear out of recovery. What you are doing here is a blessing to us all." She signed her name with a peace sign and a heart.

When I ask Sally from Topeka what drew her and Pete here, she replies, "I'm just supporting my husband." Sally and Pete have been together "going on four years," she says. She considered herself a lesbian—when she was in college: "You had to take on a label," she says. She was never a "gold star lesbian," exclusively dating women. Now those labels matter even less, she says. Since she and Pete got together, they haven't really been part of a queer or trans community. "It has always been just the two of us doing our thing," she says.

Many of those who stay here say it's the first time they've encountered other transgender men. In one testimonial, a guest writes: "While at New Beginnings, I made lifelong friends with people who I'm happy to call my brothers, my fellows, as well as their partners and parents. I felt as though I finally belonged somewhere." Lex, visiting from Southern California, writes in the guestbook: "The opportunity you offer is such a great experience, especially for those who seem alone in this journey," who do not have a support system to help them through the transition process.

Sally, who works for mental health services for the state of Kansas, tells me she appreciates the "happy vibe" at the house. At home outside of Topeka, she says, "We don't fit in any part of the queer community really. And unless we become really verbal about what we are, who we are, where we come from and all of that, we won't fit into that." They would like to be out one day about their history and the fact that Pete is transgender, but they can't be. It would jeopardize their jobs.

Pete worked as a corrections officer before he went to college and became a customer service representative for a financial services company. In his spare time, he does powerlifting and Olympic lifting at a local gym, but he had to quit his job in order to transition. His health insurance didn't cover top surgery anyway, so they're paying out of pocket. "We've just kind of been squirreling money away," says Sally, and "couponing." And they sold their extra vehicle to help raise the cash. They're planning to have kids within a year or two, once they become more financially secure.

"Top surgery changes their lives for the better," Leland says of those who have stayed here. "They seem to be very productive, much happier. A few are even having children." He notes, however, that surgery is not a panacea. "A lot of guys are looking for something—they want to prove themselves; they want to make sure they're man enough—and that can lead to problems"—like bodies that are pumped to the extreme. Forging a sense of masculinity in a culture where men assert mastery over one another can be challenging. Men between the ages of sixteen and twenty-six must abide by a "guy code," says sociologist Michael Kimmel.[10]

Showing weakness is forbidden. Asserting their power and engaging in risk taking is expected—these are rules, he says, that are learned from male relatives or teachers. Peers play an important role too: they are the gender police who keep other guys in line.

The dominant, emotionally impoverished, bravado-filled version of masculinity masks a great deal of insecurity. Still, men can be cruel to one another, and they often direct their wrath against those who are shorter or younger—or both. These gender performances are "deadly ass serious," sociologist Sal Johnston, who underwent a transition when he was in his forties, tells me. Even though he's solidly in middle age, Johnston says he is still regularly "juniored," subjected to male one-upmanship, by guys who are actually younger than him, because he doesn't look his age, and because he "doesn't have an investment in walking into a room and trying to own it." He's not an alpha male. One of the startling realizations he had when he started passing as cisgender is that "adult males are jackasses to young men." They can also be asses to those they perceive as less manly.[11]

When he first started interacting with other men as a male, Johnston had to carefully consider how to negotiate those interactions. Although he gets kicked around a lot by men, he says, he refuses to be a "jackass to avoid it." For him, the experience of being an outsider within, a male-presenting person with a female history, offers a window into gender hierarchies that few others have access to, and he's going to make damn well sure he does his part to resist the worst excesses of masculine bravado. Still, he recognizes the privileges that accrue to maleness: people take him more seriously, and he's no longer subject to constant scrutiny for his gender nonconformity.

White trans men often speak about the ways that passing enables them to negotiate the public world with greater ease, but that's not necessarily true for transgender men of color. "I don't know that black males really have a whole lot of privilege," says Bishop S. F. Makalani-MaHee, an activist and ordained minister in South Florida, who visited New Beginnings one day when I was there. African American, he is dressed in a checked shirt and contrasting bow tie and a suit jacket, and he stands at barely five feet tall. Bishop transitioned about five years ago. He works at the Pride Center, where he does HIV education and risk reduction within communities of faith.

At a training for healthcare providers several years ago, he heard someone speak of "culturally assigned gender roles not fitting," and a lightbulb went off for him. *That's me.* He was never in a great deal of pain about his yearnings, he tells me. But he was just turning forty and thinking about his "second act." He decided that he wanted to live the rest of his life in more of a male body. "I wanted to dress like the men and smell like the men. I wanted to sound like the men and treat women in the chivalrous ways I saw men treat women," he says. He is married to a woman. "For myself, I like the binary. I like being the provider, protector, and being married to a nurturer. And I'm a feminist."

Bishop's demeanor is far from intimidating, but at a time of growing violence against black men, it doesn't seem to matter all that much. "When we talk about male privilege, you have to think about Trayvon Martin, who was shot and killed for no reason at all," he reminds me. "A couple of months ago, around here, Fort Lauderdale, there's a guy in a car accident, trying to get help. He's obviously hurt, bleeding, and he knocks on a door. He's unarmed. But the people call the police, and they shoot and kill him." The year before, police killed Michael Brown and Eric Garner, spawning the Black Lives Matter movement. "Those folk who have issues with race are even more unnerved now, because the last vestige of white male privilege seems to have fallen," says Bishop. "Folk are scared. Folk are uncomfortable." Choosing to become a black male isn't exactly a wise career move right now, he says.

Toi Scott, an activist and author, writes that after he began to identify as genderqueer and transmasculine, he "began to panic" and wonder: "Does this mean I am a black man? Should I choose to transition and present myself as male? Will I have to routinely see white women clutch their purses and turn up their noses, and white men feel threatened or disgusted by my very existence? I did not—do not—want to be a black man. But unfortunately, I do not have much choice in the matter."[12]

If white trans men often rise in status after transitioning, the opposite can be true for trans men of color, particularly African American men, who are more likely to report that they're followed by security when they walk into a store, or that people cross the street to avoid them.[13] "If it wasn't absolutely imperative," says Bishop, "who the hell would make this choice?"

———

Lucas DeMonte is a few inches over five feet tall, and has short dark hair and a scruffy beard. He thinks of his body as being non-binary, and also his gender identity. He identifies as a queer trans man, "somewhere masculine of center," rejecting the belief that the world is neatly divided into male and female. When we meet in the doctor's office, a tattoo of a phoenix rises from the upper part of his chest, poking out of his tank top, and he has a pierced septum. He is wearing dark square-rimmed glasses, shorts, and sandals. An HIV counselor who hopes one day to be a therapist, he apologizes a lot and smiles when he's speaking.

On Facebook, Lucas posts pictures of cuddly cats, appeals for aid for Syrian refugees, and condemns white privilege. He posts inspirational sayings like *My brokenness is a better bridge for people than my pretend wholeness ever was*, and poems of reassurance: *Be easy. Take your time. You are coming. Home. To yourself.* He has lots of devoted friends of every hue and orientation, and a close inner circle whom he considers family.

Among his closest friends is Oliver, a former boyfriend, who has an impressive beard and mustache. (Because Oliver has been on testosterone for a longer period, his facial hair is thicker than Lucas's.) Oliver accompanied Lucas to surgery, and both are wearing nearly identical glasses. A Facebook post pictures the two of them, side by side, accompanied by the hashtags: *#bestfriend #transmantagram #whenyoubothmorphintoeachother*. Like Parker, Lucas experienced an early sense of estrangement from his female body, childhood tomboyishness, conflicts with his parents about not being girly enough, and what he now considers his "lesbian phase." In a culture that equates maleness with having a penis, both assert their right to be recognized as male without possessing one. But that's where the similarities end. Parker strongly identifies as male. Lucas, who is around the same age, is more ambivalent.

Lucas grew up as Olivia in a large Italian Catholic family in rural South Florida. His father, who was the son of immigrant Italian parents and the first in his family to go to college, is a computer consultant. When Lucas was a small baby, his mother, who worked in the beauty industry, dressed him in frilly clothes, put big bows on his head, and tried her best to shoehorn him into her version of what it meant to be a woman: deferential and appearance conscious. Lucas says that his parents had "very specific expectations for me and my womanhood and also when I get married, have kids, what my life was going to look like. I was going to be this good Catholic woman."

In middle school, whenever Lucas asked his mother to allow him to shop for clothes in the boys' department, she told him, "This is for boys and you're not a boy. You're a girl so you're going to dress like this," and she would not let him choose his own clothes. In high school, he was not allowed to go out unless he dressed a certain way, especially at dances or big school functions, for which he was forced to wear makeup. His mother spent a great deal of time and energy focusing on her child's physical imperfections. "If you lost ten pounds, you would look really great," he recalls her telling him. If Lucas's eyebrows got too bushy, his mother would say, "Oh, you look like a guy. You need to trim those." She was as sweet as pie sometimes, and at other times, she was abusive toward Lucas, throwing him out of the house.

Lucas already learned to hate his developing body in part because of his mother's stream of invective. When he turned thirteen and got his period, the self-hatred intensified. "I felt like I wasn't supposed to bleed," he recalls. All girls and women, or very nearly all of them, learn to dislike their bodies, Lucas acknowledges. "We're told we have to hate our bodies and we're never going to be satisfied with our bodies." Was he made to hate his female body, and thus decided to reject it? Or was he never "really" female at all? Over time, he came to embrace the latter view, though he admits that the social pressures facing women indelibly shaped him too.

He began to resist gender norms through sports, jumping for a catch that no one else would jump for, and pushing his body so hard that he could feel no pain. Later, in high school, he wasn't comfortable changing during gym because he didn't want others to see his body. "I didn't feel that I was 'born in the wrong body,'" he tells me. "But I was definitely dysphoric. I just didn't know it." He has few memories of his early life, he tells me, because he "was not really there."

Looking for a place to belong, Lucas attended meetings of the Gay-Straight Alliance at high school. Bullying was rampant at the high school, yet the principal proclaimed: "We do not have a problem with LGBT bullying because there are no LGBT students at this school." Lucas started dating girls in secret. By this time, his parents had divorced, and he was moving around a lot. He lived with his mother, who brought home a succession of abusive boyfriends.

Eventually, Lucas left for college in Gainesville, where he became a women's studies and psychology major and was exposed to feminism and queer theory. He learned about "heteronormativity," the widespread belief that people fall into distinct and complementary genders (man and woman) with natural roles in life. We assume that heterosexuality is the only sexual orientation or only norm and that sexual relations are supposed to take place between people of opposite sexes. But this norm was "socially constructed" and therefore can be challenged. The term "queer" spoke to him as a way to resist heteronormativity. *I am queer. I am a feminist.* When he visited his parents and shared some of these new, exciting ideas with them, they mocked him, calling him "their little feminist."

After coming out as a lesbian a year and a half later, Lucas began to date Oliver, who had decided to transition and go on testosterone a few months earlier. They became active in the university's Pride Club (where they were known at the time as "the Olives"— Oliver and Olivia) and were held up as a model queer couple. They were a very popular pair around town and had a lot of close friends. At the time, most people thought of Lucas (then known as Olivia) as a gay woman; but when he tried to interact with lesbians in town, they seemed to hold him at a distance, he recalls. They were put off by "this hairy woman."

Lucas chopped off his long hair, hoping to become a member of the club, but he never seemed to be feminine enough in their eyes, and they never seemed to remember his name. He never felt like them, even the butches, because he wasn't a player: they slept with as many women as they could, but he liked to take it slow. Plus, he was too masculine (and hairy) to be a femme lesbian, but not enough of a "bro" to qualify for butch status.

Lucas was also attracted to "lots of different genders," at times identifying as bisexual and pansexual. "You're obviously not a lesbian," people told him. With time, he began to think that maybe they were right. A pivotal moment came during junior year, when a friend talked about transitioning. "I feel a certain way about my gender. I feel like a man. I don't really feel like I'm a woman, and I feel like I'm a trans man," said his friend. Lucas replied, "Me too."

And then one night, as they were lying in bed talking, Lucas told Oliver, whom he was dating, that he didn't like having his chest touched. "You remind me a lot of myself," Oliver replied.

Lucas responded: "Well, I don't know. I'm not really very sure about that. I don't know." That was all that he had to say about it then. They eventually broke up. Six months later, Lucas declared that he was genderqueer. He couldn't lie to himself anymore, he says. He began to see a therapist and talk with him about what it means to be transgender, and he changed his name to Lucas.

Lucas's parents reacted very badly to his announcement that he was going to transition, blaming boyfriend Oliver for giving him "the trans-like infection." They stopped speaking to their child. But "Oliver easily saved my life," says Lucas. Their relationship helped him come to terms with the signals his body was giving him and begin to identify as transgender. Now they're best friends.

Over the past year, his parents—really his father and extended family (he does not speak to his mother)—have begun to come around. They now call him by his new name and use the correct pronouns. His father still sometimes says things like: "Oh, man up, men don't cry," to which Lucas responds: "What are we, in the 1950s?"

Though Lucas identifies as a man, he distances himself from men like his father, whom he sees as emotionally shut-down, racist, and misogynistic. "They brag about sexual exploits in locker rooms," he says. But a lot of the trans men Lucas knows aren't much better, he tells me. "They believe that in order to be a man, they need to reject everything that's feminine." The buff dude who wants to be stealth and very male identified who is vying to be a men's magazine model, the transmale websites that glorify those who are "very white, straight, able-bodied"—they are not his model of masculinity. "That's not me. We don't all look like that," he says.

When he looks for images of those like himself in the culture, he has a hard time finding them. "A lot of people say that I'm not trans enough. I'm not man enough. They say I need to look a certain way to be a trans man. But I want to make my own kind of masculinity."

Transgender men are uniquely able to craft masculine selves that are much more complex and self-conscious. The experience of having once lived as a female offers insights into a "toxic masculinity" many try to avoid at all costs.

Lucas tells me he likes being both/and, retaining aspects of his femininity while embracing his maleness too. Even after his breasts are gone, he says, he will be bigender. He sees gender as a spectrum, made up of shades of gray. He claims he is not female—but he's not sure that he is male either. Choosing one gender is, as he sees it, a compromise. To be intelligible to others, we must appear to "have" a gender. "Coherent gender is a precondition of humanness," writes feminist theorist Judith Butler.[14] Still, Lucas can't help but feel a sense of loss for the part of himself that must be cast away in order for him to "become" a coherently gendered person, someone who is legible as male in social contexts. So as he prepares to have his chest masculinized this week, Lucas will mourn the loss of the female part of himself.

Months before his top surgery, at an open-mic night in Gainesville in a fluorescent-lit storefront, Lucas delivered a spoken-word piece addressed to Olivia, his pre-transition self. Wearing a T-shirt, a chest binder, and shorts, his hair cut very short, he sat on a wooden chair facing about a dozen people. "This is probably really intense, and emotional," he told the crowd. "I wrote this letter to myself before I was Lucas, so there are potentially going to be a lot of 'gender fuels' [triggers] and dysphoria for trans folks in the audience, I need to warn you: bear with me." He paused and began reading, his voice shaking at first:

Dear Olivia, you never made it to your 22nd birthday. I did. Thinking of you is both strange and familiar, as if we bumped into each other at a bus stop, exchanging friendly smiles.

He reads dramatically, and with a heartfelt passion, addressing his former self while gesticulating with his hands.

You were always so warm. I hope I have inherited that from you. I am startled when I look at the mirror, because the man staring back at me has your eyes, he has your smile, he has your cleft chin, the first thing the doctor saw when you were born, before you were announced to be a beautiful baby girl. Olivia, I have lost so many of your memories, and for that I am sorry. I often wonder what your life would look like 10, 20, 30 years from now. What would your laugh be like? Would you let someone hold you while you cry? Would you still be just as fearless? I have buried you alive six feet under. I gave your eulogy and no one could hear as I wept and placed a vase of tear-stained lilies on your grave. Olivia, I love. You terrified me. You held the hurt and the secrets, the aching. You are my guilt and sorrow. You are what could have been and wasn't. I feel like I have not done you justice, but I am indebted to you. You have given me life. You are part of my being. As I breathe, you breathe too. Our heartbeats are one an*d will always be. Thank you.*

If there are transgender men who are more than willing to renounce their former lives and pass as cisgender men, Lucas is clearly not one of them. Even as he takes on a more masculine embodiment, he refuses to renounce his past as Olivia, and he is intent to display the multiple layers of his personal history for others to see. He lives in a community and has a circle of friends who support his desire to live "in between." Other trans men choose to conform, or they feel that they must conform to the ideal of cool, unflappable strength, projecting masculine authority, developing bodies that mimic cisgender ideals—at least from the waist up. But even those, like Parker, who seem to embrace more conventional understandings of masculinity, do so fully aware that they're performing a role in an unequal system in which men are still on top.

SEVEN

Last Butch Standing

Attend me, hold me in your muscular flowering arms, protect me from throwing any part of myself away.
—Audre Lorde, *A Burst of Light,* 1988

Unlike Ben, Parker, and Lucas, Nadia isn't undergoing a gender transition. She's a gender bender who wants to modify her body and still be recognized as female. For a while, she considered simply getting a breast reduction. "Maybe smaller breasts would do the trick," she says she wondered. "Then I thought that if I'm going to go through a procedure like that, I don't want to still have to wear a binder. Why would I just settle on a breast reduction?" Scanning the Internet for the stories of others like her, Nadia found a couple of women who also decided to remove their breasts, but who didn't identify as trans.

Some butch lesbians have top surgery too; twenty-eight-year-old Nadia is one of them. From the start of their relationship, Nadia told her girlfriend, Flora, her breasts were off-limits, making it clear that she didn't want them to be a part of their intimate relationship, and that "she didn't get enjoyment from them," Flora tells me. Less than a year into their relationship, Nadia started binding—first using a sports bra, then two sports bras at a time, and then, for the past couple of years, a binder. The practice was painful.

When Nadia announced that she wanted to remove her breasts, Flora wondered whether it meant that Nadia wanted to become a man. Nadia assured her it didn't. The term "dysphoria" never really spoke to Nadia, and she didn't identify as transgender. She wasn't seeking to change her gender. "My breasts just don't reflect who I am," she said. A former girlfriend once asked her if her breasts were fake. "Nadia, you have great boobs," others told her. But "I didn't want great boobs," she says. "I didn't want those things at all."

When we met at Dr. Garramone's office, Nadia had short hair and was dressed in a T-shirt and jeans. Her cats' names are tattooed on her arms. She works as an employment coach for a nonprofit that helps low-income people who have been laid off retool themselves and get back into the job market. She helps assemble their résumés and manage the financial and emotional barriers that prevent them from getting permanent work. Nadia grew up in the South. Her mother is Mexican, and her father is Lebanese. She (like Ben, Lucas, and Parker) was raised Catholic. Although the family didn't go to church on a regular basis, "being Catholic didn't leave a lot of room for flexibility," says Nadia, especially around gender. Confirmation, communion, having to wear a dress and feminine shoes were a struggle for her.

Her immigrant parents don't know she is having top surgery— "It seems like too much to explain to them," Nadia says. "They wouldn't understand." They know she's a lesbian, and they're fond of her girlfriend, Flora, but Nadia hasn't told them she's having her breasts removed; she imagines they wouldn't really notice anyway: she's been binding them for years, and they haven't said anything. "They don't know very much about me," she says.

To Nadia, being a butch lesbian means looking masculine and having a "masculine demeanor." She says, "I don't feel that I present as a typical female." She doesn't smile that much, and she's not super expressive. People don't think of her as a huggy sort of person. In relationships, she says, "I'll be tender to people, but on a day-to-day basis I don't really show people that." Being a masculine female is not something she thinks about much—it's just intrinsic to who she is, she says. She feels like a bit of a throwback to an earlier era, a "dinosaur," she says. "Trans" doesn't really describe her experience. Nonetheless, the successes of the transgender movement have enabled her to address her estrangement from her breasts.

To undergo top surgery, Nadia needed a letter from a primary care physician, so she went to a queer health clinic and told them she was scheduled for top surgery with Dr. Garramone. They said "great, good, you'll be fine," and dispatched the generic letter they had on file for such occasions. When they asked which pronouns she wanted to use in the letter, she told them "she." But when she received the letter, she saw that the gender-neutral pronoun "they" was used. And that she was identified as having gender dysphoria. That wasn't an error: few health professionals will support the removal of a healthy body part unless doing so is intended to address a gender identity issue—the clinic was covering itself legally. While large-breasted women routinely undergo reductions, the idea of removing healthy breasts entirely is widely unpopular. "Breasts have been so sanctified in our culture," psychologist Katherine Rachlin tells me. "The assumption is that if you're born with them, you would want to keep them."

When Dr. Garramone asked Nadia why she wanted the surgery, she told him that she hates her breasts but identifies as a lesbian. "Are you sure this is what you want?" he queried. Later on, he mistakenly referred to her as "he." In this, as in many other aspects of her life, Nadia is an outlier. "She's an uncompromising individualist through and through and is troubling the very categories of gender," says Flora, her girlfriend. Transgender activists created a story about top surgery that sees it as a "productive movement toward a new gender identity, or a gender identity you've always felt but could not claim. What Nadia's doing is even more destabilizing than claiming a new identity," says Flora. "At first, I didn't really understand it, but now I think what she's doing is really cool."

Removing her breasts, Nadia hopes, will help her feel more comfortable in her body. Still, she worries that the ranks of those like herself are thinning to the point where she'll soon be the "last butch standing." Are transgender men essentially different from butch lesbians like Nadia, or are they simply making different choices with their lives? That question has a long history and few definitive answers.

———

An ashtray from the first known lesbian bar in the United States, established in San Francisco in 1933, reads MONA'S 440 CLUB: WHERE GIRLS WILL BE BOYS![1] The largely working-class world of lesbian bars offered masculine women and those who loved them a space in which to congregate, a place of refuge. They were factory workers, elevator operators, laborers who managed to find jobs that allowed them to dress as they pleased, or secretaries, nurses, teachers who counted the minutes until they could shed their office drag and change into pants after work. Within the lesbian world, "butches" became handsome swans, coveted for their masculinity and for their ability to please a woman. But it was not an easy life.

Leslie Feinberg's 1993 semiautobiographical novel, *Stone Butch Blues,* documented the world of "he-she's" who lived proud, precarious lives in the early 1960s—when they weren't being beaten up by police or being harassed in the street. But in those early pre-Stonewall days, before the rise of a visible movement for gay and lesbian rights, bars could be pretty dangerous places. Bars catering to homosexuals were regularly shut down, and patrons were arrested and subjected to public humiliation. Cities swept streets to rid beaches, parks, and neighborhoods of gay people, even outlawing the wearing of clothes of the opposite gender. Periodic police raids on bars meant that those who congregated there were likely to be swept up if they weren't careful, and they could end up in jail—or in a psychiatric institution.

Esther Newton remembers those days. A retired professor of anthropology who teaches part-time at the University of Michigan, she is a pioneer in the field of sexuality studies, having authored influential studies of drag queens, the gay resort of Cherry Grove, and a memoir about her life, which is titled *My Butch Career.* She is married to Holly Hughes, a diminutive performance artist who achieved notoriety as one of four artists whose National Endowment for the Arts grants social conservatives tried to revoke in 1990 in a case that eventually made its way to the Supreme Court. When I interview her in her Manhattan apartment, Newton, a distinguished-looking woman in her mid-seventies, recalls how embattled it felt to be a butch lesbian in the early 1960s. She was regularly "gawked at on the streets, made to feel like a pariah," and lived in fear of police harassment. "I started to feel more comfortable with myself," she says, when she had her first lover when she was in her early to mid-twenties, in the mid-1960s, a few years before the revolt at the Stonewall Inn in New York thrust gay rights into the public eye.

When feminism and the counterculture came around in the late 1960s and early '70s, things became much easier for Newton. Feminists declared that they would change society to accommodate diverse bodies and desires rather than the other way around, and that everyone could be "free to be . . . you and me," as the popular television special, narrated by actress Marlo Thomas, proclaimed. If the culture revered large breasts, hairless bodies, and pouty lips, feminists found beauty in naturalness, in the embrace of a femaleness unencumbered by oppressive body expectations. Dress codes relaxed, and many women cast off makeup and dresses in favor of a more androgynous style, blurring the distinctions between lesbians and heterosexual women. Masculine women like Newton began to feel more at home, more attractive.

"We were empowered by feminism to believe that we could create our own lives and possibilities," recounts the artist Kate Horsfield, who is a contemporary of Newton's. A critique of gender essentialism—the belief that women were equivalent to their bodies and were best suited to be wives and mothers, rather than doctors, lawyers, soccer players, or astronauts—was a central theme. Some, like author and philosopher Ti-Grace Atkinson, went even further, proclaiming in 1972: "Feminism is the theory; lesbianism is the practice."[2] Loving women, she declared, was the only choice for those who wished to live their feminist principles.

It was a period that blew open settled ideas about how Americans should live. All major social institutions came under question. Radical social movements emphasized the art of possibility. Much as one could become an artist by calling oneself one and creating art, one could be a lesbian by loving women and making them central in one's life. Lesbianism was not in fact fixed at birth or in early childhood. Like artistic talent, it wasn't something one did or didn't have. These were untapped potentials in all of us that we could choose to embrace if we wished. In the 1970s, young feminists came out in droves as lesbians, entering what was mainly a working-class subculture and expanding the lesbian world to include many formerly straight women. I was a beneficiary of their efforts—and of cheap rents.

When I landed in San Francisco in the early 1980s, I found a room in a shared apartment for $100 per month together with other young seekers who were influenced by feminism, gay liberation, and other movements for social justice. My well-worn copy of the *San Francisco Bay Area Women's Yellow Pages,* which cost fifty cents, offers a window into the spirit of the time. There are listings for woman-run and woman-owned services, businesses, and resources: realtors, health product reps, and the caveat that no listings or ads that "clearly promote sexist, racist, classist, or ageist attitudes are included."[3] If you were looking for battered women's shelters, a women-only hotel, rape hotlines, support groups for fat women, or sadomasochists, and even those in feminist group marriages ("We are heterosexual women who sleep with the same men, share income, promote world peace, and experience a higher level of trusting friendship than any of us has ever felt before"), you could find them along with female career counselors, dog groomers, attorneys, tax preparers, music teachers, and carpenters. There are ads for a women's ice hockey team ("no experience or equipment is necessary, and somebody usually has an extra hockey stick"), amazon kung fu, and the women's health collective where I got my first—and only—pregnancy test.

There are dozens of listings for feminist therapists. "I see women's problems as a mixture of social oppression and individual reaction," reads one entry, reflecting their general tenor. "I help women get in touch with their own power to effect desired changes in their lives." And on the heels of the therapy section are ads for body workers, holistic masseuses, midwives, childcare workers, and a haircutter-healer who promises to cut your hair in accordance with "your particular energy field." There is, too, a do-it-yourself ethos, and a distrust of experts: male doctors, male teachers, male shrinks. They will do you wrong, rob you, manipulate you, and make you unhealthy. A podiatrist advertises that she is "not interested in surgerizing [sic] you. Ninety-five percent of foot complaints can be alleviated without surgery."

There were moments of goofiness, to be sure, but there was also a dreamy sense of possibility, of the boundless energy of young women remaking the world. It was a world comprising women of all races, classes, and sexual preferences, who were dedicated to the radical proposition that women were better than men: kinder, less violent, more empathetic. By infusing the culture with feminist values, they—we—believed we were creating a world in which gender roles would be irrelevant.

We second-wave feminists tried to create a more forgiving culture, one that would accept all kinds of bodies, which would make the world safer for big women, disabled women, women of different races and ethnicities, women who love women, poor women, boyish women. But women who would be men were never part of this plan. If women were the superior sex, why would one ever want to be a man? While giving license to gender benders, feminists cast a skeptical eye toward those who were too "male identified," leading some masculine women who felt spurned by the lesbian feminist world to seek out other options.

In the mid-1970s, a few years before I landed in San Francisco, someone named Lou Sullivan had also arrived, in search of sex reassignment surgery at Stanford University. Because he openly identified as someone with homoerotic attractions, Sullivan was unsuccessful in convincing medical gatekeepers (who maintained that homosexual transgender people did not exist) that he was a good candidate for surgery. He nonetheless began to live full-time as a man and created a support network for other female-bodied people who strongly identified as male, calling themselves FTM. They didn't have their own bars or coffeehouses, so they met in people's living rooms, where they shared information about how to pass as men and survive in the world, and how to access testosterone and chest surgery outside of university-based gender dysphoria clinics. Today's transmale subculture can trace its lineage, more or less, to that moment, and to Sullivan's efforts.[4]

Still, the question remains: are butches and trans men fundamentally different groups of people? On this there is little consensus. Early transsexual narratives distinguished between transsexual men and butch lesbians, arguing that homosexuals who cross-dressed (or butch lesbians, in current parlance) and transsexuals were different categories of persons. A butch might be able to hide out in a dress when forced to do so, and she could masquerade as a feminine woman in order to survive. For a woman who knew herself to be a man, on the other hand, no such option existed: they needed a body to fit their mind. Dr. Harry Benjamin, who is often credited with coining the term "transsexuality," agreed, more or less, and saw it as different from homosexuality or transvestism— phenomena with which it was often confused, in his opinion.[5]

The belief that gay/lesbian and transgender people are essentially two separate populations is especially strong among medical professionals. When I asked Dr. Paul Weiss, a New York surgeon who has worked with transgender people for the past twenty years, how he sees the relationship between the two, he tells me: "They're completely different." Transgender people, he says, "are attracted to the same sex, but are the opposite sex in their brain." He and the other surgeons I spoke with tended to assert that there are clear, enduring, and natural boundaries that separate homosexual and transgender people, and males and females.

Trans people sometimes agree with this view, at times to gain access to the medical interventions that will make them more comfortable in their bodies and less vulnerable to violence in a society that enforces gender distinctions. Even trans activists who are critical of the medical model frequently embrace the view that gender nonconformity and homosexuality are conceptually separate phenomena. Being transgender is "not about who you want to go to bed *with,* it's who you want to go to bed *as,*" writes trans author Jennifer Finney Boylan.[6] In other words, while transgender people may have some interests in common with gays and lesbians, they are defined by their gender rather than by their sexual orientation.

Ben, Parker, and Lucas each called themselves gay, at least for a while, before they came to identify as transgender. Like many if not most (white, middle-class) transgender men who are today in their twenties (or older), many identified as butch lesbians at an earlier point in their lives, before they discovered the transgender world and came to identify with it. (People of color and sometimes working-class and poor whites are somewhat more likely to identify as "studs" or "aggressives.") Today Ben, Parker, and Lucas say that the label "lesbian" never really fit them; it was at best a temporary stopover on the way to claiming their authentic trans selves— and acknowledging the fact that it is gender, not sexuality, that is so salient for them. As Ben told me, "Gender and sexual identity couldn't be further from one another. It's like one is an apple tree and one is an orange tree, but they just happen to be in the same garden."

But at least one study, by sociologist Henry Rubin, shows in painstaking detail how individuals, once they come to identify as transgender men, distance themselves from their lesbian pasts. Rubin interviewed twenty-two transgender men in Boston and

San Francisco in the early 1990s, who ranged in age between twenty-three and forty-nine, and who were part of the first significant wave of transgender men who transitioned. He asked them how they identified, what changing sex meant to them, and why they chose to transition. A majority of those he interviewed said that they once identified as butch lesbians, but they told him they were never really lesbians at all, in retrospect.[7]

Today, we tend to distinguish between transgender men and butch lesbians. But in the late nineteenth century and early twentieth century, homosexuality was synonymous with "sexual inversion." As articulated by sexologist Richard von Krafft-Ebing, the concept referred to the reversal of gender traits: male inverts were, to a greater or lesser degree, inclined to traditionally female pursuits and dress and female inverts to traditionally male pursuits. Popularizing this concept, Radclyffe Hall's 1928 novel *The Well of Loneliness* told the story of Stephen Gordon, a mannish woman. "I can't feel that I am a woman. All my life I've never felt like a woman. . . . I don't know what I am; no one's ever told me that I am different and I know that I am different."[8] Was Gordon (who, by all accounts, was a representation of author Hall) a masculine lesbian or a transgender male? It's impossible to know. The technology of transitioning was only beginning to be developed then, but the language that accounted for it, and the culture that enabled it, was not available then.[9]

Humans like to classify, to decide what ought to go together and what ought to be separated. We draw conceptual distinctions between things we perceive as different (such as the Danish and Norwegian languages) and group together things we consider similar (such as grapefruit juice and orange juice). These cognitive distinctions are always somewhat arbitrary.[10] Experts such as psychologists, medical doctors, and even activists carve up reality in different ways. But it is difficult, if not impossible, to prove the existence of "real" differences between trans men and butch lesbians, and there is certainly a great deal of overlap between the two populations.

When I spoke with Henry Rubin, the sociologist, in a Boston hotel coffee shop, he told me that he received a lot of push back from trans men after his book *Self-Made Men,* a study of transsexual men, came out in 2003. Some were uncomfortable with Rubin's claim that the boundary between lesbians and transgender men is malleable and not at all clear and enduring. Trans men are men, and lesbians are not, they charged. "People experience anxiety about things they do not entirely understand," he tells me. "They feel better and are more grounded if they have a clear identity." Trans people, unlike presidential candidates, don't go around talking about building walls to separate populations, but they do engage in what sociologists call "identity work," emphasizing the things they have in common with other trans people, and also what sets them apart from others. *I am gay, not transgender. I am transgender, not gay.* "Society puts some limits on the infinite ways people make sense of their lives," says Rubin. It provides categories (male, female, woman, man, transsexual, homosexual, intersexual). But these categories can never fully do justice to the complexity of our lives.

In the 1950s, when Esther Newton was growing up, "there wasn't the sense that sexual orientation and gender are totally different. It was kind of all one thing," she tells me. As a tomboy who liked boys' sports and was attracted to girls, Newton often sees her younger self in the trans men she meets today. Like them, she says, she was happier with her body before puberty. She hated getting her period, and she never particularly liked her breasts. "Most butch lesbians experience dysphoria," she tells me. She is not convinced that butches and trans men are essentially different from each other.

"It's hard being a lesbian, but being a butch lesbian means you're a flashing red banner to the world at large. Either you're read as a man, which leads to problems using the bathroom, or you're just read as a lesbian who's out 24/7. It takes a toll and affects your life chances." People stare at you on the street, and they don't take you as seriously at work. It's still a daily struggle for Newton, even at age seventy-four. In addition to being "sirred" and thrown out of women's restrooms, she has strangers tell her to "smile more," she says. " 'Come on, smile.' Masculine women are still treated as other. Some people just get tired of it."

———

In the 1990s, the crunchy-granola college town of Eugene, Oregon, was a pretty easy place to flout gender norms. Blue jeans, hiking boots, and Gore-Tex was (and still is, as far as I can tell) the unisex uniform. There were a couple of gay bars, a women's bookstore, a tolerance for freethinkers and tree huggers. And with a population of about 120,000, Eugene was big enough that you could find others like yourself, but spread out enough that you could hide if you really wanted to. Alex Grayson went to graduate school at the university there, and I was one of his professors. When we first met, he had fled working-class Michigan in search of a different kind of life. He was a butch lesbian in a relationship with Julia, a fiery East Coast Jew who dubbed him Alex. The name stuck.

From an early age, Alex had what he calls a "secret boy life." With his guy friends, he had a guy name that the grown-ups didn't know about. When he was eleven or twelve, "things started getting weird," and he could no longer be one of the boys. He knew he was attracted to girls. After several years of being isolated, he eventually found the lesbian world, which offered a place of belonging. Alex was able to live fairly comfortably as a butch woman, except that he often felt judged by others for his appearance. He had very short cropped blond hair and wore men's button-down shirts. When he walked into a room at the university or into a gay bar, he always felt that he was pushed to the edge, that he didn't really belong, and that he was "bumping into something, and somewhere he shouldn't be." His self-presentation was always more masculine than that of most of the others around him. Sometimes he seemed like a butch lesbian, but other times he seemed more like a man. "I never felt right. I always felt pushed to the margins," he says.

At the time, feminists tried to soften gender binaries, promoting an androgyny they hoped would submerge gender distinctions. The butch lesbian, having a marked lesbian body, enjoyed privileged status as the "authentic" lesbian—as long as she was recognizably female. Gender expression was tamped down. It was okay to be butch—but being too butch veered into maleness, which was verboten. Alex says he always worried about being "too male." Although he found girlfriends in the lesbian community, and it was "a social space that made for a livable life," he never felt that he fully fit into the lesbian scene. "But at the time it was the only social category out there that seemed to describe who I was," he says.

After finishing his doctoral degree, Alex moved to Los Angeles to take a teaching position. Shiny L.A., which mirrored the celebrity-obsessed culture that surrounded it, was a challenging place to live as a masculine woman, particularly during the rise of the "lipstick lesbian." "No butches or fatties" read the typical lesbian personal ad. One evening, Alex and his best friend, Kristin, also a butch woman, went to a "lesbian-only night" at a gay bar in West Hollywood, and the bouncer asked them: "Do you know what night this is?" He didn't admit them until they handed him their IDs, proving they were female. Once inside, they realized that they were the only butches there; the bar was filled with glammed-up dykes. Work shirts and combat boots were no longer the uniform of the Lesbian Nation. Femmes were taking over the scene in some cities, including L.A.

Alex's unapologetic masculinity often isolated him and made him feel like a freak. In a warm climate where people wore fewer clothes, it was harder for him to hide his gender variance, or to bind his breasts without feeling uncomfortable, and he was regularly kicked out of public restrooms. "My ability to pee organized my daily life choices," he told me. The constant need to figure out how to present himself in public drained him, and he was always frustrated with himself. "I didn't want to stay in that socially murky space of neither male nor female. I constantly felt as though I'm the problem. It's exhausting to feel wrong all the time. It's corrosive."

He also worried about being victimized by violence if someone didn't like how he looked. "I think that because I mostly passed as a young boy/teenager, or possibly as gay, I felt particularly at risk. I felt like a very easy physical target for groups of younger men," he says. He looked much younger than his age, so dating proved to be difficult. "At forty or forty-two it is a problem to look like a fifteen-year-old boy. It was un-sexy to be on a date with a forty-year-old woman and have the server assume you're her son." He was exhausted by "the amount of work entailed in managing [his] body"—staying out of certain places, trying not to take up too much space in others. "Gotta fix it, gotta manage it. It's corrosive to feel wrong all the time."

Alex and I lost touch over the years, but about ten years ago I heard through the grapevine that he had transitioned and begun to present himself as male, so when I began to research this book I contacted him to see if he would speak to me, and he agreed.

When we meet on Skype, he has a modified crew cut, is wearing a plaid button-down shirt, and looks a lot like he did years ago, though with a thicker neck and deeper voice, a light beard and the beginning of male pattern balding. If you saw him on the street, you would never know he was once considered female—which was also true of just about every other female-assigned person who had undergone a gender transition whom I interviewed for this book. If they wanted to, they could pass pretty seamlessly as men— that is, they could be "stealth" in public, presenting themselves as cisgender men if they so desired.

Alex tells me he had long been aware of the existence of trans- sexuals, and he had even contemplated transitioning earlier in his life. He had known a couple of people over the years who had tran- sitioned, but he had no idea of how to go about doing so, and he lacked the money and the wherewithal.

In the early 1990s, "the conversation changed," he says, making it possible for him to contemplate transitioning. He heard about support groups for transgender men. FTM groups were form- ing in San Francisco and Seattle. A burgeoning "queer" move- ment was challenging the dominance of radical feminist ideas and was offering female-assigned individuals who wished to embrace their inner maleness a way to do so affirmatively, with a sense of pride. Writers and activists like Sandy Stone and Kate Bornstein were talking about a different, more expansive understanding of the radical potential of gender switching, rejecting medicalized notions of trans people as having the "wrong body," or as being mentally deficient. The term "transgender" was established as a way to move beyond the medical model of "transsexualism" and to include a broad array of gender-variant persons who wished to challenge the binary. It enabled Alex to call himself transgender.

"I did not want to have to say I was 'crazy.' I don't even like saying

I'm dysphoric, though I fit the narrative," says Alex. "I didn't start T until I found a very good doctor who didn't demand a letter from a therapist. I wouldn't confess dysphoria in order to get access to top surgery. I won't do it. Why would I want to make myself even more marginal?" However, once there was a "weakening of pathology, of judgment," he decided to move forward.

Meanwhile, Kristin, Alex's closest friend, settled in Seattle after graduation, where she found an accepting culture and a lively butch presence in the lesbian community. She worked for a state representative, and when she visited the state capitol to lobby on his behalf, people sometimes perceived her "as a boy." But mainly she felt okay about looking different, and she fell in love with a woman, Jennie, who affirmed her right to be who she was. Kristin is pretty flat chested and small hipped, and "looks like she wants to," more or less. She presented as a masculine female. It helped that her family tended to be supportive. "Even though I don't really operate as a woman, I operate in the sphere of women, and there were a lot of really strong women in my big Polish family!" Also her dad, now deceased, was queer, and her brother (who appears in this book) is a transgender man.

Because Kristin, unlike Alex, received a lot of support for her gender nonconformity, she said it never became a major source of distress for her—which isn't to say that it hasn't been a challenge at times. She contemplated transitioning for a while but eventually made peace with her body. Being in therapy helped. "I thought that my anxiety was special and everyone else was normal," she tells me. But as she found ways to ease her generalized sense of anxiety, she became more comfortable with her body and her gender nonconformity. "I thought, 'Why do I care so much about what other people think about my gender?' I have a right. I have a fucking right to be who I am," she tells me, her voice cracking.

And as she became more comfortable with herself, she found ways to deal with bathroom confrontations. "Now when people come up to me and tell me I'm in the wrong bathroom, sometimes I look my body up and down and look at them quizzically and say, 'Oh, really?' Thanks!" She makes light of it. "The more comfortable I am, the more likely they are to think I'm in the right place and leave me alone. Now it's even funny at times." But airports, she says, are still particularly challenging. Heightened security seems to extend to the policing of gendered bodies in bathrooms.[11] The other day, a blond woman in her fifties came over to her as she entered a bathroom stall and started yelling, "You're in the wrong place—the men's room is over there." Kristin just smiled and said, "Thank you," and the woman left in a hurry.

"I get why some people transition," says Kristin, "to be normal, and not have people gawking at you all day. It takes a whole lot of energy." Still, she came to the conclusion that transitioning would not solve her problems, and that it might open up new, unknown challenges. Alex, on the other hand, made the decision to modify his body and present as a male, and it has made his life much easier. He no longer gets harassed walking down the street, and he's no longer as angry. "I still look young," he tells me, "but at least the beard and receding hairline prove I'm through puberty!"

He is much happier now, he says. "I honestly don't feel I've changed that much. That is, 'transitioning' didn't change me so much as it forced others to see me as I saw myself. Yes, the bodily transformations were welcome and comforting. I felt that I was finally 'home.' But how do you separate that feeling from the sense that you're finally recognized by others for how you see yourself?"

For her part, Kristin sees herself as someone who "embodies something different, who is on the edges of womanhood." She loathes it when she's in a group of women and they are addressed collectively as "ladies." "I hate that," she says. "But I do like embodying the space I'm in and being okay with it, and showing other people that you can be a woman who looks like a guy, and, guess what, you can be okay! You can be healthy and not crazy!" One day, Kristin and her girlfriend, Jennie, devised different gender identities for all of their friends. Jennie became "riot grrl," after the Northwest feminist punk subculture of the same name. Kristin is "gay boy nerd." Their friend Christine, who identifies as male but who is not modifying his body, is "nerd nerd." Kristin says she wants to see all of those differences. "I'm not interested in erasing them. The differences are what makes things interesting."

As Alex and Kristin's stories suggest, decisions to transition or not are very personal ones, and they are also shaped by the contexts in which people live. What categories are circulating in the culture? What are the personal and political consequences of affiliating with one category over another? How can we move through the world relatively unimpeded, without attracting undue attention and the threat of harassment or violence? Will our parents disown us? Will we lose our jobs?

Gender and sexual identities—as cis, trans, gay, straight, and an ever lengthening list of others—don't simply emerge from within. While they are shaped by a host of factors over which we have little control, we make choices about how best to live our lives, and these choices have a great deal to do with historical and situational factors. WPATH acknowledges this too. "Even if epidemiologic studies established that a similar proportion of transsexual, transgender, or gender-nonconforming people existed all over the world," it says, "it is likely that cultural differences from one country to another would alter both the behavioral expressions of different gender identities and the extent to which gender dysphoria is actually occurring in a population."[12]

Arlene Lev runs a clinical practice in Albany, New York, and teaches at the State University of New York campus there, training people to work with lesbian, gay, bisexual, and transgender clients. She is the author of a 2004 study called *Transgender Emergence,* which was the first book to suggest that being trans is an identity, not a diagnosis, and to advise therapists to understand their trans clients within the context of their families, as children, partners, and parents. Lev tells me a story that illustrates her perspective. Recently, she traveled by plane from New York to California, hunched between two large men. Lev is very short—four foot nine—and describes herself as a "fat woman." At one point during the flight, she placed a suitcase on the floor of the plane so that her legs wouldn't go numb. It pressed her legs together and made her feel "fatter and uglier by the second." But when she stepped off the plane in San Francisco, "all these people are looking at me, just smiling and checking me out," she recalls. "All of a sudden I was cute again, attractive even. It was a fascinating moment."

"I noticed how much my self-esteem and sense of self was interactional. How comfortable I feel in my body is also a reflection of how I am seen by others." For her, the experience was a metaphor for the challenges facing gender-variant people, including the decision of whether or not to transition. Transgender people are unique individuals, who are embedded in different social contexts—families, communities, workplaces, and also history— and must be understood in relation to those contexts. "It's never just a question of who I am," says Lev, "but also a question of how do I fit into the times that I am living in."

———

When I lived in San Francisco in the 1980s and early '90s, there were half a dozen lesbian bars. Amelia's, on Valencia Street in the

Mission District, was one of them. It was my neighborhood bar. There I could find a rainbow mix of Sapphic sisters on any night of the week. LaBelle's "Lady Marmalade" seemed to play on an endless loop. During those days, every major city and most college towns had at least one lesbian bar, and some places, like New York, Chicago, and San Francisco, had a handful or more. But today such bars, which were once among the very few places women who loved women could dance, flirt, and socialize publicly, are fast disappearing—driven out by gentrification, the mainstreaming of gay and lesbian culture, and the uncoupling of lesbianism and feminism.

Rents in San Francisco and other major cities have skyrocketed, pushing young dreamers out. If you're looking to find others like yourself, you no longer consult a typewritten booklet lovingly produced by a volunteer collective of feminists; you can look on the Internet, where you will find countless versions of different ways to live. Women can legally marry each other, and men can openly make their lives with other men, too, but the androgynous anything-goes style of the 1970s has given way to a renewed body consciousness. Taking personal responsibility for one's health, one's body, and one's career advancement is the new normal—a practical strategy at a time when nearly half of the U.S. workforce is now made up of contingent workers who enjoy little job security.

The last of San Francisco's lesbian bars, the Lexington Club, closed recently, and in Manhattan only two hang on. Younger women and trans men are more likely to identify as "queer" and less likely to seek out women-only spaces. It's easier these days to live openly as a lesbian in much of the United States—especially if one is white, affluent, and gender conforming (think of comedian and talk show host Ellen DeGeneres). For many people, claiming a homosexual identity is not nearly as risky as it once was. After all, you don't have to worry about being arrested for visiting a gay bar or wearing men's clothes. People meet each other online. Some observers say we are entering a "post-gay" era, when being queer is less likely to determine major life choices, such as where one lives or what kind of work one does—or even whether one's family is accepting. "We should no longer define ourselves solely in terms of our sexuality, even if our opponents do," says former *Out* magazine editor James Collard. "Post-gay isn't 'un-gay.' It's about taking a critical look at gay life and no longer thinking solely in terms of struggle. It's about going to a gay bar and wishing there were girls there to talk to."[13] In a post-gay world, lesbian bars are no longer necessary because being gay or lesbian is no longer a very big deal. Of course the reality is much more complex. Although social attitudes toward homosexuality have certainly become much more liberal over the past few decades, sexuality continues to define many individuals' lives.

As yet as I researched this book, many millennials told me that they didn't like the word "lesbian" and couldn't identify with it. They saw the project gay women of my generation worked so hard to achieve—affirming the L-word and the women-who-love-women it described—as largely passé. Today women still sleep with other women; they simply are less likely to claim an identity on that basis. Sometimes they call themselves queer. While only 1.3 percent of women actually identify as lesbian, according to the U.S. Department of Health and Human Services' *National Health Statistics Reports,* 17.4 percent have had same-sex sexual contact.[14] The shifts in language and identity were largely generational.

If millennials I spoke with were less likely to identify as lesbians, baby boomer lesbians continued to strongly identify with the category. As the most visibly identifiable lesbians, butch baby boomers who came of age during the heyday of feminism, the 1970s and

'80s, were particularly vocal about naming their existence publicly. Identifying as a lesbian, writes cartoonist A. K. Summers, "marks me squarely in my middle age and as invested in a sexual culture which is less common than it used to be."[15] Esther Newton is even more adamant: "Lesbians are never in style no matter what. Never in style. It's never easy to be a butch, especially." Butches still exist, of course. Some call themselves "studs," or "aggressives," particularly if they're from African American or Latina backgrounds. Others embrace terms like "boi." But the decline of the lesbian bar means that these subcultures are somewhat less visible.

While I was researching this book, femme lesbians often expressed fears to me that their pool of potential dating partners is rapidly diminishing. An academic friend of mine, a stylish woman in her forties who never leaves the house without lipstick, said that if she and her partner, a proudly butch woman about her age who knows how to build furniture and is a fierce baker, ever broke up, she might have to go back to men. And, in fact, while researching this book, I had to admit that I, too, found myself unnerved at times by the sight of handsome women transforming themselves into dudes with stubby beards, thick necks, and deep voices, people who were passing out of the zone of my own attractions. Of course, I realize that it's not about me—it's about them. Still, at times it's hard not to feel a sense of loss.

When we met, Angie Terry, a metalworker who lives on a farm in southern Arizona, inhabited a liminal zone between genders. Angie went by the pronoun "they." In appearance, thirty-two-year-old Angie resembled any number of boyish women I've known throughout the years. But unlike them, Angie didn't identify as a lesbian and described being estranged from their body, particularly their breasts. "My breasts feel like a deformity on my body," Angie tells me. "I feel like there's a big disconnect between my brain and my body." Angie feels somewhere between male and female—closer to male, they said. They get "very upset in social situations, when I'm 'ma'am-ed' or 'lady-ed.'" Sometimes when dealing with people at stores Angie tells people to refer to them as doctor or another gender-neutral pronoun. In relationships, they are always "the husband, boyfriend. Never the girlfriend or wife."

After having top surgery, Angie wanted to keep their given name but live as a male, for all intents and purposes, and go by the pronoun "they"—to remind people of the limitations of gender binaries. "I have a lot of anger and distrust of men, and I have a lot of empathy and sweetness toward women," Angie tells me, expressing ambivalence about transitioning to maleness. "I like the idea of having a female name, and looking gender-neutral or genderqueer." Angie has no plans to take testosterone. The goal is to stay in between. One of Angie's role models is Zackary Drucker, an actor and trans woman who retains her male name. "I really like the idea of confounding the idea of gender," Angie says. "Now, I'm not confounding gender at all. In my head I am, but not socially."

A few months later, Angie became Carson. Their voice was still female sounding, and their face was smooth, but they had given up living in between genders, and were planning to go on hormones. "I'm more comfortable being seen as male than female. In a perfect world, I'd like people to refer to me as 'they,' but at this point that's asking too much of people. The mass public just constantly reverts to seeing me as female. That's what they see, so that's what they do. They're not really paying attention."

As appealing as it may have been to try to live in between, especially as someone who identifies as a feminist, and a gender bender, it was too difficult to pull it off in a world that continues to divide people into male and female. So, even as Carson would prefer to live in between, as neither male nor female, our culture makes that very difficult. Since he is more drawn to masculinity, Carson has chosen to embrace his maleness and undergo a transition. In a more perfect world, gender wouldn't matter. But in this world, he'd rather be recognized as male than as female. For Carson, and for many others I met, seemingly personal choices such as these have profound political implications.

Baby boomer feminists tend to share that conviction. But having come of age in a "woman power" era, they are more likely to feel ambivalent toward masculinity, and toward a younger generation of individuals who were assigned female at birth, who seem to gladly embrace maleness. "Everybody now wants to be a man, or be with a man," laments a fifty-eight-year-old feminist writer and critic who did not wish to be identified. Others are even less forgiving. A sixty-three-year-old retired schoolteacher in New York secretly wonders whether transgender people are dupes of the medical establishment, and whether it's all a "big science experiment." And Esther Newton tells me, "It just pisses me off that trans is what catches [younger people's] imagination now. That's where the energy is. From a lesbian perspective, that annoys me."

Some (but certainly not all) feminists of this cohort imagine that the rise of the transgender movement is part of a broader backlash against the gains of feminism—along with the assault on reproductive rights, the sexualization of teenage girls' bodies in the media, and other less-than-desirable developments. While some refer to such attitudes, and those who hold them, as TERFs (trans exclusionary radical feminists), they remind me of the laments I heard in the late 1980s about the growing numbers of lesbians who were "going straight," leaving the lesbian world in search of "heterosexual privilege." They signal a sense of loss rooted in a nostalgia for one's youth, fears of demographic decline, and the real challenge of creating a different kind of life when the community that supported it is no longer. Lesbian subcultures still exist, of course. These days, Brooklyn is a haven, of sorts, for women-loving-women. So are college towns like Ann Arbor, Northampton, and Ithaca. But transgender is the hot new thing—which means that younger people are as likely to question their gender today as their sexuality.

"It's a generational divide. I can understand that," says Macauley DeVun, a forty-two-year-old activist and artist who lives in Brooklyn. DeVun masculinized his chest but never went on testosterone. DeVun identified as a butch lesbian prior to the rise of transgender, but now as "gender-nonconforming, queer, trans." Any of the above. DeVun doesn't identify fully as "male or female" and "uses all pronouns and enforces none." His four-year-old son calls him Daddy. They're gender non-binary and bi-gender, but not adamant about any of it. DeVun believes that many transgender men are actually quite ambivalent about maleness and would choose to be gender-nonconforming if they could.

When we spoke at a café in Greenwich Village, DeVun told me that he sees himself as a member of a "bridge generation." Having come of age during an era when lesbian feminism had more clout, he was also influenced by the rise of transgender, so DeVun understands some of the misgivings older lesbians feel about the decline of butch space, and knows older lesbians who have tattooed teardrops on their bodies to signify that loss, the fear that the butches would be no longer. "But the times they are a-changing," says DeVun.

For DeVun, being transgender is a means of survival, of being true to oneself and affirming a deep sense of gendered self. At a time when more and more gay and lesbian people seek out respectability, identifying as transgender also has the capacity to challenge many of our taken-for-granted ideas about the relationship between bodies and identities, and the differences between the sexes. It doesn't mean being transgender is easy. Studies show that trans folks confront violence, family abandonment, job insecurity, and levels of precariousness that far exceed those in the general population.[16] And yet that hasn't stopped Ben, Lucas, Parker, and thousands of others. Only a few decades ago, being a transgender man was practically unimaginable. That's no longer the case.

Would some butch lesbians of the feminist generation who are now in their fifties, sixties, and seventies have chosen to transition, too, if the technology—and cultural approval for using it—had been available when they were younger? Esther Newton says she would have willingly gotten rid of her breasts if it were an option, though she probably would not have transitioned. "I certainly spent a lot of time, especially as a child, wishing I'd been born a boy. But feminism profoundly affected my life," Newton says; it made her "feel very differently about being a woman." Feminism gave her the strength to beat back social disapproval and proudly assert her femaleness, even if she never felt all that womanly. She, too, wonders if lesbian identity is disappearing.

"If I were growing up now, I might consider myself trans too," says my friend Kate. She grew up in the Texas Panhandle during the 1950s and gravitated toward feminism in the 1970s like many of her peers. She adds ruefully: "I'm glad I didn't have that option."

———

Nadia has absorbed those fears, and she wonders whether her friends will see her top surgery as an act of betrayal. Before they left for Florida, Nadia implored her girlfriend, Flora, not to tell lesbian friends of theirs that she's "getting rid of [her] boobs," joking that she'd "be out of the club." Flora says she feared losing access to her lover's body. Never having undergone surgery before, she was afraid of the unknown. "Will it really solve her problems?" she wondered. Why put yourself through that? And why go to a doctor who specializes in transmale top surgery if you're not trans yourself?

Nadia has stayed in touch with some of the lesbian-identified people she met online who told her they were having top surgery. A few have since "decided to go on T and now identify as male," she says. It led Nadia to question her own motivations: "Will I begin to identify as trans? Is removing my breasts some sort of internalized misogyny? Am I betraying the lesbian community?" The fact that transitioning is now an option for women who identify as male means that Nadia must consider how she wishes to identify herself. Flora reassured her: "Having tissue removed from your body is not going to make you a man."

Several months after she had undergone top surgery, Nadia still sees herself as a woman—albeit a woman without boobs. She has a new job and a new girlfriend—someone she used to work with at the employment counseling nonprofit, who worked with her in her union. Her involvement in the union has energized her in new ways, renewing her commitment to social justice organizing. When we speak, she seems happier and more at ease with her life. Top surgery hasn't changed her life radically, though it has helped her intimate relationships, she says, and has made her less self-conscious about her body. She goes to the beach or to the Y locker room topless now and no one bats their eyes. "I now look how I'm supposed to look," she says.

Recently, when she was at a union conference in Las Vegas, Nadia spotted another person at the hotel pool who also had the familiar scars of someone who had had top surgery, who was also there with a girlfriend. Though they didn't say anything to each other, they looked at each other and shared a glint of recognition.

Her story suggests that after being estranged from one another, younger butches and trans men are finding one another and making common cause, welcoming gender-crossers into the Lesbian Nation. In an effort to blur the boundaries between butch lesbians and transgender men, some have suggested the label "transbutch."[17] When I ask Nadia whether that label is meaningful to her, she seems unconvinced. "It seems too 'second wave,'" she says.

Nadia sees herself as part of feminism's "third wave," which is more aware of queer issues and racial diversity, and which refuses to "put people in categories." Unlike her second-wave feminist foremothers, who, in their enthusiasm for remaking the world, seemed at times pretty prescriptive, she'd prefer to "let them decide for themselves how they identify," she says. So for now, she's calling herself "butch and queer." Or "whatever."

EIGHT

Waiting for the Big Reveal

Borders are set up to define the places that are safe and unsafe, to distinguish us from them. A border is a dividing line, a narrow strip along a steep edge. A borderland is a vague and undetermined place created by the emotional residue of an unnatural boundary. It is in a constant state of transition. The prohibited and forbidden are its inhabitants.

—Gloria Anzaldúa, *Borderlands/La Frontera*, 1987

After surgery, Ben stays with his parents at a timeshare at Disney Vacation Club, where, surrounded by Donald, Mickey, and others, Gail tends to Ben's wounds, conscientiously cleaning out the bulbs on either side of his chest that collect blood and tissue after surgery. Every four or five hours, she unpins the drains from the surgical wrap, pinching the tube connecting them to Ben's body, and carefully pours the blood and other fluids that had collected into a measuring vessel, diligently recording the amount of fluid.

Lying on his back, Ben takes deep breaths every few hours to expand his lungs. He cannot raise his arms overhead or extend his arms. On meds to ease the pain, he is loopy for most of the week, while the Shepherds watch bad TV, text, and talk with friends and family in Maine. Ben drinks plenty of fluids. He also takes a daily arnica supplement to help reduce swelling and speed healing.

Ben posts a picture of himself on Facebook, two drains poking out of his bandaged chest. A friend replies: "Now you see 'em, now you don't!" Another writes: "Sooo metal!" And a third shares the fact that her mother, who had lung surgery, also went home with drains, telling him: "Ick. Heal fast." The next few days are a jumble of naps, drains, pain meds, the occasional bit of food, and nausea.

"Feeling a little better every day!" reports Ben six days after surgery. "Tomorrow the drains come out and I get to take off this painful wrap and see my chest for the first time! Super stoked! Then we start the long drive home." Friends and family offer him encouragement. "Ben, actually we hit the jackpot with having you and all your endless bundle of energy and kindness!" says Bob. "You do make each and every day an adventure." They are a family who communicate with one another through Facebook—even, on occasion, when they're sitting across the table from one another. "Appointment for the big reveal in 30 minutes!!!!" Ben announces at breakfast at the Waffle House with his parents. He can't wait to see his new chest. Bob and Gail are nervously anticipating Ben's bodily transformation and eager to return home. "Ready for Ben's unwrapping," posts Bob.

Meanwhile, Darby cares for Parker at an apartment in Fort Lauderdale, Oliver nurses Lucas during his recovery week at the nearby house of a friend, and Nadia and Flora are staying at New Beginnings, the cavernous guesthouse that accommodates individuals having top surgery, in a gated community a short drive away from the surgeon's office. They all have appointments at the doctor's office the same day.

As efficient as the surgeon's office is, there is always waiting, and more waiting. Sitting nearby to Ben and his family are Lucas and his good friend (and former lover) Oliver, who underwent top surgery with Dr. Garramone last year. They strike up a conversation with Ben, while Bob and Gail Shepherd have little choice but to listen in. Lucas and Oliver talk about the limited ways people tend to view gender transitions (as a medical fix) when there is much more going on beneath the surface of these body modifications. The process is complicated and emotionally demanding.

"A lot of people say, 'I'm going to get rid of my boobs and that's it,'" says Lucas, "but they don't really sit and think and reflect." There's an emphasis on "you get the surgery, you're a man. Done. That's it." A health educator, Lucas says that whenever he does presentations on transgender matters, people always ask him: "Did you get x, y, or z surgery?" "They ask about my body and want to know what's between my legs," he says. "But they don't want to know about my life." Transitioning is about more than simply physical changes, he says, because "there is all that stuff underneath it too." In other words, medically transitioning is neither the beginning, nor the end, of one's story.

Lucas has "huge problems with the idea of passing," he says. He has encountered many trans men who either are not out or don't identify as trans. "They are like, 'I am a cis man.'" On at least one Facebook group, Lucas tells me, trans men post photos and pose the question: "Do I pass today—yes or no?" and people weigh in, advising them about how to better conform to mainstream notions of what men look like—such as which hairstyles are least revealing, what stand-to-pee devices work the best, and so forth. The claim that "I'm a trans man but, oh, I'm straight is just not our experience," he says. He resents the fact that many trans men successfully pass as cisgender. It makes educating people more challenging and leads naïve people to say things like: "Wow, I would have no idea that you were trans." He's critical, too, of sexism wherever and whenever he encounters it.

"Some trans men say terrible things about women," Lucas says. They embrace a "toxic masculinity" that rejects all that is feminine—including their own feminine pasts. "I'm like, 'That make no sense,'" says Lucas. "Hey, if that's your journey, I'm not going to say that's wrong, but that is not my experience. That is not my journey." Lucas admires Laverne Cox and Janet Mock, who represent an out and proud trans sensibility. "I look up to them very much so and they do amazing work," he says. But where are the transmale spokespersons, he wonders? There's Chaz Bono, but Lucas says that Chaz doesn't speak for him. Nor does muscle-bound Aydian Dowling. "I mean, it's great to finally see a trans man out there," Lucas says, "but he's very into himself and his image. The only reason he is accepted is because he looks like a cis man. I'm very out and very proud of who I am and love who I am. But we're not all just beautiful butterflies."

In the liberal college town of Gainesville, when he encounters people who don't know him and who assume he's a cisgender man, Lucas makes a point of coming out to them. Sometimes it happens in the context of a transphobic comment, or a joke about women using men's bathrooms—and he quickly intervenes, informing the person: "You're talking to one." He's out at work, to the extent that he can be—his co-workers all know he has a "female body history," as he calls it—but when he traverses rural Florida doing HIV testing at clubs, bars, tattoo shops, and community centers, he's stealth. In one small Florida town where Lucas works sometimes, there's a gay bar where the drag queens say "really transphobic things all the time," he says. There's no stall door on the men's toilet, so he never pees there, he says, fearing someone will walk in on him. "I have to keep that under wraps because I feel like it gets me in a lot of trouble." It can be "really, really lonely being a queer trans man when you have to navigate the professional and the personal, very weird," he says.

As queer trans men Lucas and Oliver are willing to do what they need to do to gain access to medical technology to modify their bodies so that they align with their masculine identities. They embrace the concept of gender dysphoria ("my sexed body causes me distress") when they need to get access to medical modifications. While sharing some of the anguish of their transsexual predecessors—the trauma of growing up in a culture that denies their realness, and the struggle against family rejection—they claim the right to modify their body. But they refuse to identify fully as either men or women. Rather than go stealth, they are unwilling to tell a story that isn't true to their experiences.

Accordingly, they're skeptical about all the emphasis on the now-you-see-it "reveal," the "money shot" of home-made gender transition videos. In these videos, which are a staple on YouTube, trans men offer visual records of their own surgery and advice for those who are shopping around for a new, masculine chest. "On a lot of trans videos you find on YouTube, people just talk about their physical appearances changing," says Lucas. "But they don't talk about the male privilege that comes with being a trans man. They don't talk about your emotional state. They don't talk about anything. They just go, 'Oh, I look different. I no longer have breasts. Or I have a beard now.'"

Rather than imagine his trajectory in terms of neat resolutions that culminate in a "cure," Lucas speaks of ambivalence, of being both/and, of living on the borderland of gender. That's not a particularly easy space to occupy. He has been learning to love his body and himself, he says, but "it has been a very bumpy road, for sure. It's very, very complicated, very gray and complicated, and there are a lot of questions we don't have answers to."

College-educated millennials are schooled in the belief that gender is a performance rather than an essential, unchanging aspect of the self. They are cognizant, too, of the limits of thinking in binary terms about gender. That doesn't necessarily mean they shun surgery or hormones, as Oliver's and Lucas's stories suggest. The availability of these critical theories enables them to imbue their body modifications with a different set of meanings. They see themselves making empowered choices to alter their bodies and unsettle notions of gender as fixed and immutable.

―――――

In the early 1950s, George Jorgensen traveled to Denmark and returned as Christine, becoming an instant celebrity. "Ex-GI Becomes Blonde Beauty" roared the front page of the *New York Daily News*. *Voila!* It was a twist on the classic American theme of the penniless striver who invents a miracle elixir and makes a mint, the beautiful bride who marries a millionaire to escape her immigrant roots. We are never truly stuck with the hand we are dealt, the story tells us. We can reinvent ourselves.

Even as Christine Jorgensen publicized the possibility of transitioning, early medical protocols for gender transitioning required patients to live as heterosexuals after transition, and to obscure their bodily histories. It was a strategy that was well suited to mid-twentieth-century America. Writing of that period, the sociologist Erving Goffman describes how those who possess potentially "discreditable" characteristics, such as being deaf, or homosexual, or even having a history of divorce, were forced to manage their identities in order to minimize stigma. Those who could "pass," such as light-skinned African Americans, Anglo-looking Jews, or

gender-conforming homosexuals, were bound to present themselves as members of the dominant group of "normals" lest they
be shunned. That female-assigned individuals who were gender-
variant might try to pass as men as a way of eluding stigma, or
gaining some of the privileges of men, never entered his analysis.
Nonetheless, he offered a powerful indictment of social inequality, and how stigma forces individuals to conceal their identities in
order to survive in society.[1]

Doctors who devised the first protocols for gender transitions
during this period assumed that successful gender transitions
meant people would shed their old life, like animals who molt,
and operate in the world as their chosen gender. They were told
they must break off connections with most of those who knew
them prior to their gender transition and become largely invisible as transgender people. Entering into a viable marriage with a
member of the "opposite" sex was considered the test of a successful transition. "To be assessed good, the total life situation had to
be successful as well as the sex life," wrote Harry Benjamin, who
assumed that the potential for social ostracism doomed those who
would dare to be openly transsexual.[2]

For an earlier generation, who came of age before Internet transition videos, *Orange Is the New Black, Transparent,* and antidiscrimination laws, going stealth was the only option. It's still true for
many transgender people. A closed Facebook group for trans men
in South Florida, for example, has about two hundred members—
those who are willing to be out, online at least. But according to
local activists, they're a small fraction of the total number of trans
men in the region. Many live wholly stealth existences in suburban
communities with wives and kids and do not publicly identify as
trans, even online. (As of this writing, only eighteen states and the

District of Columbia clearly prohibit discrimination against transgender people.)[3]

Still, my interviews suggest that few younger trans men imagine that they will go "stealth," or pass at all times. In contrast to an earlier generation, younger transgender people are less likely to see secrecy as desirable or necessary. They are more likely to see passing as cisgender as a situational strategy rather than a permanent solution. To be safe in the daily activities most of us take for granted, like using public restrooms, or going swimming, or even walking comfortably down the street, they must present as cisgender. And they must be acutely alert to the different contexts they travel through. If you're living in a conservative part of the country, are at risk of losing your job if you disclose, or are subject to violence if you don't pass well enough, you have no choice but to go stealth. But even for those who are stealth, accusations of deception are an ever-present risk.

Trans women, particularly low-income trans women of color, tend to have less access to the technologies they need to pass effectively as their chosen gender. But even if they do undergo surgery and receive hormones, it's more difficult for them to pass as cisgender women. Their bodies are bigger. Estrogen is not all that effective in changing the pitch of one's voice. Transsexual women are also much more visible in popular culture and are therefore more recognizable in public. At some point in their lives, many trans women engage in sex work in order to make ends meet, and are therefore more vulnerable to violence. Transgender women of color are therefore more likely to be the victims of hate crimes than any other group of Americans.[4]

Depending upon who you are, and where you live, stepping out of dominant conceptions of gender can be dangerous. It often takes a considerable amount of privilege to openly flout binary gender categories without fear of violence. Lucas and Oliver, in different ways, embody that privilege, and they are acutely aware of having it. They are white, college educated, and live in a fairly liberal place, Gainesville, Florida. They have access to enough money to modify their bodies as they wish. They have jobs that enable them to be out as trans men, more or less. They are casting off the old label "transsexual" and all that it symbolizes, rejecting the scripts that required individuals, once they medically transitioned, to hide the fact that they are trans—now commonly described as going "stealth." Lucas and Oliver are able to openly question our cultural emphasis upon spectacular body transformations, and they admit that even after their female breasts are gone, they still retain aspects of their female selves. They carry in their bodies and their minds the legacies of feminism, the gay and lesbian movement, and the queer revolt.

In the late 1960s, a brash, vocal gay and lesbian movement transformed same-sex desires from the "love that dare not speak its name" (as Lord Alfred Douglas, Oscar Wilde's lover, described homosexuality in an 1894 poem) into the love that would not shut up. Radical gay activists made coming out—declaring one's sexuality boldly and publicly—a central political strategy. They reclaimed the eccentric cousin who never married and lived with his "friend," and the spinster aunt who was once doomed to a secret life, and they forced them out of the closet. If everyone who had ever harbored same-sex desires or who had engaged in homosexual relationships came out, they argued, homophobia would no longer persist. In many respects, that strategy worked: today, there are fewer and fewer families for whom homosexuality is completely unknown, and marriage equality is now enshrined in federal law. The majority of gays and lesbians are much better integrated into mainstream American life than they were even twenty or thirty years ago; their sexuality is less likely to define their choices, where they can live, what kind of job they can have, whether they can have children, and so forth.

Is being gay or lesbian becoming more like being Italian American or being Jewish American—a status with particular customs, rites, and rituals rather than a category that carries the weight of stigma or the promise of transgression? As gays and lesbians have inched toward legitimacy, becoming the boys and girls next door, they're entering what anthropologist Gayle Rubin once called the "charmed circle" of sexual respectability.[5] It helps if one is white, middle-class, and gender conforming. In exchange for greater acceptance, many gay and lesbian people choose to define themselves largely in the terms set by the dominant culture—closer to the heteronormative ideal of monogamous coupledom.

While the mainstream gay and lesbian movement, for the past four decades, demanded the same rights as everyone else, including the right to marry, its anti-accommodationist wing, calling itself "queer," emerged, celebrating the misfits. In the early twentieth century, "queer" was a derogatory term for those who refused to abide by gender norms, especially effeminate men; the word came to be associated with homosexuality, and with mental instability. In the 1970s, some radical activists reclaimed the word as a kind of "reverse affirmation" of that which was despised by the dominant culture, and during the following decade radical "queer" theorists introduced new ways of thinking and theorizing about sex and gender.

Drawing upon the queer practices of drag, cross-dressing, and butch-femme, philosopher Judith Butler developed a conception of gender as performance, and of gender parodies as subversive acts. Literary critic Michael Warner coined the term "heteronormativity" in 1991 to describe the dominant cultural belief that heterosexuality is the only normal and natural expression of sexuality, and "the institutions, structures of understanding, and practical orientations that make it possible"—such as legal marriage.[6] A system of heterosexual privilege extends power to those who live in the monogamous couple form and subjects those who remain single by choice or necessity, or who construct alternative forms of intimacy, to stigma. While hard-nosed activists fought for inclusion—in the institution of marriage especially—queer theorists instead emphasized the primacy of language and the power of the imagination.

Queer theory is a revolt against norms that decree how we should live our gender and sexuality. It suggests that things aren't as simple as masculinity and femininity, gay or straight. Speaking of such binary ways of dividing up the world, Judith Butler asked "whether these norms produce distress and discomfort, whether they impede one's ability to function, or whether they generate sources of suffering for some people or many people."[7] Thanks in part to the influence of the queer revolt, the landscape of gender and sexuality looks different today. More and more people attend college today than ever before, and if they take courses in gender, sexuality, literature, or history, they're likely to be exposed to these ideas. Twenty-five-year-old Oliver Klicker is among them.

———

We meet in the outpatient clinic the day of Lucas's and Ben's surgery. Oliver is here accompanying his good friend and former lover Lucas. Oliver hears that I teach at a university and immediately engages me in a discussion of my research. He is eager to tell his story. A spirited talker and an eloquent one, he tells me that he underwent top surgery two years earlier at Garramone's office, and has been presenting as a male more or less since then. Oliver is an artist based in Gainesville. In the waiting room, he tells me about some of his work: two linked videos titled "What Makes a Man," which examine the notion of gender as performance.

In one video, Oliver, with an impressive beard and dressed in a black suit and tie, slowly undresses. The other video begins with him nude and captures him dressing himself. Installed in a gallery and positioned next to each other, the two videos "suture a transgender temporality while confronting viewers' own biases about manhood," says the artist. In this simple gesture, he says, "I ask the audience to consider what actually makes a man, beyond assumptions about his body or appearance." Oliver's willingness to reveal his naked body, including his female genitals and his hairy, masculine chest, challenges viewers to confront their discomfort with nonnormative bodies. His general approach, reads the artist statement, "embraces the possibility and reality of existing as both and neither." The art explores the spaces in between, and the difficulties of assuming one gender when you feel rooted, emotionally and physically, in more than one.

"When I started transitioning," Oliver tells me, "I thought I wanted to do everything I needed to do—hormones, surgery—to align my body visually with how I saw myself." And in many respects, he has done that: "I have facial hair, my body fat redistributed. I'm much more masculine looking in general." And still, he says, "Whenever I have to check one of those boxes, male or female, I don't know necessarily that I fit in either of them." He sees himself as in between. Yet he feels much better about his body now, and about himself (as data suggest, the incidence of regret among transgender individuals who've medically transitioned is very low). After Oliver underwent top surgery, he and Lucas cried together, mourning the lost breasts and all they represented. ("I've had these all my life. Just because I don't want them doesn't mean I'm not going to grieve them," Lucas tells me.) Even as they saw it as a triumph that symbolized their capacity to take control over their lives, they were also grieving for society's inability to tolerate the in-between.

Oliver grew up a tomboy in a small Florida town where everybody knew everybody, and where belonging meant being a good Christian. While his parents were somewhat more liberal than others around them, it was important to them that their only daughter conform to expectations of how girls should look and act. Appearances were particularly important to his mother, who loved fashion and was a devotee of *Vogue* and other style magazines. One of Oliver's earliest memories is when he was really young, and everyone kept telling him that he was such a great mother to the family cat. He remembers thinking that he didn't want to be a cat mother; he wanted to be a cat father. By the time he got to middle school, his mother wanted to know "Why aren't you wearing makeup?" Kids began to bully him.

At some point, he and his mother negotiated that if he had his ears pierced, he could cut his hair short; "otherwise I would look like this little boy." His parents (his stepfather is a doctor) even sent him to etiquette school once a month for six years, which was designed to socialize local girls into the ways of Southern female gentility. Oliver recalls the "ball gowns, white gloves, dance card, the whole shebang." Such rituals of upper-middle-class respectability had fallen out of fashion in most of the country, but you could still find them in small-town Florida. If boys asked you to dance, says Oliver, "You couldn't say no."

Oliver felt out of place in the world of his parents and his town, and at odds with the rules of behavior that were demanded of young women. He sought refuge in the small lesbian subculture at his high school, but it never felt quite right. "I started realizing that I didn't identify as a woman, one of the cornerstones of that community," he told me. "I wanted to have really hairy legs and be recognized as a man. But people perceived me as a woman." When he looked in the mirror, "I didn't see what I wanted to see," he recalls. "I wasn't seeing myself with facial hair." At home alone, he flattened his chest in front of the mirror. "I wanted to see what it would look like." He experienced a lot of social anxiety and contemplated killing himself, he tells me.

During his junior year of high school, he stumbled on some YouTube videos made by trans men and began to follow some of them covertly while he was still living at home. That was where he first learned about chest binding and top surgery, although he wasn't exactly sure what it all meant at the time. He told his friends he thought he might be on the "trans spectrum" and recalls, "I wasn't quite sure if I super identified that way, but I knew that it felt more correct than being a young lesbian or a young straight woman." He wondered: "What do these words mean and do they fit who I am?"

A few years later, while studying at the University of Florida, he found a therapist who could help him to explore his gender issues, and he convinced his parents to let him see her. He was nineteen. He didn't know whether he wanted any medical interventions at the time, and he battled with his mother about it. But the therapist affirmed his understanding of himself as trans. "There wasn't any negotiation. She was like 'Okay if this is who you think you are, what are you doing right now?' She began to refer to me as Oliver." In retrospect he describes her as "more of a cheerleader therapist than an actual therapist who was working through these things with me." She responded to his interest in exploring gender issues by saying, "You are obviously transgender, which is great." She told him at their first session: "You're not here because there is something wrong with you. You're here because the world doesn't understand you, and I'm here to help you deal with that."

While she was very supportive, and that was tremendously important to him, the therapist, he says, was "not super helpful in figuring things out," he tells me. Oliver felt that calling himself male was the best way to describe how he felt, and he says that at the time "I couldn't live authentically and feel good about myself as a woman." He was having trouble relating sexually to people because others saw him as a woman, which is not quite how he saw himself. He had his doubts, but he felt that he couldn't tell his therapist "because I didn't think she was going to write my letters if I expressed them," and he admits that she may have pushed him to transition more quickly than he may have done if left to his own devices.

He couldn't tell his parents either, fearing, he says, that they would "invalidate this new identity and this new footing. They were very black-and-white. It's like you either know or you don't know." They told him, "If you don't know, then let's put a stop to all these things. Why would you want to be in-between in the world?" While they had become comfortable with his lesbianism, they considered his being a masculine woman, or a butch lesbian for that matter, to be more problematic. But why, they wondered, would one want to undergo invasive medical procedures and transition to maleness? He had his own worries and doubts. Was he "really" a man? Why else would one transition?

He began taking testosterone supplements in May 2012 and had top surgery that August. "I don't know how I did it, because I wasn't super sure. I wasn't sure of anything," Oliver says. But once the train had left the station, there was no going back. He changed his name that summer, too, with his mother's help. Within three months, it was all done: the surgery, the hormones, the name change. "It was a huge emotional shock. I wasn't sure it was right after I had done it."

He made a video of himself injecting testosterone and posted it online. He was scared of needles, and it was not easy for him to inject himself, but doing so online was important, he says. "If I had an audience, I knew I could do it. Otherwise, I wouldn't have been able to get through it." Performing the injection for others made him publicly accountable to them—a bit like getting married in public, surrounded by one's family and friends. "Wow, you're so afraid of needles that if you were willing to do this, this is obviously important," his parents said. "I was trying to get their approval," Oliver says. But he was so nervous at the time that he almost passed out while giving himself the hormone injection.

It's not that he has regrets or wishes to turn the clock back. He is much happier in his masculinized body, which he feels aligns, more or less, with how he sees himself. In fact, he believes that transitioning saved his life, and that he may have committed suicide had he not had access to surgery and hormones. (According to at least one survey more than 40 percent of transgender Americans have attempted suicide, compared with 5 percent of the general population.)[8] "I feel very lucky that I am still alive," he tells me. Like other trans people, he's searching for authenticity and the feeling that his body reflects himself, more or less. He's disappointed by the fact that he rarely sees non-binary identified people, like Lucas or himself, who question the gender binary, reflected in the trans male community.

When they were at the University of Florida, Oliver and Lucas were exposed to queer theories. Now, empowered by those ideas, they refuse to see being transgender as an individual problem, a pathology that deserves (or could be resolved by) a simple medical fix. Such thinking sustains existing gender norms and encourages people to conform to them, they believe. Instead, Oliver and Lucas call into question the ways we divide the world up into binary gender categories and force people to fit into them. Rather than see medical fixes as a solution, they ask whether there is a problem with the gender norms we feel that we must abide by.

"It's not easy yet," says sociologist Sal Johnston, who is in his fifties, and the longer people wait to transition, the more damage is done, he believes. "But what I think is interesting and hopeful about talking to young guys is that they're clear about who they are and what they want, and much less interested in accommodating others and pleasing them," he tells me. "And that's pretty radical. It really is."

———

Sitting in a doctor's office provides a stark reminder that it's much easier to live in between in one's art than in one's life. In order to gain access to the medical technology they feel they need in order to live their lives, people who are transitioning find that compromises are often necessary. As members of a younger generation of politicized trans men, Oliver and Lucas refuse rigid binary conceptions of gender, embracing uncertainty, indeterminacy. Yet they feel that they must submit themselves to a medical and psychiatric apparatus that forces them to choose one of those boxes, so they present themselves as men. It's not simply a matter of medical expediency; they don't want to be subjected to violence. Just about every transgender person has known someone who has been assaulted. While trans women are particularly at risk, trans men often fear that other men may react violently if they are judged as effeminate or not masculine enough.[9]

Ben's ambivalence about maleness is less focused on the fear of male violence. "I hate the word 'male' because it feels so 'sciencey,'" he says. "But calling myself a man is weird too." He describes himself as "a dude" because "it implies youthfulness," he says. Ben is less embedded in radical queer culture than are Oliver and Lucas, and more hooked into his family than just about anyone else I met in Florida who was undergoing top surgery.

In the waiting room this morning, Ben is uncharacteristically quiet. The fact that his parents are within earshot doesn't help, especially when the conversation soon moves on to the subject of dating, and the challenges transgender people confront in looking for love on apps like Tinder or Grindr.

Dating apps invite one to swipe left on a picture if you're not interested in the person and right if you are, and after each rightward swipe, one is presented with a profile. Within a person's profile, one can view additional photos, their Instagram, and more information to help evaluate whether the person in question is a "true" match. This is how people hook up. Twenty-somethings today, especially queer millennials, are more likely to find each other online than in bars—which poses unique challenges for those "dating while transgender."

Trans people must figure out how to identify themselves online: how open should they be about their trans status in their profiles? Should they stealth date, coming out to people only once they get to know them? Or should they clearly identify themselves as transgender in their profiles? Making a choice not to disclose right away can lead to awkward, if not dangerous, encounters, including what some call "trans panic"—some people freak out at the thought that they might be attracted to a trans person. It is especially likely in the South, says Oliver, and can lead to violence. That's why many trans men specify their history explicitly: "It weeds out the bigotry and intolerance," he tells me. "If somebody doesn't understand or needs basic 101 education I can't be with them. Maybe somebody else can do it, but I can't dedicate that amount of time and energy to it."

When people message Oliver on Grindr without having read his profile, he comes out to them fairly quickly. But being out as trans from the get-go diminishes one's potential pool of partners, he says. "I'm not the typical man other people would be attracted to," he acknowledges. Potential dates would have to be "more flexible in their sexuality," and probably identify as either bisexual or pansexual. There's an overlap between genderqueer and "kink" subcultures, which attract those with a more experimental, role-playing approach to sexuality. "A person might express a femme side in an encounter with a butch and express a fag partial identity with a gay transguy the next day," one study suggested.[10]

There's also the problem of those who deliberately seek trans men out as sexual partners, people who are looking for "something new, something weird and different," says Lucas. Rarely do people look at him and really try to get to know him as a person, he says. "Even in person, the people that know me, and who I've been out to and stuff, I feel like they only are interested in me because I'm a fetish, because I'm new, because I'm different." Sometimes he meets people online and presents himself as a male, though not a typically masculine one. His profile says he likes flowers and animals. But few cisgender gay men or lesbian women will date him— though more men than women express interest—because, he says, "you're kind of just in between to them." They'll think: "Ugh—oh, no, a trans person." Dating as trans can be a challenge.

Lucas's desires are open-ended, he says: he is attracted to trans women, cis-persons, non-binary people. "It just doesn't matter to me. My sexuality is just so fluid that it's more about the person for me than anything else. Gender doesn't really matter." Sometimes he calls himself "pansexual," acknowledging that there are more than two genders, that he is attracted not only to men and women but to a variety of genders, and that he chooses partners independent of their sex/gender. And yet the structure of online dating on sites like Tinder requires one to identify as male or female, and to specify to whom you're attracted (male, female, or both). In your profile, you can elaborate on those categories a bit, inserting your personality "to combat the boxes," says Lucas. "But it's still ultimately a game. A game full of boxes." The questions people address to trans people online, such as "Do you have a pussy?" or "Have you finished your procedures?" are ones they'd never say out loud. Oliver shared the text of one of those online exchanges, one that he had had with a cisgender man I'll call Ed.

ED: What do u mean by trans guy?

OLIVER: Transgender. I'm female to male, so I'm a man with a pussy.

ED: That's new. Can I see it?

OLIVER: Well, that's not blatantly objectifying or anything.

ED: K

Oliver sends him a picture of his genitals.

ED: Oh, ok, I might be down. If nothing else, out of curiosity lol. No offense.

OLIVER: Oh lord it's not as exciting to be an object of curiosity.

ED: I'm sorry! Not like that. I'm bi. But I've never been with a girl.

OLIVER: It's okay it happens! You're bi? ☺ Well luckily you still wouldn't break that streak.

For Oliver, these exchanges frequently end with little more than hurt feelings and a sense of being perpetually misunderstood and objectified. "While most conversations on Grindr and similar sites are objectifying," he tells me, "being trans in this space takes it a level further. Presenting as visibly trans intensifies the ever-present curiosity and entitlement of cisgender folks. Being a sexual object is okay, but being a dehumanized body is not." Sometimes Oliver takes screenshots of what people write him on Grindr and makes art out of them, as a way of processing his feelings and talking back to the nameless strangers he meets online.

Oliver and Lucas describe the process of transitioning not only as a physical and psychological transformation but also as a social and spiritual one—a process filled with conflict, compromise, triumph, and also sadness. Several years into his transition, Oliver has experienced an array of highs and lows. Lucas, too, seems acutely aware of the complexities, and ambivalence, embedded in the process of "changing gender."

Ben listens, taking it all in. He is just so excited about getting rid of the breasts that have weighed him down for so many years that it's hard for him to get too mired in this heady conversation. We are, after all, awaiting the Big Reveal, when Ben and Lucas (and later in the day, Nadia and Parker) will finally see their new, flat chests—the ones that they have longed for, and for which they have plunked down thousands of dollars, and have collectively traveled thousands of miles to attain. And then, suddenly, the receptionist calls Ben's name, and he and Gail are quickly ushered into a consult room.

The doctor hands Ben the drains as he unwraps his chest. First he removes the bandage, and then the gauze, revealing the new, flat chest below. Two small bandages are taped over his new, repositioned nipples, which are attached to his chest with hundreds of small stitches. Ben stands up and looks in the mirror, a big grin on his face. Gail asks the doctor: "How did it turn out?" The surgeon responds: "Awesome!" He tells them that the swelling will go down, and the tape strips covering the incisions will fall off within the next week, or they can take them off themselves. The doctor raises the chair Ben is sitting on with a whirring sound, and lowers it so that Ben is lying flat, and then removes the drains.

Ben is beaming. There is some swelling, but as the wounds heal, the inflammation will subside. The doctor instructs him to start showering tomorrow, to avoid facing the shower head directly, and to replace the dressings after showering. He gives him three weeks' worth, including two small squares to cover up his nipples for two weeks, which he will replace daily. Dr. Garramone tells him to spread ointment on the scars and cover them with gauze, and to refrain from heavy lifting for six weeks. The doctor hands Ben a compression bandage to take home in case he needs to wrap his chest, and presents him with a letter stating that he has had "irreversible sexual reassignment surgery":

Psychological and medical testing has been carried out
to determine this patient's true gender. In the case of Ben
Shepherd this was determined to be Male. Ben Shepherd has
been diagnosed with Gender Dysphoria, and has undergone
psychological treatment. Ben Shepherd has been referred for
and undergone surgical procedures of chest masculinization
performed by me to irreversibly correct his anatomy and
appearance. Ben has been treated in accordance with the
accepted medical protocol for the treatment of Gender
Dysphoria and has completed sexual reassignment in
accordance with appropriate medical procedures. On 5/12/2015
I performed and completed sexual reassignment surgery on

Ben Shepherd. From a medical perspective, Ben Shepherd
is now Male and the gender marker on all of Ben Shepherd's
identity documents should now be changed to acknowledge
this medical fact.

Bounding out of the doctor's office with his characteristic exuberance, Ben exclaims: "Look, no tits! Looks even better than I had imagined." We walk out into the parking lot and he unbuttons his shirt. His nipples, which have been repositioned, are taped, and his chest still bears the marks of the surgeon's black pen. "You'd never know I was once a DD," he chuckles. Ben quips that his former breasts are now a "little creature swimming around in the universe somewhere," and that it's a pity there is no "trans parts swap," so that he could donate them to a trans woman in need.

Bob, standing by his side, looks a little uncomfortable about Ben baring his chest in the glare of the hot Florida sun. Until just a week ago, Ben had large, pendulous breasts. Are they really gone? Bob and Gail gently load Ben into the car and we bid good-bye. "Big success for Ben!" Bob posts. "Now the road trip north to Maine begins! Ugh." As the journey home begins, Ben posts a picture of himself on Facebook looking happy. "Boom!!! On the road again!! So long tatas! Leaving a little piece of myself in the Sunshine State."

NINE

Turn and Face the Strange

An infinitely happier person is now looking for the right
outlet for his many fine qualities. His chances, I feel, are
ever so much better than hers were five years ago.
—Harry Benjamin, *The Transsexual Phenomenon*, 1966

In Maine during the months after surgery, Ben's wounds itch ter-
ribly, and he is in pain. Gail helps him care for the drain holes at
the end of the incision, and for three weeks they cover each nipple graft with Neosporin ointment and a Band-Aid. The center of
the nipple graft takes the longest to heal. At first, it looks a bit like
a hole, or crater, but it eventually fills in. The doctor had warned
that the swelling could last for three months after surgery. For a
few weeks, Ben had pimple-like blisters along the incision site that
itched uncontrollably, and he applied Scarguard assiduously in an
effort to flatten and shrink the scar tissue.

Ben is a high-energy person, but the downtime—he cannot
drive for the first couple of weeks after surgery, nor exercise for at
least six weeks—gives him some time to reflect upon his life. He
loves being freed of his breasts and is pleased with the way testosterone is deepening his voice and creating facial hair. He is looking
forward to the time when the swelling on his chest will disappear.

A few months later it does. Ben tells me he feels more like his "old self but better," and I make plans to visit him and his family in October, six months after we first met in Florida.

I drive north past iridescent blue lakes framed by orange and red leaves. After a day, I reach the Shepherds' house in Maine. Ben greets me at the front of the house.

"Hi Arlene!" he says, smiling.

"Great to see you, Ben," I reply.

In the past, he hadn't really called me by my first name. Perhaps it's because I'm his parents' age and he didn't want to offend me. Maybe it's because I'm a college professor and he felt a bit intimidated by my status. But through our Skype conversations during the past several months, we've gotten to know each other better—and I've gotten to know his family and close friends too.

As I've come to know Ben better, and the other subjects of this book, I've also changed. At the start of this project, I regarded women—who don't start wars and rarely beat their spouses, who have smooth skin and tend to smell nice—as the superior sex in many respects. I had difficulty wrapping my head around the fact that some female-assigned women wish to embrace maleness. But now I have a deeper understanding, and respect, for why someone might make the decision to transition.

No longer swathed in baggy clothes, back hunched over under the weight of his large breasts, Ben holds his body differently. Those weighty, oversized breasts never seemed to fit. "I love being able to run around without a shirt," he says. He can pass more easily as a man. He seems relaxed.

"OMG the roller coaster is over. I absolutely think testosterone is the best thing for my body ever." He doesn't have the crazy mood swings he once experienced. After top surgery, many trans men speak of dysphoria giving way to euphoria. The bodily changes feel right to them, and they are seen as the person they've long wanted to be—by family members, friends, people on the street. Testosterone also gradually gives them more energy, smooths them out, and calms them down. Removing one's breasts can be a more dramatic measure, clearly marking a before and after.

Could a relatively simple procedure like top surgery have such a dramatic impact? Transgender men report that top surgery enables them to navigate public places, like bathrooms, more easily, and marks a new phase in their lives.[1] The sense of distress some once felt about living in a body that seemed inauthentic and false diminishes. "There are thirty, forty years of studies that tell us that people are much happier after surgery, and that regret is minimal," says Katherine Rachlin, the New York–based psychologist.

Ben leaves for work, and I chat with Bob and Gail over coffee and homemade scones. Ben is "more focused, more directed" than he has ever been, Bob says. In the past, he'd sleep "real late," until late morning. "He wasn't happy, and he wasn't doing a lot." For a moment, though, Bob slips and refers to Ben using female pronouns. "She never knew from one day to the next what she was doing. You'd wake up and be scared to say, 'How's it going, Bess? What's new?' We never knew what to expect. She always had a new idea," says Bob.

He then catches himself and begins to refer to Ben as "he" again. "He did two semesters" at Boca Raton, and then went to Lynn University "and then left." Then he said he wanted to be a teacher, so he went to the University of Farmington. A couple of weeks into it, he changed his mind and didn't go to class. Then he said he wanted to study art and graphic design. "He was constantly switching colleges," says Bob, "and with every switch, it was costing us more." Gail would say: "He's evolving; it's okay." Bob put his foot down and said that "all this evolving has to stop." Ben's bedroom was a trashed wreck too. He would leave stuff around and walk away. It was a major source of conflict at home. "It was ridiculous," recalls Gail. "How can you live like this?"

After his transition, Ben went back to school at the University of Southern Maine, which he's paying for himself, and he even made the dean's list. He's been keeping his room fairly orderly, and his car too. The other day, an old college friend of Gail's came to stay for the weekend, and Gail asked Ben to clean up the basement so the friend could sleep there. Ben couldn't do it that night because he had plans, but said he would clean it the following evening. When he got home that night he went straight downstairs, and half an hour later the basement was shipshape. "That wouldn't have happened before," says Gail. "There was no follow-through. We'd nag and nag and nag and nag, and then we'd have a fight, and something would happen. His follow-through has been amazing."

When I asked them how they account for the change, Gail says, "It's Ben's self-esteem. I just think him being Ben is helping him to get things done." Bob agrees: "I think he's found his space, his focus. People look up to him. He's running a statewide campaign for 'ranked-choice' voting, a process in which voters prioritize candidates rather than simply picking one. People look up to him. He's organizing others, which is just amazing." In the past, says Bob, "I would've said, 'No way. He can't make it through the day.'"

I sit with the Shepherds at a long oblong wooden dining table in a room that could be anywhere in America. The decor is familiar, unpretentious. Family photographs figure prominently on the walls. "For us, family is key," says Gail. They've provided well for their kids, taking them on family vacations to Disney World and beyond. Ben's transition has tested them in so many ways, but at no time did they ever think they would abandon him because of it. "I've heard of cases where kids get kicked out," says Gail. "But that was never in the cards." They still stumble on pronouns. When we speak about top surgery, Bob mentions all the support "she" had from friends in Maine, and from people at work, and Gail corrects him and says "he." Bob repeats, for emphasis: "he."

Gail has adapted more seamlessly than her husband, though she's not immune to such slips either. Ben is quick to forgive them, acknowledging that his parents lived with Bess for thirty years, but they've lived with Ben for only one. If bodily transitions take time, social transitions can take even longer, and the fact that Bob and Gail gave their blessing by accompanying him to Florida and driving through the night to get there has created a family contract, of sorts. By supporting Ben in changing his life, they expect him to be accountable too: more reliable, organized, focused, and above all, less self-destructive. A friend of Ben's attempted suicide last year, and Gail is well aware that transgender men are at heightened risk, even after transitioning.

Gail savors memories of mother-daughter manicure and pedicure excursions, but she has given up her "plans of weddings and dresses." In retrospect, she acknowledges, "It must have been tough" for Ben to join her on those female-bonding rituals, but that "he did it because it made me happy." She tears up, apologizing to me. "I thought I had it all together today and I wouldn't cry. But it still sits there. These things I have to give up because he needs to be who he is."

As Bob and Gail grapple with figuring out how to integrate Ben into the family, they've also gone to some lengths to figure out what to do with the reminders of Bess, the daughter they once had. While you don't remove dead relatives from the family photo album, what do you do with a child who is both present in the family and, in a way, now absent? Their living room walls are lined with dozens of family photographs in which Bess figures prominently.

"This is a self-portrait that she did when she was in high school," says Gail. "This is her in 2010" at Disney World with Jo, her girl-friend at the time, "when she came out as gay," standing in front of a banner that reads WHERE DREAMS COME TRUE. "This is her at seven years old," says Gail, and "that's a cruise back in 2000." There are photographs Bess took of different images of water, when she was a water sports photographer, and there are extensive docu-mentations of family vacations, which tend to involve boating.

When Gail asked Ben what they should do with the photos, he told her to keep them. "Are you sure?" she asked. "Yes," Ben said. "That's who I used to be." But Gail and Bob ended up moving many of them to another part of the house. There's a large portrait of Bess as a senior in high school "that used to be in the family room, but we moved it here because we never come into this room," Gail says. Anyway, it's "not who Ben is anymore."

The experience of having a transgender child has changed Gail and Bob. Having grown up under modest circumstances, and having built good lives for themselves and their kids, they once believed that the Republican Party shared many of their values. Gail tells me she even signed a petition against marriage equality a few years back that their church had circulated. "I thought to myself, I didn't know anyone who's gay, so I thought what the hell, and signed it." It seems like a very long time ago to her. Ben's expe-rience has transformed her views.

As trans men craft post-transition identities, those who remain close to them are crafting new identities too. The relatives are all on board, more or less—even Gail's ninety-year-old mother, Erma, who lives in central Vermont. Gail has become an activist for trans rights at her middle school, where there is at least one transgender student. When the physical education teacher, whom Gail describes as "kind of old-school," insisted upon referring to

Malcolm as "her" and prevented him from using the boys' locker room, Gail suggested that Malcolm use the private bathroom, and she encouraged the PE teacher to talk to the parents and get permission for Malcolm to use the boys' locker room.

Recently, Gail's school held a staff training concerning transgender issues and showed a film featuring a mother who spoke about her feelings about losing her daughter. As principal, Gail has a supportive staff, she says, but she broke down and had to leave the room. And even as she and Bob have come to accept and respect Ben's decision to transition, it's difficult for Gail to figure out what to do with reminders of the daughter they lived with, loved, and struggled with for nearly thirty years. You can shift old family photos around, but there's lots of other rearranging to be done too. Gail says that being a Catholic was always a difficult balancing act, and that she learned to "hold on to some pieces that made sense to me, even if all the other crap they told me didn't make any sense at all." Over time, Gail has realized, there is less and less to hold on to.

"If we're going to shed the costumes we're wearing," Gail told me, "then I have to shed this big one about the Catholic Church. There's no way I believe anything they say anymore." A few months ago, looking for a way to be together and express their spirituality, Gail and Ben began going to a Unitarian church together in Portland. "Everyone's accepted, no matter who you are, and everyone has something to share," says Gail. There's even a trans woman named Lisa who sings in the choir. "Everyone's like, whatever."

"I had blinders on," says Gail. "Now I have more empathy for everyone. I realize there is no such thing as normal." These days she has a hard time listening to the news. "When they talk about the need to monitor Muslims, it makes me sick, the pigeonholing of people." Ben has a friend who's an American Muslim, she says, who has faced difficulties getting into the country on a number of occasions. "I can't believe this is happening," says Gail. "What have we learned?" Having a kid undergo a gender transition has taught her that "everyone is different, and everyone has a story," she says. "Instead of putting people in boxes, we need to stop and listen to their stories."

Bob, ever the pragmatic one, still worries about details like the fact that Ben never legally changed his gender markers, and his driver's license, birth certificate, and social security card still reflect Ben's birth name. The laws for making such changes vary by state. To obtain a legal name change in Maine, an applicant must submit a petition to the probate court. "If she wanted to go to Montreal right now, could she? I don't think so," says Bob, momentarily reverting to Ben's assigned name and pronouns. "She's Elizabeth Shepherd and she's got a beard, but her name is Ben. It's all over the place. His ID problems alone are going to give him a headache," he tells me. In order to update his name and gender on his driver's license, Ben would need to submit a document demonstrating the name change, such as a birth certificate, passport, or court order, or a form signed by a licensed medical provider certifying that his gender identity is male.

Gail's main concern is that Ben find someone to share his life with. "Be who you want to be," she says. "It's even fine that he's still living at home at age thirty. But I want him to be happy with someone else in his life." Sometimes if Ben mentions a name of someone more than once or twice, Gail will ask him: "Is this someone who is important to you or not?" She doesn't want to make a big deal of it, but she does think about it from time to time.

The other day, when Ben went on a date, Bob asked Gail: What does that mean? "It means he went on a date," said Gail. "With a guy or a girl?" Bob asked. Gail responded: "A girl." Bob replied: "Oh." Transitioning alongside your kid means confronting questions you didn't even know you had, stretching parts of yourself you never knew existed. I asked Gail what she hopes Ben will be doing in ten years' time. She pondered the question for a moment and replied: "All bets are off."

The Shepherds are trying very, very hard to do right by their child, and they're pioneers. When Ben first announced that he wanted to transition over two years ago, they did not know what it meant. "We didn't know anyone who had any transgender people in their families," says Gail. Ben had thought about quitting school and "putting a pause on life" while he transitioned, but he decided to move back home to save money, and so that his family could "be a part of the process." If he had separated from them, even temporarily, he says, "there would be a distance we could never bridge."

While many people separate from their family and friends as they transition, others, like Ben, want family members to accept them on their own terms, without apologies. It doesn't always go smoothly: old conflicts come up. For instance, sometimes Bob and Gail resent the fact that Ben, who is rarely around, treats the house like a hotel. He can still be exasperating at times, and disorganized. Ben and Bob are on a volleyball team together, and Chrissy and Allison, who live nearby with their husbands, occasionally stop in to hang out. "I'm still the same person," says Ben. "Who I am, my mannerisms, how I carry myself hasn't changed. The way I talk hasn't changed," he says. Dealing with the outside world, however, poses a bit more of a challenge, and the fact that he now "presents as a dude" has been an eye-opening experience.

———

Ben and I drive about twenty minutes, over the Casco Bay Bridge, until we reach Higgins, a beautiful small beach near Portland, his favorite spot for surfing. In the summer, Ben and his friends used to meet in the wee hours of the morning to catch the best waves. He points to a large rock, showing me where surfers line up with their boards. On crisp early mornings, you can see huge fish jumping right off the shelf, and the occasional seal. Later in the day, the beach is packed with locals and some tourists. But on this October afternoon, the tide is low, and rocky outcroppings pop out of the sand, forming pools where small sea creatures roam, and there are only a few people. Walking along the beach, one can see pieces of shipwrecks from eras past. It's a beautiful place. Ben comes here when life gets hard, such as when he and Jo broke up and when a friend had a mental health crisis last year.

In the winter, he can hear the sound of snow hitting the water at Higgins, which is the "coolest thing in the world," Ben says. Lately, he's been working sixty-hour weeks and hasn't had time to come. We pass a crowd of young people and overhear one young woman say to another, "She's ready to transition." What kind of transition were they referring to—a job, a move, a gender transition? "You never know," Ben says, laughing. "Life is full of transitions of all sorts. You never know where it may take you," he muses.

Since I saw him last, Ben's become more vocal, and while he presents as a cis man in public, he discloses his transgender status to others when he can. Unlike Oliver and Lucas, he's not all that concerned with deconstructing gender binaries or troubling the categories, though he is eager to educate others through his own example. At this point, his biggest challenge is whether and how to disclose his identity to those outside of his inner circle. "I know I'm trans, and all the people in my life know, but the new people in my life don't know that, and that's hard." But the activist in him believes that "visibility is really important." He says he wants people to know "we're not scary monsters." He believes that disclosure is a central task for transgender people, as it was, and is, for gays and lesbians.

A couple of decades ago, few of us could have imagined that same-sex marriage would be legalized. Shifts in public opinion are often hard fought. Ben, who worked as an organizer on several statewide marriage equality campaigns, knows this firsthand. "We won marriage equality by talking about love and commitment, and by connecting that to voters' friends and family," he says. Over the years, more and more Americans have come to know a gay or lesbian person, or they have come to recognize that family members and intimates they have always known have same-sex preferences. As Ben recalls, "We moved straight people by flipping the script, challenging the view that lesbians and gay men were an 'abomination,' to getting people to see them as ordinary people who also love others and are committed to them." Now, he says, the challenge is to apply that strategy to transgender people. Few voters know any transgender people, "which is why coming out is so powerful and important. It can be a reference point for people, humanizing what many don't understand."

On a recent political campaign, a couple of legislators came into the office to chat with the team. Whenever they do introductions, they go around the room, introduce themselves, and identify the pronouns they wish to go by before they talk about a question of the day. One of the legislators was an older gentleman who asked, "What is this pronoun hoo-ha?" and Ben was silent. The woman who followed him, a legislator in her forties, said, "You know, I've never been asked to say my pronouns out loud, which makes me realize how privileged I am never to have been forced to think about them—until literally right now."

When it was his turn to speak, Ben announced: "I'm Ben, my

pronouns are he/him/his, and I want to thank you so much for appreciating the privilege cisgender people have, because I am a trans guy, so it has impacted me a lot in my life, and I appreciate you calling that out." Half of those who were present, Ben recalls, "were like 'What!?'" Many of them had worked with him before and didn't know his history. The legislators had never met him before. The organizer in him enjoys the challenge of engaging people during these teachable moments. "So many people think they don't know anyone who's trans. Or they think it's a mental disease or something," he says. When you come out to people who are strangers, or who are not part of your intimate circle, and they connect with you as a person, and they "have this moment of holy shit, wow, okay, you can see them get it." That's why being visible is important to Ben. He attributes the passage of marriage equality to how activists changed the conversation. "We didn't win because public opinion changed. We won because we changed public opinion."

Though most people now see him as male, occasionally strangers mistakenly use female pronouns when addressing him (some transgender people refer to this as "mis-pronouning" someone) despite his facial hair and newly flat chest. On line at the Quick-Chek convenience store in Portland recently, a guy behind Ben told someone else who was waiting, "I just let her go ahead of me," referring to Ben. He was corrected by another customer waiting on line, a man behind him: "You mean he, or sir," he said.

"That was *different*," says Ben.

And he still struggles with bathrooms. "If there's a guy in the stall, do I wait?" It's a relatively minor problem, he acknowledges. He's still scared when he first walks into the men's room at times, until he looks in the mirror and realizes that no one can tell he's not a natal male, and he reassures himself: "It's fine, nobody knows."

He uses family restrooms whenever he can. But he's not as fearful of such public places as he once was, and no he longer constantly feels frustrated, wrong, out of place. He is clearly enjoying his masculinizing body and exploring his new identity as a man. But sometimes it's difficult to figure out how to just *be*.

The transition process has a clearly defined script: first you change your name and go on hormones; then you have top surgery and legally change your gender marker. But there's no script for living as a trans person. How should he be in the world now? Ben is figuring out what it means to be a social male with a female history in a society where men still dominate, now that most people see him as a "white cis dude." He alternates between feeling powerfully liberated and also burdened, at times, by a new sense of responsibility.

When he was a sports photographer in Florida, presenting himself as female in a male-dominated field, he was forced to be "the loudest voice in the room," he says. He had to "be obnoxious in order to get shit done" or no one listened to him. Now that he presents as male, and is armed with "male privilege," Ben feels he must challenge sexism when he sees it. When he's out with his girlfriends, strangers—servers in restaurants, for example—look to him to make decisions about what to order. "They don't even realize they're doing it; they just see me as the dude in the room." Now, he says, he has to learn how to turn it down, take up less space, and remember not to mansplain.

In his current job as a campaign organizer for ranked-choice voting, which would streamline the electoral process, eliminating the need for run-off elections, "rather than speaking first I'll wait until everyone goes," Ben says, "and then if it hasn't been said, I'll throw it out. Or if somebody comes to me, I'll say: Don't talk to me, go to Erin, she's running this shift. That feels really important."

Last semester at the university, while he was waiting in front of a classroom, some guys made a reference to a hot girl who had just walked by, and then acknowledged Ben's presence, saying, "You know what I mean?" Ben responded that he didn't know what they meant, and that what they were saying was sexist. "No guy had ever checked them before," Ben says. "They responded: 'Oh dude, you're probably right.'" Now that he presents as male and no longer feels "like there's a character I have to play," Ben has become more and more conscious of the ways we perform gender. And he has come to realize that "cis dudes need to check one another on their sexism."

Before his transition, nearly all of his friends were female, and he "connected more with women," he says. But now that he's passing, "it seems like I bond more easily with guys." He's not acting any differently, he says; people are responding differently to him, and more males than females are drawn to him. He's realizing that he has "as much fun with dudes." And yet, he tells me, "Men are so weird. And it feels weird to say that because technically I identify as a man."

Ben says his masculinity has softened and become less defensive. While we're driving, he points to a pink water bottle sitting in the car that belongs to his mother. "I would never have been caught dead drinking out of this," he says, "but now I can." He feels more strongly than ever that it's important to challenge sexism on the job. He never identified as a feminist before he transitioned because he associated feminism with being "feminine." At times he would even say things like "This is a man job" or "Let's get some guys to move the furniture." Now he has greater empathy for women, and he has come to recognize his own sexist attitudes— and his former aversion to everything feminine in himself. As I've gotten to know him over the past year, he does seem calmer, more at ease with himself.

Recently, Ben and his BFFs Chrissy and Allison took a road trip together to Vermont, and they all went for pedicures, just like in the old days. Ben used to tag along on such excursions grudgingly, always feeling like an imposter. Now, he says, for the first time he enjoys them. "Femininity doesn't scare me anymore. There are no longer boundaries." Recently, he had his nails painted a sparkly purple. "It was really fun," he says. "When I look in the mirror now, I like what I see. I no longer have anything to prove."

———

Parker, back home in Austin, is also basking in his newfound gender euphoria. When we spoke shortly after I visited Maine, he told me that he now passes as male in many aspects of his life. He feels so much better about his body, and he says: "I can finally breathe." The sense of relief is physical and emotional. In the past, he said, it physically hurt him to have breasts, even small ones. When he stretched during his workout routines, he said, there were a couple of muscle groups he kept tense. "Now I just keep looking at my chest in the mirror and feeling happy," he tells me. "It's crazy to look at yourself sideways and just look like a man, like how I want to look. I don't have to push or tape or suck anything in. It's just how I want to look."

After the bandages came off, Parker posted a picture, scars and all, of his chest on Instagram. In a second photo, he is wearing a NASCAR T-shirt cut off at the midriff that shows off his abs. He is wearing sunglasses, a cigarillo hangs from his lips, his head is cocked, and his dirty-blond hair is slightly tousled. A friend writes: "Bro, where the fuck have you been?!? Give your homie a call sometime." A third photo shows him in a reversed baseball cap, gold chain, muscular chest (with scars barely visible), stud in ear, looking a bit like Mark Wahlberg, with tattoos and a light mustache. A plastic penis, or maybe a dildo, hangs off his key chain. "Only you can create the life you want for yourself," he posts. He works out, lifting weights three or four times a week, and it shows. He tells me his friends are "eating it all up and trying to pimp me out," introducing him to girls and making a fuss over his manly good looks. On his Instagram feed they comment: "You're hot."

He responds: "Getting there."

Another writes: "holy manly . . . 'sup studly . . . looking fly."

"If we're talking body, you got a perfect one so PUT IT ON ME. . . . Damn."

A few months later, on Facebook he posts a suggestive photo of himself, bare chested, his middle finger pointing to himself, proclaiming, "I wish I was Tyler Durden." Bronzed from the sun, his chest scars show, though they have faded, and his abs are toned and muscular. Fine, dark hair surrounds his navel. It's a sexy image.

While Ben transitioned with all of his significant relationships intact, Parker isn't as lucky. His girlfriend, Darby, whom he describes as "the love of my life," split up with him shortly after he had top surgery. Once he started passing as a man, she felt that their relationship was no longer viable. "Darby wanted to try lesbianism full-on, and I couldn't deny her that," he says. Now, he says, she's hanging out with all the "cool L.A. chicks." When one partner transitions, it can test even the most solid relationships. Parker and Darby had been together only a few months when Parker began to present as a male, so perhaps it's little wonder that transitioning posed a challenge. Before modifying their bodies, trans men tend to partner with individuals who are attracted to masculine females. As they become more masculine, they sometimes move out of their partner's zone of attraction.[2]

Parker hasn't seen his parents since he had top surgery and hasn't spoken to them in a year and a half or since he disclosed to them that he is transgender. The other day, he texted his mom to tell her that he's making her the beneficiary of his life insurance, and he sent her a podcast about a woman whose daughter is trans in the hope of initiating a conversation about his decision to transition. He wrote her: "There's a part of the podcast that gave me a good understanding of the loss you must feel toward Kate, and I want to recognize that." She never responded. His dad, the military man, texted Parker the other day when he saw a photo of him at a club making out with a girl; he told him he thought it was inappropriate.

Parker loses his composure and his voice cracks when he talks about his parents. He says he's thinking about writing them an e-mail and starting a conversation that way. He heard "it's a good way of keeping a connection with your parents." Transitioning has meant moving away from his parents and trying to create a chosen family with friends and workmates. It's one of the reasons, he says, he works so hard. "If I don't make my own money and have my own shit together, I have no one." And yet he believes that it has all been worth it. Now that he "passes better," he says, he's treated more or less like a guy would be. His friends on social media may know his story, and many of his work colleagues do, too, but "most people see him as cis male," and that's just fine with him. "I'm really happy with my identity now," he says.

Before Parker transitioned, men he worked with would sometimes ask him for advice about dating women. "You're a woman, they'd say," and then they'd hem and haw and eventually come out with "What do women like? How do you please them?" Now that they perceive him as a man, the talk goes "straight to sex," he says. "They'll say, 'Hey man, did you see what Kramer said last night on *Seinfeld*?' and then go into 'Oh man, I totally ate this girl out last night for two hours, and she didn't come. I think I suck at it. What should I do?'"

Parker's got nothing against sex talk; he tells me he recently hooked up with "a really cute girl" named Kiley who grabbed his chest, ripped off his shirt, and informed him that "it's been so long since I've been with a guy and it feels good." During sex she says: "I want to suck on your cock." He loved it. "It made me feel like fucking Gandhi," he says. There have been other advantages, too, including unexpected financial ones. "I think people take me more seriously at work now as a man than when I was a butch lesbian, especially since I cut my hair," he tells me. His boss wouldn't see it that way, he says. "He would say: 'Parker has grown up, is more mature now.'"

Sociologist Kristen Schilt studied the workplace experiences of more than fifty transgender men and found that "some trans men find employer support" for "transitioning openly" and manage to secure employment as "one of the guys"—if they are white, educated, and "physically passable as men." If they're visibly gender-variant or a racial minority or they work in entry-level retail jobs, they have a much more difficult time integrating into the workforce. So do trans women, who often encounter "extreme harassment" and in some cases face termination if they transition. "It is the logic of the workplace as a gendered organization," Schilt writes, "that encourages everyone to adapt to masculine expectations and devalue femininity." There seem to be clear benefits for doing so. Two-thirds of the individuals she interviewed, some of whom were open as trans men on the job while others were stealth, reported that becoming men led to increases in workplace authority, a perception of competence, and more rewards and recognition for their hard work, including higher salaries.[3]

Parker never went out searching for male privilege, but once he realized it was possible to transition, going through with it became a driving force in his life, and he felt he had no choice but to do it. That he's treated better now on the job is just icing on the cake—he'll soon be moving to Scottsdale, Arizona, because of a promotion. The fact that he's white and passes well as male is not incidental to his enhanced status on the job, according to Schilt's findings. It isn't all smooth sailing, however. Now that he is perceived to be a man, cisgender male colleagues are more apt to compete with him for status.

"There are so many stupid fucks in Texas who talk without thinking," Parker told me. "One of them is this guy I work with, another manager, who's got like four inches on me. He uses it to his advantage. He puts it in my face. We fight about the littlest things— even about five dollars. I can't stand it when he says, 'Parker, you're my little brother. Let me give you some advice.'" That same guy dismissed and disrespected Parker before his transition. Now that his co-worker sees Parker as a man, "he's much more about one-upping me." He hits Parker in the chest and says, "'You're a dude, dude! You got like man pecs!' He's tripping out." Parker doesn't disguise his disdain for him.

Men, particularly taller men, dominate over those of lesser stature, and even though Parker passes well now, at five feet six inches tall he is acutely aware of being short. When he began transitioning, he wanted little more than to become a guy's guy. Afterward, he feels like a "regular white dude" and someone who "knows what it's like to feel marginalized and uncomfortable in your body." He says he has more compassion for women and people of color now.

He's trying to "take up less space" and "is relating to women better now," he says. "Even my podcast playlist has totally changed." He's listening to more stories about African American lives and police violence.

"I've had such a great transition. I've gotten everything I've wanted. I almost feel selfish. It has changed me," he says. He feels more empathy for boys, he says, because they "get shat on by older men" and called every manner of insult. The other day, he watched a boxing match on television with some friends who have kids of middle school age. When a commercial came on, the younger one, who is about eleven and has no idea Parker was once assigned female, called something "really gay," and Parker reprimanded him for it. "Dude, that's not cool," he told him. "Where I'm from, you'd get your butt beat for that." The eleven-year-old looked at him curiously. His older brother replied: "Well, other kids say it at school." Parker told him that calling something you hate "gay" is "almost as bad as using a racial slur." Being able to teach those kids was "awesome," he said. "I feel like I'm bringing some good to the world."

Before he transitioned, Parker said he often hit on cute girls by going up to them and complimenting them on an article of clothing—"Oh, I really like your boots"—as a way of making contact and luring them into bed. Now, presenting as a man, Parker says he feels a responsibility not to be "douchey."

Dating can be a dog-eat-dog world, and Parker tends to be attracted to extremely feminine straight women—"'top shelf' sexual partners," he tells me. On the way home one evening last August, Parker decided to stop and have a drink with some co-workers. "This super-attractive blonde sitting across from me caught my eye and I guess I caught hers too," he tells me in an e-mail message. "I saw her look at me, then whisper something to her roommate, and in the next second I was being invited to their housewarming party. Her name is Susan—I really like her. One night after having made love I asked her how she was feeling and what she was thinking. After some nudging and encouraging we finally talked about sex. She asked if I had ever been with a girl who had only been with cis guys. I told her no. . . . It is kind of like a first for both of us."

At first, Parker said he wanted to go stealth and fade right into the woodwork. But over the past year, as he became more transgender identified, he decided to try to attract women who are comfortable being with "a dude without a dick." He wants his partners "to love [his] body in the current form it's in." His current girlfriend, Susan, doesn't "think about the fact that I am not an anatomical male when we are having sex," he says. She really likes it. "We are taking it slow." But the other night she asked him: "What if I start to touch you and get uncomfortable and want to stop?" Parker says he "laughed in the way that you are supposed to when something is not a big deal and told her, 'Then of course we would stop.'" While he said that Susan "never makes me feel bad about not having a dick," the truth is, Parker wrote me, "I was flooded with a wave of dysphoria and disappointment. I am so sexually attracted to her and I want her to touch me. But I don't want to be reminded of what I am not working with when she does. I want to be able to kiss her while I'm inside her and when I am on top and she's grinding against me from below and kissing me—it makes me feel like she wants that too."

For now, he says, they're using a strap-on. "I don't think she's used to sex with a partner focused on her pleasure first and foremost," says Parker. "Lucky me!" But he eventually wants bottom surgery. His story, and others I heard, suggests that once transgender men enter the dating scene, if they're mainly attracted to cisgender women who have little or no experience in the queer world, they can feel inadequate. Sometimes, Parker says, he "feels dysphoric" about his lack of a phallus. However gender-fluid or along the gender continuum they may feel, transgender men who wish to be known as men must define themselves in relation to a system where men are still on top, and heterosexuality remains the standard.

Like many twenty-somethings, Parker's a work in progress. During the year I've known him, he has changed more dramatically than any of the others I interviewed for this book. When we first met, he wanted nothing more than to be Tyler Durden, a cool guy with an attitude, and to be seen as a cisgender man. But more recently he posted a time-lapse video of his body in transition on Facebook, showing his evolution from Kate, the butch lesbian, to Parker, the buff dude, and sometimes, he admits, he's nostalgic for his old lesbian life.

"Rebelling against all that bullshit male power was fun and sexy and mysterious. Sometimes I miss it. I am proud of my female-bodied history." In fact, after longing for a phallus, and feeling inadequate in several of his relationships with straight cisgender women who had only ever dated "cis white men," he says he's now "honestly starting to really enjoy and embrace the genitals I naturally have." He's taking it slower these days, partying less, dating more discriminately. "The choice to get bottom surgery should be weighed with how you feel about yourself—not prodded and pushed by how a sexual partner makes you feel," he says.

As Parker has become more transgender identified, his masculinity has softened—as much as Ben's has. "I'm more sensitive to how women feel now. I don't say 'bitches' anymore. I can relate to women more now than when I was a woman. As a white man, I take up more space. I'm conscious of being threatening. But I remember being a woman. And I know that until women are free from sexual violence, they won't be able to participate in society equally." At the beginning of his transition, he tells me, "I thought I had to do all the right things to get in to some 'boys club.'" Now he talks about having lived "both genders at the same time," and "feels a duality."

In April 2017, anticipating his third anniversary of being on testosterone, Parker posted two photos of himself on Facebook. "I'm here to say I'm proud of my history and the feminist lens through which I view the world." One photo shows him with short cropped hair and a smooth face, staring into the camera. He was twenty-three when he started taking hormones. He looks much younger, like a teenage boy, and gazes self-consciously, his eyes downcast. The second photo pictures him in a baseball cap, with a faint mustache, months into his transition, looking somewhat more directly into the camera.

Parker sent me a photo of himself dancing shirtless at a performance of Swedish synth-pop band Miike Snow at Austin City Limits, the annual music festival held in the Texas capitol. He's sporting a stylish black-rimmed hat and tortoiseshell sunglasses, and he has a scruffy beard and mustache, and shoulder-length blond hair, and he is flaunting pecs and abs that would be the envy of any cisgender man. But beneath the supremely masculine exterior is a gender identity that is exceedingly complex.

"When I first started my journey I thought I had to conform to everything I thought or was conditioned to think that 'boy' was," he posted on Facebook three years into his transition. "But FUCK THAT. Gender is what you make it—hormones or not. Shattering/questioning gender and gender roles is our generation's revolution. One that's beautiful and wholly incomplete."

———

A year after his top surgery, I also check in with Lucas, who tells me that he has a new job as an advocate for rape victims, a new girlfriend, and a new dog—a Dalmatian–pit bull rescue who is deaf and "the biggest love-bug." He's "passing better," aided by his testosterone-deepened voice and a flat chest, he tells me, and therefore he feels safer in public presenting as a male. He has shaved off his beard and added some tattoos to his body. To the phoenix that adorned the top of his chest, he has added a half sleeve of images of lotus flowers and cherry blossoms, and a pocket watch ("because I've been obsessed with pocket watches, with the passage of time, and with childhood"). There's also a moth, which represents his Italian heritage; on the inside of his forearm, a dagger and compass ("I didn't like the direction my life was going in, and I made a change"); the word "vulnerable"; a small transgender symbol in the hilt of the dagger; and the organic chemistry symbol for testosterone over his liver ("because T's not technically good for your liver, so I'm embracing the irony"). The tattoos symbolize how he's reclaiming his body, one step at a time.

"He has already been through a lot of shit," so his body is "easy to work on," the tattooist told him. What's a little more pain? Lucas just turned twenty-four, and during this time of year, he says, he's "grateful and humbled." Celebrating another birthday is an opportunity for him to take stock of his life. "I never realized how much my breasts were killing me until they were gone," he tells me. He says he feels more "confident in my own skin," and safer too. Since he's no longer binding his chest, he says, "I feel like I can actually breathe."

Lucas's job has him helping victims complete rape kits and communicate with police, and he accompanies them to legal hearings. He's the youngest staffer there, the only trans person, and one of only two male-presenting people. He tries to model a different vision of masculinity, particularly when he's working with kids who are children of rape victims. Rather than teaching them to man up, he says, "I'm all about, let's color, let's talk about our feelings and paint our nails." Although Lucas was hired as an out trans person, his predominantly rural white clients know very little about his past. Although he doesn't deny or hide it, it rarely comes up. "I'm there for their hurt and pain, and I don't want them to be distracted," he tells me. His history as a person who transitioned from female to male, as well as his history as a survivor of rape, he says, "gives me a lot of really good insight." He will tell his clients that even though he is a man, "I'm a survivor, and I'm here for you."

White trans men who work in male-dominated fields, such as Parker, a software sales manager, say that transitioning to maleness can be beneficial to their careers. Surprisingly, it can even be beneficial if they're working in the female-dominated helping professions. People who don't know Lucas is transgender often think he is a gay man, and they are surprised when he tells them he dates women. Still, they take him seriously, he says, and speak to him differently than they do to his female co-workers. "They remember my name," he says, and they are less likely to pull him into interpersonal disputes. He feels that he's respected more. When a female staff member recently suggested a change to organizational policy, nobody listened to her. Recently, Lucas made the same suggestion. Others sat up and listened. If a guy says it, he tells me, "it must be true."

His newfound male privilege makes him even more vigilant about challenging sexism on the job, he says. When law enforcement officers fail to take victims' claims of rape seriously, sometimes even blaming them ("she was asking for it"), he makes a point of challenging them. When he encounters young men from rural communities who say things like "that's girl talk," he'll question them: "I'm not sure what girl talk is." His female co-workers speak in gender stereotypes too, he says. Recently, when preparing to attend an out-of-town conference, one woman lamented the fact that she has to pack a suitcase, while "guys can just bring small backpacks."

Lucas challenged her: "Most of the women I know pack backpacks, and most of the men pack suitcases," he said. He says he tries to "meet people where they are, but push them to the extent that he can." Now that he can pass as male, Lucas is seen as a "sensitive male," a feminist ally who can challenge "toxic male" behavior. Operating as an outsider within can at times be frustrating, requiring a lot of patience and insight, but it makes the job more interesting, Lucas says. "Every day seems like a social experiment."

A few months ago, Lucas broke up with his girlfriend, a trans woman of color who he realized "was not a very nice person." He's now dating a queer cisgender woman who is "very aware of trans things," he says, and "very validating." They met through mutual friends a while back, when she was with someone else, and they reconnected again on Tinder. "We both matched and I said, 'Hey, I know you,' and we hit it off instantly." The further along he's gotten in his transition, he says, the less he cares about a partner's physical appearance or gender: it's more about the person. As his "body keeps transforming and changing," he says, his physical attractions have also changed. "People's anatomy is the last thing I look at." Transitioning has given him permission to experiment more, he says. "I'm queerer than ever in certain respects." (A recent large-scale survey of transgender people revealed that only 12 percent considered themselves to be heterosexual. Sixteen percent identified as gay or lesbian, and 15 percent as bisexual. Eighteen percent identified as pansexual. The largest single category called them-selves queer—21 percent.)[4]

Some transmasculine people are inventing a new language for their bodies, asserting a masculine sexuality and redefining body parts and activities. One butch dyke who identifies as trans and genderqueer, when interviewed by gender scholar Robin Bauer, told her that she uses the term "boy cunt," combining masculine and female elements to create a new concept of a sexed/gendered body. Some trans men refer to their testosterone-masculinized female genitals as a penis, or they call the phallus that is not permanently attached to their body, which is in fact a dildo, a "dick." In sexual interactions, partners of trans men and gender-nonconforming people may agree to refer to their partner's clitoris as a cock, enhancing a sense of reciprocity and pleasure. Individu-als use language to "capture a material existence that shifts bodily boundaries," writes Bauer, who studied genderqueer communi-ties. "Butches, FtMs, and their partners experience 'dildos' as real parts of their bodies, with a dynamic of their own." Through sexual practices, they can change the way they experience the sexed/gen-dered body.[5]

Lucas is part of that wave of genderqueer experimentation, though he says he feels less queer over time. "As my body has come to align visually with how I see myself, I've become more binary," he says. He's preparing to have a hysterectomy in a few months. He says he's getting along better with his family these days—or at least with his father's side of the family. After he had surgery, "they're like, 'okay, wow, he's really serious,'" he tells me. "Unfortunately, that's, like, a terrible dynamic"—that it takes having surgery for your parents to believe you're "really transgender," he acknowl-edges. But they've finally been calling him Lucas and getting his pronouns right, most of the time, at least. During the past few months, he says, "my family has really started to be like, 'Okay, Lucas is a trans man.' Okay." But as he loses his "genderqueerness," he says, he must figure out what he wants his masculinity to be.

If asked to "check one of those boxes of female or male," Lucas says he still feels he doesn't "fit in either of them." "I still very strongly identify as a transgender man or a trans man, but I feel like the longer I'm on hormones or the more surgery I get, or the longer I explore what gender means and deconstruct what gender means, the more non-binary I become. My body feels so non-binary, so gray in comparison to other folks." After his transition, he "both does and doesn't fit in even more" than before he transitioned. "The more that I am in this process," Lucas says, "the less gender makes sense to me, and the less I understand why we enforce such strict binaries of gender and why we're still afraid of breaking that binary and deconstructing what gender means." But that's okay, he says, because "it's more interesting living in the gray. Living in the gray, that's what makes sense to me. Or at least that's where I am right now."

TEN

I Am Enough

> How to explain, in a culture frantic for resolution, that
> sometimes the shit stays messy?
> —Maggie Nelson, *The Argonauts*, 2015

The cavernous convention center is a sea of genders, colors, and ethnicities. Trade shows, political conclaves, and pin-striped attendees are a typical sight here. Today the place has been outfitted with gender-neutral restrooms for the annual Philadelphia Trans Health Conference (now called the Trans Wellness Conference), a gathering that attracts upward of four thousand attendees. Gender-bending and gender crossing are the order of the day. The median age is perhaps twenty-five, and there are lots of pierced lips and dyed coifs, and an abundance of facial hair. A young white person of indeterminate gender with pink-and-blue streaked hair is wearing a short skirt; another wears a men's button-down shirt. A strikingly tall African American trans woman is rocking a T-shirt emblazoned with the slogan THE FUTURE IS FEMALE. A mobile testing unit offers free HIV and STD screenings, along with Reiki and massage. Community organizations and health providers—plastic surgeons, fertility experts, and endocrinologists—and small-time entrepreneurs are hawking information and "merch" for trans people, including books, prosthetic devices such as packers and strap-ons, and T-shirts emblazoned with slogans like TRANS MEN ARE REAL. Bathrooms are refitted with gender-neutral bathroom symbols—a silhouette of a figure, half of which has a skirt on, and half of which is clad in pants.

A year after Ben's top surgery and six months after my visit to Maine, I arranged to see Ben here. We never specified a meeting place, and I cannot find him amid the throngs. Our phones are not cooperating. As I scan the crowd, I bump into Dr. Russell Sassani, who has come from Fort Lauderdale to drum up business. He greets me and proudly flashes a picture of his eighteen-month-old daughter. Although many of the largest and longest-running transgender conferences around the nation, such as Southern Comfort, which moves throughout the Southern states, have tended to be dominated by trans women, trans men are highly visible here; trans male poster boy Aydian Dowling is selling trans-themed T-shirts and posing for photographs with his fans.

While I wait for Ben, I peruse the 120-page program, choosing among sessions on "Reclaiming the Transgressive Traditions of Christianity," intersexuality, the power of positive thinking, healthcare planning, and issues facing transgender people in higher education. "Dating 301: The Trans Masculine Experience" focuses on the "unique circumstances associated with dating as a trans man." Most workshops are open to anyone who wishes to attend; some, like "Transgender Muslim Lives" and "Father's Support Group," are restricted to those who fit those categories of identity. I settle on "The Fluidity of Attraction," which promises to give "participants of all genders" the opportunity to enhance their understanding of the "spectrum of complex, interacting, and fluid factors that make up our sexual orientation."

In a packed room that seats at least a couple hundred people, health educator Terri Clark, a sporty middle-aged woman, approaches the subject of sexual complexity with evangelical fervor. She lays out what psychologists call the Klein Sexual Orientation Grid, which looks at different variables in attraction—behavior, fantasies, emotional preference, social preference, lifestyle, self-identification—and ranks them on a scale of one to seven. A one means you're attracted only to the other sex, a four means that you're attracted to both sexes, and a seven signifies same-sex attractions only.

Clark asks participants to stand at different points of the room, under signs numbered from one to seven, representing different moments in their lives. "Stand at the number that defines your sexual orientation before you were sixteen," she instructs the crowd. Most stand near two, three, and four. A few gravitate toward four, five, and six. Nearly no one stands beneath one or a seven, which marks exclusive heterosexuality or homosexuality. Then Clark asks people to stand near the number that represents their sexuality in the last month.

Audience members move in waves across the room, and a few shift toward the number 7—the gay zone. One man says, "I'm a minority here, but that's okay." Most gravitate across the numbered spectrum. Finally, the facilitator asks people to stand by the number that represents their ideal: "What do you think you would eventually like?" The crowd pushes in different directions again, dispersing across the seven numbers, and most people gravitate between the numbers three and five.

A female-presenting person in the audience says: "It shows that people are evolving, even day to day." Clark agrees. "We're used to this word 'opposite,'" she tells her, "but it doesn't really fit. Our language is always evolving, and we make it our own."

A cisgender man offers that when he was in high school ten years ago, "straight, gay, and bisexual were the only options." He says, "Today, I've heard a lot of terms I've never seen or heard before. This is a framework for understanding, but it's not a box. Not either-or."

Another audience member muses: "Linking sexual orientation and gender identity is like mixing oil and water."

Alfred Kinsey's massive survey of American sexual habits in the mid-twentieth century pierced the secrecy surrounding what people really did in bed, and pushed "ordinary" Americans to begin to see sexuality as a continuum. Plotting people on a scale from one to six, where "ones" are entirely heterosexual and "sixes" are entirely homosexual, Kinsey revealed that the vast majority of Americans, if defined by their actual sexual experiences, lay somewhere between homosexual and heterosexual. His radical reimagining of sexual orientation, which scandalized 1950s America, seems rather quaint today.

Kinsey's idea of a sexual continuum was "monosexual," says Clark. He devised a scale on the basis of sexuality alone (rather than in relation to gender and sexuality), and he believed that individuals' desires are pretty fixed over time. That is, while there is typically some change over the course of one's life as most people veer toward heterosexual marriage, Kinsey's model, says Clark, "didn't really consider past, present, ideal future, and didn't encompass a lot of variables." Clark tells the crowd that in 1978, Fritz Klein, a Viennese-born psychiatrist and sex researcher, published *The Bisexual Option*, which imagined sexual orientation as a dynamic, multivariable process, one that involves sexual and nonsexual dimensions that change over time. By adding the element of temporality, it complicated Kinsey's findings.

When gender variance enters discussions of sexuality, it mud-

dies sexual categories beyond Kinsey's wildest dreams. If heterosexuality means that you're attracted to the "opposite" sex and
homosexuality is defined as attraction to the "same sex," what happens when "the opposite sex is neither," as Kate Bornstein once
put it—what if you don't feel that you're male *or* female? How do
you even speak of heterosexuality and homosexuality in relation to
individuals who experience their gender identities as non-binary,
or fluid at different points of their lives?

In the conventional model of transitioning, one moves from
male to female or female to male and stays there. Done. But for others, gender and sexuality become more complex over time. There
are even those who undergo gender transitions, who then decide
that they were happier in their assigned gender and then revert
back—"detransitioners," they're called. Sometimes these individuals (who comprise a small percentage of those who undergo
transitions, according to experts) had harbored unreasonable
expectations about what their lives would be like once they transitioned, or they were unprepared for the transphobia they would
encounter once they started living in their new identity, or they
simply couldn't get access to the hormones they needed to live. If
we see gender as something that is fluid rather than fixed, as multidimensional rather than singular in definition, the choice to move
from one gender to another and then back again appears somewhat
unusual—particularly after all the time, energy, money, and physical discomfort entailed in transitioning—but it is not altogether
unimaginable. "Just as trans individuals' identities and personal
understandings of gender may shift over time prior to transitioning," writes trans woman Julia Serano, "they may do so afterwards
as well."[1] In the brave new world of gender, we're all on a journey.

———

I spot Ben across the crowded room wearing a T-shirt with the words I AM ENOUGH written across the front, and we greet each other with hugs. After the "Fluidity of Attraction" session ends and the audience disperses into the convention center lobby, we walk together past the Reiki and T-shirt booths and into the warm Philly sunshine. When I ask Ben about what the slogan on his shirt means, he explains: "Whoever we are, whatever we look like is okay. We don't have to be somebody we're not. I don't have to be some jacked guy to feel good about myself." He has come to Philadelphia to feel the energy of others who are figuring things out, too, and to learn from them. He seems somewhat more subdued than he was when I last saw him a few months ago, but he is more open to sharing his struggles, as well as his triumphs.

"What's going on with you these days?" I ask him.

"I'm a hot mess," he says.

Some of the problems that predated his transition—his struggle with his weight, and his depression—have returned. He's now unemployed, having left his campaign job. He recently ended a relationship with a woman that was great while it lasted, and which left him wanting more. He's still sleeping in his childhood bedroom, at his parents' home, and there's no alternative in sight. "I'm just living the dream," he says facetiously. Although he is grateful for his parents' hospitality, he doesn't know how he's ever going to afford a home of his own.

In many respects, he is wildly successful. As Gail once told me, "Ben is the only person I know whose five hundred Facebook friends are really friends." I saw firsthand how devoted those friends are. Still, Ben says he has always felt like a misfit. Never a proper girl, he had trouble conforming to the settled ways of Brompton, where people tend to know their place. He was always a big person, disheveled and disorganized. Because he was lovable, devoted to others, and had a supportive family, it all seemed to work—more or less. But over time, as his peers learned to find their place in the world, Ben felt left out. While others coupled up, had children, and pursued careers, he never had an intimate relationship that he considered successful, and he longed for a different way of being in the world.

Transitioning was a quest to find a place for himself, and it has helped him to sort out some of his issues. He feels better about himself now that he has more of a male body and is seen as "a dude," as he puts it. But some of his old challenges have yet to vanish. New ones have reared their heads too. Six months ago, Ben was taking it slow, focusing on his campaign work and not paying a whole lot of attention to matters of the heart. He imagined he would present himself in the world as a straight trans man and date women. His "target demographic" was queer women, he told me. There are a "lot of rad queer women in Portland who would be into a trans guy," he said, though he wasn't quite sure. But he was working long hours, leaving him little time to date anyone, and he felt fine about being single. He had a brief fling with a woman at work, which was really nice, but for the most part, he put his love life on hold.

"Relationships are a lot of work," and the last thing he wanted, he said, was "one more person needing things from me right now." That was new. Before his transition, Ben wanted to be with someone and lamented the fact that he had long had trouble connecting with people sexually. Then he was sorting out what kind of intimate life he wanted. But testosterone made him randier. He longed for new connections, so he began to think about dating again. He set up an online profile where he was up-front about his trans identity and talked with a few potential dates, but none of them seemed right. It would be difficult to find someone he's interested in who would also be interested in him, he imagined. Also he's very aware of being a man and doesn't want to be a jerk. "I kind of just want to wear a sign that says 'I promise I'm not a creepy man,'" he said.

And then a woman he had met in the campaign world unexpectedly resurfaced, and they connected. Though he doesn't easily become attracted to people, he said, something clicked. Jen identified as queer, and she had been with both men and women in the past, including trans men. It was thrilling at the time. But once he and Jen became intimate, Ben's old insecurities reemerged. It wasn't simply a matter of not having the right parts; there were other issues, too, including Ben's ADHD. Still, it was his most fully realized relationship since the one with Jo, which had ended nearly five years before.

Ben's beginning to wonder whether he might be queer or even pansexual. Ben began as a trans man who had a pretty clear sense of himself as a heterosexual male. Now as he passes better as a man, he sounds queerer, more like Lucas, and his sexuality has become more open-ended. Might he even actually be with a man in the future? He doesn't know. The categories of gay, straight, bi seemed to grow fuzzy.

During the early phase of the transition process, matters of identity typically come to the fore: Am I "really" transgender? If so, what should I do about it? What kinds of medical treatments, if any, might be appropriate for me? There's a clear script that tells you how to proceed if you want others to recognize you as your chosen gender. But after their body comes to align better with their sense of self, trans people are faced with figuring out how to manage a tremendous array of life changes. High on that list, says Marilyn Volker, a Florida therapist, are body issues, and "mating, dating, and relating." Many trans people find that when they modify aspects of their bodies, in this case their chests, other body parts may become problematic.

"There's this dysmorphia even post surgery," Volker told me when we spoke in Florida a few months earlier, using the psychiatric term that signifies a negative fixation on a part or parts of one's body. It's a bit like renovating a house: once you've removed that kitchen wall unit that's been bugging you, you're suddenly aware of the 1970s-era range next to it that you never really noticed before. "Those body-image issues can complicate the search for intimacy," Volker said, and they can lead one to ask: "How do I present myself, and how do I date?" Such questions are fraught for many of us, but they can be particularly so for transgender people, according to some mental health professionals. But while some individuals find that transitioning introduces new challenges into intimate relationships, others experience a newfound capacity to forge different, more meaningful kinds of connections. For Ben, both are true.

Today, he says, he's not sure what he wants, or even what sort of person he wants to be with. Some trans men seem to have an easy time articulating who they are and what they're attracted to, he says, "but fuck if I know." He's pretty sure he "prefers female folk," he says; he's not going to "rule anything out." At the conference, the second time Ben has come, surrounded by all the other square pegs in a round-holed world, he feels at home. "I love coming here," he says. "It's where I truly feel that I can be myself."

Writing more than fifty years ago, Harry Benjamin acknowledged that even after transitioning, individuals are "not boundlessly happy and free of disturbance," though he believed they were "better able to find a satisfactory niche in life, perhaps in a job or profession as a bachelor or as a married man." Conforming to a middle-class, heteronormative lifestyle was, he believed, the key to a successful gender transition. Today the 1950s ideal of a breadwinner husband and stay-at-home mother, the context in which Benjamin was writing, is no longer. Middle-class lives look different. For growing numbers of millennials, the traditional markers of adulthood—the promise of a stable relationship, a permanent job, even a home of one's own—are becoming unobtainable longings, quaint reminders of bygone days. As all of our lives become less fixed, and somewhat less certain, once stable gender categories are being sliced and diced and shattered into a million little pieces.

———

"Within the current limiting gender binary culture many people are 'uncategorizable,'" says Leo Caldwell, a writer, activist, and self-described "invalidator of the gender binary." In a workshop called "Gender Cube: Redefining Gender," which promises to enhance my understanding of the "multidimensional elements of gender," Caldwell, who is in his early thirties and wears a button-down shirt and khaki pants, says he wants to devise a different model, one that we can use to speak with people "who don't have any experience except with the binary." In speaking about his youth in Indiana, he says that since he never felt like a woman, he thought, "I must be a man." And yet, "I've never felt quite male either. But I did always feel like me." He always had, he says, "an unshakeable sense of self." Yet, in order to live in the world, he needed to conform, so he "journeyed through styles, hormones, and surgeries." He received diagnoses.

"It all felt so natural, so real, so me. Until I was labeled. Until I was diagnosed." He never felt dysphoric, he says. Still, he felt that he needed to alter his body to conform to the dominant gender binary. It led him on a quest to complicate our models of gender. "People are so stuck in the binary, I wanted to move beyond it, but I want to be understandable to people," he tells the crowd of about three hundred. "There's a great deal of pressure to identify with the binary that comes from the outside world—media, our families, our schools," says Caldwell. (Caldwell goes by Leo; his website identifies him as Leo Natasha Caldwell).[2] Some trans narratives, such as the surgical Big Reveal, feed into the binary as well. "Why are we stuck in a binary which fails to describe how many of us think about and experience gender?" he asks. His presentation relies on masculine and feminine concepts but "uses boxes to think outside of them."

A few years ago, people were talking about the gender spectrum. Gender was seen as a continuum, with masculinity on one side, femininity on the other, and androgyny in the middle. But that's so last week. Different continua operate simultaneously, and gender isn't simply one thing, says Caldwell. In his schema, there's the social, or contextual dimension: the ways people are perceived differently here at the conference, or in their workplace, at home, or among friends. There's also the cultural dimension: "how a stranger sees you," which is shaped in part by "gender props"—hair, ties, et cetera—objects we use to manage the impressions others have of us. And finally, there is "personal, or self gender": "how you feel when you're alone," says Caldwell. Caldwell takes the idea of a spectrum, which is how many trans-identified people speak of gender, and represents it three-dimensionally. On a PowerPoint slide he presents a multicolored graphic of a cube. Each side of the cube represents a different axis of gender: a *self identity* axis (x), a *social identity* axis (y), and a *cultural identity* axis (z). Each axis, in turn, is visualized as a spectrum: masculinity on one side, femininity on the other. The exact middle is gender-neutral. It all seems fairly logical, if a bit unwieldy.

Caldwell asks audience members to rank themselves, choosing a number that corresponds to where they would place themselves in relation to three dimensions of gender: personal, social, and cultural. To get the discussion rolling, he describes his own gender identity: 3Xm, 2Yf, 3Zm, which he breaks down into "how I see myself, how I want to be seen, and how I am seen." He explains that while he sees himself in the middle of the masculine side of the spectrum (3Xm), when it comes to how he presents himself to others, he is closer to the middle of the feminine side of the spectrum (2Yf). But others tend to see him as fairly masculine (3Zm)—both more masculine than how he himself "feels" and more masculine than the ways he presents himself socially.

Members of the audience join in enthusiastically. One young feminine-looking person with green streaks in her hair asks: "How can you capture fluidity?" A more masculine-presenting person queries: "How will you talk about people with more than two genders?"

Another audience member suggests that the best way to picture gender is as a galaxy: "Every gender is unique." Caldwell responds: "Yes, clearly, gender is a much more complex social system than simply male or female."

A young feminine-presenting person suggests that Caldwell take a look at the "unicorn" model, which complicates things even further. Instead of three axes, it has five: gender identity, gender expression, sex assigned at birth, physical attraction, and emotional attraction. It shares, with Caldwell's model, a rejection of binaries, and it conceives of gender and sexuality as a series of continua—except for the category "sex assigned at birth," which consists of female, male, and other/intersex. Everyone has their own gender unicorn, their own relationship to gender plotted along multiple axes. Some school districts have begun to use the gender unicorn model to educate teachers and staff about gender identity and expression. (In August 2016, a Charlotte, North Carolina, school district came under attack after conservative parents declared that the unicorn model "penalizes those of us who believe we were created male and female and should be able to use those terms.")[3]

Caldwell's multidimensional attempt to visualize gender suggests that gender is both highly subjective and also socially embedded. How we feel, how we experience our "authentic" selves, is never simply a matter of "who we are." We make sense of our embodied desires and feelings in relation to the messages others give us about our bodies, the categories societies create to order those bodies, and the ways we make sense of ourselves in relation to those categories. These efforts to build a better, more complex model of gender stem from the desire to visualize, and verbalize, gender's complexity, and to achieve recognition from others for that complexity. Without names, and ways to describe ourselves to ourselves and to others, we do not exist.

But for some members of the audience, even gender spectra, unicorns, grids, or continua fail to tell the whole story. "Different cultures are less binary than the West, and yet your model doesn't acknowledge that," says an androgynous audience member who appears to be of South Asian descent, and who pronounces the gender cube Eurocentric.

"You define yourself." Caldwell nods approvingly. "You don't have to fit into the boxes." Still, we must be intelligible to those around us, he tells her. Acknowledging the power of social regulation and the complexity of gender, Caldwell proposes that we should be able to legally file our gender at eighteen, and we should be able to revise that identity every ten years. Clearly, the meaning of transgender is in flux. The language of pathology that underpinned the notion of "gender identity disorder" and still haunts the idea of dysphoria, which calls upon people to adapt to the society

that surrounds them, is giving way to a more subjective and affirmative understanding of transgender identity.

There are those who migrate from one gender to another, who
embrace the gender "opposite" to the one they were assigned at
birth, and who seek to permanently assimilate as a member of
that gender. Many transgender people continue to subscribe to the
medical model because it speaks to their sense of difference and
provides access to medical interventions. For a younger, college-
educated group of trans folks, who have come of age in a postfeminist, queer, and Internet-savvy age, the idea that one starts at one
place (as female, in the case of trans men) and ends up at another
point (male) without ever looking back is looking passé. More and
more people are refusing to identify clearly as male or female and
are remaining "in between."

To openly identify as transgender is, in a way, to stake a claim for
in-betweenness, which acknowledges that one was assigned female
or male at birth but has made a choice to embrace a different gender identity. Calling oneself genderqueer or "masculine-of-center"
gestures toward this as well. The various bodily transformations
that "used to form a complete package have been unbundled,"
observes sociologist Rogers Brubaker. "One can now mix and
match elements or experiment with different forms of embodiment at different times"—a stance that was clearly on view at the
Philadelphia conference, and to a great extent in the lives of Ben,
Parker, and Lucas, and even Nadia.[4] Others seek to transcend
categories altogether. They see all categories as traps and gender
as something one *does,* rather than something one *is.* Some call
themselves "agender" or "ungendered" and are experimenting with
language that seeks to do away with gender altogether. In Japan,
for example, there is a growing movement of "x-jendā" (x-gender)
people who identify as neither male nor female.[5] The "postmillen-

nial" generation seems to be even more open to gender diversity. A 2015 survey of a thousand thirteen- to twenty-year-olds in the United States reported that 56 percent knew someone who used gender-neutral pronouns such as "ze," and more than 80 percent agreed that gender does not define a person as much as it used to.[6]

"The whole idea of the gender binary has been shattered," psychologist Margaret Nichols tells me. A revolt from within is energizing the trans movement, leading to a proliferation of categories that are ever more fine-tuned. For example, a recent survey of nearly thirty-five hundred transgender-identified people asked them how they identify. Among the choices were transsexual, transgender, cross-dresser, transvestite, genderqueer, or "other." Few transgender people identified as transsexual or cross-dresser, the binary-bound terms of choice for an older generation, and among those under thirty-five, "genderqueer" was the most popular identifier. While the vast majority of respondents classified themselves as male, female, or transgender, close to 8 percent chose the "other" category, which included at least a hundred separate identifying labels, including "queer," "fluid," and "third gender," to name a few.[7]

One of the most striking findings of the study is the degree to which gender categories are generationally based. For an older cohort of trans people, these categories are bound by the gender binary. For a younger generation, or at least for those who are part of the conversation at conferences like this one, gender is fluid and variable, which means that their positioning within a multiplicity of genders depends upon context. One of the other interesting findings is that those who were assigned female at birth were more likely to report being comfortable with non-binary identity categories—I am neither male nor female.

"I'm an agender individual with multiple transition experiences," an audience member declares at the end of the workshop.

"My first transition was transmasculine (I lived in Kansas so I didn't have access to information). In my first transition, I went hyper-masculine. In my second transition—I was bi-gender—I identified as both male and female. I'm this today, and this tomorrow. People didn't know what to make of me. My third transition: I wouldn't deal with any of this gender bullshit if I didn't have to." Today, they say, "I'm agender. I gave up gender clothing entirely and just go with a medieval-style monastic gender tunic [a formless brown outfit, belted at the waist]. So that's me, adding the dimension of time and complicating it to the nth degree."

"This is an evolution, a revolution," enthuses Leo Caldwell. "We are the catalyst for reaching past a binary. The takeaway is that there is no standard."

I've been studying gender and sexuality for nearly three decades, and yet right now, sitting in this workshop, I feel a bit like Rip van Winkle, having suddenly awoken after a deep sleep to find that the landscape of gender has changed so radically that I no longer recognize it. As the session ends, I text my partner, Cynthia: "You would not believe how many names there are for gender these days. You and I are dinosaurs." I feel a swirl of mixed emotions. On the one hand, there is relief. The menu of limited choices with which I grew up—be a wife and mother or be destined to be an outsider, a lesser woman, a spinster, or a dyke—has been replaced by a supermarket of gender options. Finally!

Facebook recognizes fifty-six custom gender options. New York City now recognizes thirty-one genders: bi-gendered, cross-dresser, drag king, drag queen, femme queen, female-to-male, FTM, gender gender, genderqueer, male-to-female, MTF, non-op, hijra, pangender, transexual/transsexual, trans person, woman, man, butch, two-spirit, trans, agender, third sex, gender fluid, non-binary transgender, androgyne, gender gifted, gender blender, femme, person of transgender experience, androgynous.⁸ Here, at the conference, there are even more categories to choose from, so many that it often seems that our gender identity is so deeply personal that the only thing each of us can say for sure is that we alone possess it.

I am relieved and also, quite frankly, a bit bewildered by it all. My generation of feminists tried to tamp down gender as a way of minimizing its oppressiveness. We emphasized the similarities between men and women, embracing androgyny and unisex style, giving boys and girls the same toys, changing the language we used to refer to men and women as well as the messages we gave young people about what kinds of jobs are appropriate. My generation believed that gender is imposed on us by advertising, scientific experts, parents, teachers, and other influences. By taking control of how society defined gender, we believed that we could create a world where gender differences would play an insignificant, or at least minimal, role. We thought we could undo gender's hold on our lives.

Most of the younger people I interviewed for this book, in contrast, seem to have little interest in obliterating gender altogether. They acknowledge, quite rightly, that gender is institutionalized through norms, routines, and laws; and that it is shaped by those who have the power to define those norms, routines, and laws. Societies define gendered possibilities, affirming certain ways of living in the world and diminishing others, making some ways of being men and women more acceptable than others. They provide a template for imagining how we should or could live. Biological processes rooted in the body also help make us who we are. In addition, we also draw from a rich storehouse of unconscious fantasies, memories, and feelings, some of which we learn in our families, as well as from widely recognized cultural values.⁹ "Each person personally inflects and creates her 'own' gender," as the feminist psychoanalyst Nancy Chodorow has written. Individuals are not simply reflections of the culture. We push up against it, adopting some of its values, resisting others. The people I write about in this book find the courage to defy the rules, challenging authority figures and undergoing painful, expensive body modifications, often at great risk to themselves: they feel that they need to be true to themselves, and they know that society isn't necessarily going to accommodate them.

My generation of feminists thought we could undo the constraints of gender by casting off high heels and constraining bras, and refusing to abide by "gender roles" in the family and without. We tried to conjure a world, through talk, through community building, and by passing civil rights protections, in which women and men would become more fundamentally similar to each other. We made it sexy and fun to be lesbians, whom we often saw as the vanguard of resistance to "the patriarchy." Today's generation continues some of those projects. It, too, is acutely aware of the limitations of the ways we organize gender, and the ways the powerful have the capacity to define what is and isn't normal. But the younger people I met in researching this book are much more willing to let a thousand genders bloom, and to see the modification of bodies, and language, as the foundation for such projects. For them the struggle for greater freedom of gender expression is the focus.

Language is changing at a breakneck pace, describing new, previously unknown forms of identification. Lee Naught, who identifies as mixed-race, Chican@, and genderqueer, writes: "I live in a space of gray, which is what queerness is all about to me: defining oneself rather than being trapped within unchangeable categories."[10] A younger generation of gender activists, who have come of age in a consumerist society of seemingly endless choices, is developing new words to describe how bodies, selves, and feelings collide. The proliferation of categories in evidence here at the conference is an attempt to translate the cornucopia of gender options, and the shattering of the two-gender model, into language. The *Oxford English Dictionary,* which charts a thousand years of changes in the English language, recently added Mx., a gender-neutral replacement for titles such as Mr. and Mrs. One day, if Leo Caldwell has his way, perhaps we'll say: *Just call me a 3Xm/2Yf/3Zm. Or a non-binary transgender gender gifted androgyne.* Good riddance "men" and "women"!

Categories can be useful. In a world where people increasingly interact via social media, categories seem essential. When we have words to describe distinctions among things, we can more easily differentiate among them. Speaking of popular music, the journalist Tom Vanderbilt writes, "We listeners are endless and instinctual categorizers, allotting everything its spot like bins in a record store. The human brain is a pattern-matching machine. Categories help us manage the torrent of information we receive and sort the world into easier-to-read patterns."[11] But categories don't just reflect distinctions; they also create them. When we put things in a category, they become more alike in our minds. Things we might have viewed as more similar become, when placed into two different categories, more different. "The tendency is always strong," John Stuart Mill wrote in 1869, "to believe that whatever receives a name must be an entity or being, having an independent existence of its own."[12]

Today's generation of gender dissidents argues that becoming transgender isn't simply about altering one's body, or fitting in to some preconceived notion of how we should live; it's about creating a meaningful life. For some people, that means changing one's body, including one's chest, to align it with a subjective sense of gender, assimilating into existing social categories that divide the world into gendered bodies. But for others, it means something different. And that something different can change over time.

———

Certainly transgender people are forcing many of us to rethink what sex and gender mean. The old division we used to draw between "sex" and "gender," where the former is a matter of chromosomes or genitals, which are fixed at birth, and the latter is a matter of how we were brought up, and is therefore more malleable, now seems exceedingly blurry. It turns out that one's sex, if we believe that it is located in the body, is fairly malleable, at least if we have access to the right tools. Gender, on the other hand, may or may not be as changeable on the level of the individual. Some of us identify strongly as one gender or another. But for others, gender is in flux.

It's not simply gender that is in flux, according to the late sociologist Zygmunt Bauman: everything is. Bauman characterizes the postmodern world in which we live as a "liquid society." We once thought of marriage in terms of "till death do us part" and imagined that we would spend our lives working for one company, or in one profession. Now we are more likely to see marriage as temporary and relationships as somewhat more fleeting, along with careers. In the past, we would furnish our homes with things that we inherited from grandparents and other relatives. Now, the *New York Times* reports, older people are having a difficult time downsizing because their children and grandchildren don't want their things: they can buy new, inexpensive furniture at Ikea.[13] It's not only work, or things, or love that is liquid. So are social relationships. I hardly know any of my neighbors, but I have nearly five hundred friends on Facebook. Liquid jobs, liquid friends, liquid gender.

Writing this book challenged many of my assumptions about gender and its fixity. I no longer assume that there is a simple congruence between people's gender presentation and what's beneath their clothes, between appearance and reality. Passing through airports, I now find myself looking at people, questioning whether the statuesque thin blonde in a white dress or the bearish man in a Gators baseball cap is all that meets the eye. I'm more likely to question the assumed naturalness of the normal and the mysteries that lie beneath the surface of the bodies that surround us. If Theo, the buff tattooed male I met in South Florida, began his life assigned female, how can I be sure that the same isn't true of the tattooed gentleman in front of me on line at the supermarket? I find the uncertainty reassuring.

Feminism enabled me to cast off makeup, dresses, and deferential behavior, freeing me from the compulsion to perform extraordinary feats of femininity. Why, I wondered when I set off to write this book, couldn't others make the same choices? Wasn't modifying one's body a bit extreme? I was once among those who wondered whether transgender reinforces rather than subverts gender categories and the binary gender system. On occasion, that may indeed be true. But over the course of the past year, I've also come to appreciate how this generation is embracing gender's complexity. I wonder how I would feel if I were coming of age today, faced with so many choices, when one's experience can be optimized if the right "search terms" are found. What gender would I choose, and once I'd chosen one, would I feel that I had got it right? What are the implications of knowing that one's gender is something one can always revise? And how does one make time for the mundane tasks of everyday life, like flossing one's teeth or raising children?

In the future, if we become more accustomed to diverse gender presentations, individuals may be more likely to move away from their assigned gender without undergoing body modifications at all. Or we may see the proliferation of body modifications that have little to do with transitioning to one gender or another. "I think we're going to make choices about our bodies, and how we want to look, that aren't going to have to do with gender identity," Bishop, the South Florida trans activist, tells me. "People are going to be operating outside of a physical binary." Bishop knows men who are bi-gender and married and sexually intimate with their wives "who play with estrogen," he says. They like having some breast tissue. He also knows lesbians "who don't want breasts anymore." It's not easy to walk into a surgeon's office and do that, but it is getting easier. "More people want the option just to be comfortable in their skin, and that's empowering." Recently he met a queer activist from South Africa who told him that she woke up every day wondering whether she would have enough food to eat that day. "Being able to express her gender identity is maybe number six on her list of daily priorities," he says. Gender expression is important, and it may even be a matter of life and death for some people. But it is, he acknowledges, a "First World problem."

Many of the transgender men I met in Florida who were awaiting top surgery, who live in places like Wichita, or Calgary, or small-town Tennessee, have little interest in embracing their inner unicorns, or plotting themselves in relation to gender cubes. Beyond the world of trans health conferences, queer theory courses, trans-affirmative therapists, and certain corners of the Internet, the gender binary is still alive and well, and many (if not most) trans people are still quite wedded to it. They want to live lives that make sense to them, and they want to use public bathrooms in peace. The folks I met who were recovering from top surgery at the guesthouse in

Florida were mostly medical technicians and workers in corporate back offices, not rebels or people who want to make art about their gender journeys. Some believed in their hearts that the two-gender model is highly limited, and that it fails to do justice to their lives, yet they desperately wish to move from one clearly defined gender to another. They're preoccupied with figuring out how to make a living, and with repairing the bonds that were frayed with their families by their transitions, or by their partnering with someone undergoing one. They simply want the right to be ordinary.

Since I've known him, Ben has looked for a way to live in the world as a male, more or less, without attracting too much attention, while also educating people about his transgender identity. He has one foot in his small Maine community, where traditional assumptions of what it means to be a male or female rule, and the other foot in the proud tribe of gender-slashers at this conference. He's clear about feeling masculine and wanting to embrace a clear gender identity as a man, but he's also a relentless seeker, someone who tries to be the best person he can possibly be. "On a scale of one to ten, ten being a man and one being a woman, I feel physically like a nine or ten, and mentally, more like a six," Ben tells me. Even without a phallus, he says. Yet he acknowledges the limitations of language.

"I can't even say that I can neatly put my finger on exactly what words describe who I am. Trans man, yes, that's typically the box I fit into. But does that really describe who I am? No. I think that it's more complicated than that. I'm sure more words will come out in time, or maybe they will be a better fit. But the act of identifying with others means that, oh God, I'm not alone. Not being alone gives me the space to think and explore those possibilities."

———

These days, Ben feels much better operating in the world as a man. But the place he once imagined as a destination looks hazier and a lot less clear than it did when he began his journey. For a while, figuring out whether to transition at all and then how to go about doing so—how to access hormones, pay for top surgery, disclose his intentions to friends and family, organize his top surgery trip, and recover—was a preoccupation. It defined him, gave him a focus and a road map for remaking his life. Today, having transitioned, he has lost some of that focus and the excitement and sense of purpose it introduced into his life. Some of his old baggage is weighing him down.

Being at the conference is a reminder that there's a small but growing transgender "industry" that provides medical, legal, cultural, and emotional support for transitioning. There are the surgeons who have developed lively, lucrative specialties serving transgender clients. There are the corps of therapists who meld psychology, feminism, New Age philosophy, and old-fashioned American individualism to serve their trans clients. There are networks of support and advocacy organizations, an extensive array of print and web-based support literature, and makers of transition paraphernalia and swag.

"I've been saving for this conference," Ben tells me before we part ways. "The 'merch' area is my favorite part." He purchases a copy of *FTM* magazine and some books published by something called Transgress Press: an anthology about transgender men's bottoms called *Below the Belt*, and another called *Hung Jury,* and some "packers"—which trans men use to give the illusion of having a penis. He also picks up a trans man's memoir, a book for partners of trans men ("to loan to my future partners"), a bunch of kids' books ("if I ever have kids or for friends' kids"). He takes a selfie with Aydian Dowling and buys lots of T-shirts emblazoned with trans-affirmative sayings like "This is what trans looks like," "Transtastic," and "Own your journey, tread stealthily." There are the vaguer, more spiritual ones, too, such as "You are as important as all things in the universe, including the stars and the trees" and "Less Human, More Being."

There's a lot to appreciate about his life. Moving through the world as a male feels better, truer. His family and friends have stuck by him during his transition, and he still vacations with his parents—recently in the Pacific Northwest, where they gazed at the majestic Mount Rainier, and they saw orcas. Bob barely stumbled on the male pronouns. Ben's beginning a new venture too: a skills-building exchange for community organizers. And he has a new dog, a mutt named Remy. But had he placed too much confidence in the belief that changing his body would transform his life for the better?

When I put that question to Ben, his response was emphatic. "Oh my God, this might sound cheesy or silly or something," he told me, "but I feel like my whole self, finally. I always had this picture of myself as an adult that looks like me now. And I feel like I've finally grown up." When we first met more than a year ago, he described himself as a "late bloomer." Today, even as he has yet to achieve many of the traditional milestones of middle-class adulthood, he feels that he has finally come into his own. Instead of going through the motions, he is living his life, trying to inhabit it as fully as he can.

It is the improvisational nature of this process that is so striking today. Gender benders become gender-crossers. Gender-crossers start out wanting to "pass" as their chosen gender, and then they decide to bend gender, emphasizing ambiguity, blurring boundaries between male and female. Although some individuals are content to move from one gender to another, a growing number of gender-variant individuals see their identities as temporary stops on a much longer, circuitous journey, rather than as a destination that was fixed in advance.

"We all change. All we can know is what we know at any given point," therapist Arlene Lev tells me. "Many people explore and experience gender in different ways, at different points in their lives. These are people who are continuing to grow," says Lev, referring to the shape-shifting character of many young people's identities. "They are saying: this is not the end of my story." For Ben, Parker, and Lucas, medical transitioning is neither the beginning nor the end of their story. Though Nadia is not undergoing a transition, she shares some things in common with those who do: the belief that bodies are malleable, and that individuals should have the right to change them if they wish. In fact, it seems to me now that the very frame of "transition" that so intrigued me at the beginning of this project may hide at least as much as it reveals.

The mid-twentieth-century model of medical gender transitioning was originally designed to enable individuals to create new lives and assimilate into a fixed gender order. Women who felt at odds with their gender could become men, and men could become women. It assumed that to be successful one needed to pass as either a man or a woman and fit into what was then a highly polarized gender system. Because our ideas of progress are so intertwined with science and our notions of gender so rooted in the body, we tend to believe that once medical sex reassignment procedures became available, they settled the matter of gender variance. But transitioning is about a lot more than the surgery one undergoes. Even if it were possible to modify the body to have all the "necessary equipment," transitioning entails much more than simply moving from one gender to another, as I learned in my travels through one corner of the transgender world.

It's still true that most of us feel that in order to get along in the world we need to present ourselves as "either" male or female. Not doing so can place us at risk of familial rejection, employment discrimination, and violence. But by openly identifying themselves as transgender, today's gender dissidents are saying that male and female are not enough. Gender, sex, and sexuality have become the focus of self-conscious choices and political claims. We don't yet live in a postgender world. But we do live in a world that is opening up the possibility of making gender more personal and flexible, calling into question the very basis of the categories we once took for granted. They are trying to build a culture that makes it possible to feel affirmed in one's body—the body one inherits or the body one chooses to modify.

Say good-bye to *Ozzie and Harriet,* the television sitcom that once beamed a white, middle-class, heteronormative ideal of family into millions of living rooms in the country. So long to *Modern Family,* a show that introduces family diversity, at least in relation to sexuality and race, to mass television audiences in the new millennium. One can imagine that in the family sitcom of the future, the fatherly figure sitting at the head of the table will be someone who spent the first twenty years of his life known as a female. And when a gender-nonconforming child takes their place among the assembled rainbow mix of kin, it won't be the point of focus, or big reveal, or plot twist, but an unremarkable aspect of family life.

In that day of the not-too-distant future, we may take for granted the fact that identities given to us at birth are actually quite malleable. "My generation opened up all sorts of possibilities of living in one's body, and loving whom one chooses," said my seventy-five-year-old friend Kate, who first got me started on this project, "and this generation is opening it up even more."

Afterword

One evening in mid-November 2016, Ben drove down Route 9, a few miles away from his house. Alongside him a car traveled at about thirty-five miles an hour. Ben passed the other car, which was operated by a white man in his fifties, and when he did, the driver of the other car sped up and tried to run him off the road. Ben pulled into a nearby gas station, out of breath, and then proceeded to drive home. When he arrived home, the man in the other car was there waiting for him. "Is that guy stalking me?" Ben wondered. He pulled out his cell phone and took a picture of the other car's license plate, and the stranger sped off into the night.

Ben immediately drove to the local police department. It turned out he knew the dispatch person on duty, who was the mother of a high school friend. He didn't know if she recognized him or not, but he was too embarrassed and shaken "to tell her it's me." He had never been so scared in his life.

Ben had been as out as anyone I met while I was writing this book. A transgender-pride bumper sticker gleamed on the back of his car, and he'd happily tell anyone who asked what it meant. He felt that it was his political duty to challenge co-workers, friends, family, and even strangers at times, to recognize him as a transgender man, rather than to try to blend in seamlessly. But in November of

2016, right after the presidential election, Ben began to hear about hate crimes sweeping through small towns and cities throughout the nation, targeting people of color, suspected Muslims, and Jews. He wasn't naïve enough to imagine that transgender people would be immune from the growing atmosphere of intolerance. Despite the fact that he passed, for all intents and purposes, as a white cisgender guy, he suddenly felt more vulnerable than ever before.

When I spoke with him shortly after the incident, he told me that he would be taking the trans-pride sticker off his car. "All my stickers are coming off this afternoon. I can't do this. I don't know that I am as strong as so many others."

Although the Obama administration had moved farther than any other to enshrine transgender rights into the law, that didn't make it suddenly safe to be out as transgender, and trans people— particularly trans women of color—reported high levels of harassment and violence, according to a recent survey of more than twenty-seven thousand transgender and gender-nonconforming individuals by the National LGBTQ Task Force and the National Center for Transgender Equality.[1] Transgender populations are disproportionately poor because of employment discrimination, family rejection, and difficulty accessing school, medical care, and social services. These factors increase individuals' participation in criminalized work, such as sex work, in order to survive, which means that they experience higher levels of incarceration too. As lawyer and activist Dean Spade reminds us, the gendered organization of society exerts "an especially strong presence in the lives of poor people."[2]

Transgender people also encounter widespread institutional discrimination. More than half of those who sought insurance coverage for a transition-related surgery in the past year were denied, and more than a third who saw a healthcare provider in the past year reported having negative experiences related to being transgender. Those who are disabled, imprisoned, or undocumented faced ongoing challenges. But the survey also revealed that more than half of respondents who had disclosed their transgender status to their immediate family reported that their family was supportive of them, and more than two-thirds of those whose co-workers knew their status reported that co-workers were supportive. And while many social and legal barriers still exist, some recent openings, including growing federal support for antidiscrimination laws, were making a difference.

Ben, along with Parker and Lucas, and even Nadia, too, was among the beneficiaries of these cultural and political changes. Their willingness to share their stories with me, and to do so very openly, without fear of reprisal, testified to that. Of course, the fact that they have grown up with social media and reality television, which makes the personal eminently public, may have played an important role as well. But just as the culture has opened up, it could also easily constrict again, making it more difficult to be transgender. Activists knew this. Anticipating a possible Trump presidency, transgender people were cautioned to protect themselves legally while they still could, and in the fall Ben legally changed his name, along with his gender marker, completing the process right under the wire. Still, he never anticipated the kind of fear he would feel that night, confronted by a stranger in a car.

Days later, armed with the license plate number of the driver, Ben was able to trace the identity of the person who had followed him. When he did so, he concluded that the other driver's actions were not politically motivated, but an incident of road rage—he was not harassed for being transgender after all. Chances are, the guy who followed him might not have even known the meaning of the bumper sticker, which contained a transgender symbol that mixed symbolic representations of female, male, and androgyny. "Of course, it's still not okay," said Ben. But, he acknowledged, "I have noticed that my temper has been running hotter since the election. My patience is shorter as my stress runs higher."

Just because I'm paranoid doesn't mean they're not out to get me.

And, in fact, Ben, who was adamant about using his real name in this book, was so shaken up by that incident that he decided to go by a pseudonym, fearful that being out in this book might attract undue attention, and possible violence. A couple of other subjects in this book decided similarly. They did so reluctantly, despite their conviction that it is important for transgender people to be out, as a way of educating others and throwing off shame. And yet today, suspicions run high, and fear, like hate, is easily inflamed. When I spoke with Oliver Klicker, whose artwork is unapologetically genderqueer, he talked about the sudden shift in the rules of public engagement. Railing against so-called political correctness, growing numbers of Americans now feel entitled to speak their mind—even if it threatens the well-being of others, he said. "In our current sociopolitical climate," he told me, "I find my fears intensifying as people are encouraged by our new government leaders to 'tell it like it is,' regardless of what 'it' is and where their opinion came from."

I've spent much of life taking for granted a belief in the forward march of progress, at least when it comes to matters of gender and sexuality. I know that not so many decades ago, an out gay or lesbian person had the potential to land in jail, or in a mental institution. I don't remember those days firsthand, but I can certainly recall a time when loving one's own sex meant being disowned by one's family, and living in a culture of self-loathing, at best. In my lifetime, we have seen enormous movement in this area: unprecedented freedom and the expansion of possibilities for self-determination and the celebration of human difference. As the British historian of sexuality Jeffrey Weeks has written, "The contemporary world is a world we are making for ourselves, part of the long process of the democratization of everyday life."[3] The rise of transgender people represents a new stage in this evolution.

A few decades ago, in San Francisco, New York, and other cities, female-assigned people began to gather and take tentative steps to affirm their right to live as masculine persons. More recently, empowered by the Internet's capacity to connect them instantaneously, they (and their MTF counterparts) pushed medical gatekeepers to view them differently, and they made common cause with lesbians and gay men, who came to see the transgender struggle as separate from but connected to theirs, and part of a larger movement for self-determination. Transgender people began to gain greater visibility and power, not only on the coasts and in cities, but in small towns and rural areas too. An earlier generation of transgender people aspired to pass as completely as possible and were convinced that their well-being depended on their ability to fade into the woodwork. Today, in contrast, more and more individuals wish to be known openly as transgender. Twenty states and the District of Columbia offer protections based on gender identity, and the legal recognition of gender-nonconforming people is now on the agenda too.

In 2016, in a groundbreaking ruling, an Oregon judge decided that Jamie Shupe, a retired army sergeant, should be able to identify as neither sex and be classified as non-binary. Shortly after that, both Oregon and Washington, D.C., added a gender-neutral identifier to drivers' licenses. In 2017 Canada began to offer a "third gender" option on passports or national identification cards, following the example of India, Germany, Australia, Bangladesh, Malta, Nepal, New Zealand, and Pakistan, which already did so. A third gender category confers official recognition to those whose gender identity or gender expression deviates from the binary model. With time, changing gendered social classifications could make it easier for people who refuse to choose one gender or who behave in ways that fundamentally deviate from the sex/gender they were assigned at birth.

But the door that recently opened, enabling more transgender people to come out and access medical interventions if they wish, as well as legal protections that recognize their right to autonomy and inclusion, could close. In November 2015, voters in Houston repealed an antidiscrimination ordinance that included gender orientation as a protected class. In March 2016, North Carolina prohibited people whose gender presentation does not match the sex specified on their birth certificate from using public bathrooms. And then a president who has promised to restore national greatness and white male dominance took office.

Weeks into his presidency, Trump rescinded Obama-era guidelines that protected transgender students from discrimination. Emboldened by the administration's stance, twenty-two states introduced religious exemption laws to limit LGBT persons' rights, effectively allowing discrimination against LGBT people in relation to adoption, as well as to accessing healthcare and social services. And then, in August 2017, Trump announced that he would reverse a policy that enabled transgender individuals to serve openly in the military and that he would cut off funds for gender-reassignment surgery for military personnel. The Family Research Council, a conservative Christian group, praised the decision. "Our troops shouldn't be forced to endure hours of transgender 'sensitivity' classes and politically correct distractions like this one," it declared. Another wrote: "The purpose of the military is to defend the U.S., not to be a test tube of liberal social experimentation."[4] President

Trump's attempt to repeal the Affordable Care Act, which made it illegal for health insurance companies to refuse coverage to patients with pre-existing conditions, including "gender dysphoria," also threatened the well-being of transgender people. Transgender people continued to battle with health insurance companies for coverage for transition-related surgery and hormones, even while the ACA is in effect. But its repeal would certainly exclude many more people from receiving body modifications.

While some suggested that the president's decision to go after transgender people was a distraction, it was very much in keeping with his campaign's promise to restore an imagined past—where men and women know their place. At a time of heightened economic insecurity, the promise to restore simpler days is a temporary balm to some, even as it threatens to make others second-class citizens. Collectively, the Right stands for the reinforcement of racial, ethnic, class, gender, and sexual hierarchies and the belief that these hierarchies are natural and/or God given. The existence of transgender people is threatening to them because it suggests that many aspects of who we are as individuals aren't really fixed at all.[5]

Today's greater fluidity of identities began with industrial capitalism's massive movement of populations into factories and cities, and away from the families and communities of their birth. It meant that young women and men could make a living for themselves and stand apart from their families of origin if they wished, forging their own life path. Later, in the 1960s, as a younger generation came to champion self-fulfillment and self-expression, consumer capitalism furthered that unsettling of identities. The rise of LGBT people, which challenges the belief that our gender, our sexuality, and indeed our identities are fixed at birth, is a continuation of that long movement toward personal autonomy. It declares that individuals should have the capacity to invent ourselves and make our own choices. That is precisely what is so unsettling to those who oppose transgender rights.

Transgender visibility may well be one of the casualties of a national shift to the right, at least in the short term. Gender-variant people will continue to seek out surgery, such as chest masculinization, and access to hormones, but conservative activists and elected officials are likely to challenge efforts to expand private and government insurance coverage for gender transitions, along with laws that allow people to use the bathroom of their choice. "Bathroom bills" designed to bar transgender people from using public restrooms that match their gender identity are likely to be introduced across the country, and at least some of them will pass, leading to renewed surveillance, stigma, and policing.

Some of the people I interviewed for this book worry that being out as transgender may soon become much more dangerous, and that those who embrace non-binary gender presentations will be particularly vulnerable. A newly emboldened Far Right, which preaches racial purity, could also make life much more difficult for those who refuse to respect racial divisions, and there may be pressure for people who transgress fixed identity categories of all sorts to retreat individually and collectively. The dream of a world of greater choice and equality may be much farther away than many of us had previously believed.

"I wish I had an answer, a plan, a solution," says Ben, referring to the current political moment. "But I don't." His indefatigable optimism, so visible during the time I've come to know him, seems more muted now. "We just have to get through one day at a time," he says. "Be gentle with ourselves and others. One day at a time. One. Day. One step at a time." For most of his life, his body felt like a burden, weighing him down. For the past few years, he's been pretty preoccupied with his transition. Now he's better able to focus on other things: making a living, finding a romantic partner, and engaging in politics that matter to him. He feels more grounded in who he is, and more focused, which isn't to say he has figured it all out—he hasn't. But as larger questions loom all around, and new vulnerabilities emerge, he acknowledges, "Gender isn't all of who I am. It's just one part of my identity." However challenging the current circumstances may be, it still feels good to be able to say that.

Acknowledgments

I've accumulated many debts while writing this book. Kate Horsfield told me about her trip to South Florida, which sparked my interest in this project. Her tales of growing up as a boyish girl in Texas in the 1950s were always interesting and fun. Ben Shepherd graciously opened his life up to me, allowing me to accompany him on doctor visits and hang out with him before and after surgery and in Maine, and we Skyped and talked more times than either of us can remember over the course of nearly two years. He also read the entire manuscript and gave me feedback on it, helpfully debating with me at times about my take on things, including my interpretation of his life story. Throughout it all, he was always cheerful and wise. He also introduced me to Chrissy, Lindsey, Megan, and Allison, who spoke with me about their good friend, along with his brother, Chris. To Ben, I am eternally grateful.

I never really knew what Gail and Bob thought of the middle-aged college professor who landed, seemingly out of the blue, in their family. Was I being a pest by asking them lots of personal questions? Was I intruding upon their privacy? They said they hoped my book might "help other families going through this process." When we spoke by phone the month before my trip to Maine, Ben thanked me for spending time with them in Florida.

"I think it was really useful for my parents," he said. Perhaps my presence offered a neutral listening space. In any event, I learned a great deal from them, for which I am very grateful.

Parker, Nadia, and Lucas were more than generous to share their stories. I am hugely thankful to them for putting up with my curiosity; for their openness, good humor, and thoughtfulness, and for their willingness to go public. Getting to know each of them over the course of a year was a highlight of researching and writing this book. Thanks are also due to those who accompanied them to surgery in Florida, for speaking with me.

Wendy Chapkis, Sonja Pei-Fen Dale, Steven Epstein, Joshua Gamson, Janice Irvine, Tey Meadow, Joanne Meyerowitz, Sharon Miller, Jodi O'Brien, Jenni Olson, Julee Raiskin, Susan Stryker, Polly Thistlethwaite, and Phil Zuckerman offered helpful comments, introductions, or conversations. I explored some of the ideas that eventually made their way into this book at a seminar at the Institute for Research on Women, with Yolanda Martínez-San Miguel and Sarah Tobias at the helm. Thanks to the seminar, I met JB Brager, who became a research assistant on this project, and whose knowledge and skills were invaluable. The Rutgers Research Council and the School of Arts and Sciences gave me several small grants that made it possible for me to conduct the research for this book. I am thankful to my colleagues in the Department of Sociology at Rutgers. I am especially grateful to Sarah Tobias for supporting my work and for making the Institute for Research on Women such a wonderful space for feminist collaboration; conversations with Ali Howell and Kyla Schuller were also helpful.

In Maine, Wendy Chapkis and Gabe Demaine opened up their home to me; Lisa Sette and Liz Bradfield did so on the Cape. Debbie Nadolney and Sue Goldberg made being there so much fun. Audiences at the Eastern Sociological Society, the International

Sociological Association, and the University of Oregon gave me useful feedback, for which I am grateful. A special shout-out to Tom Linneman, Jennifer Putzi, and their students in the Gender, Sexuality, and Women's Studies program at the College of William and Mary. Thanks are also due to Heather Love at Public Books, and to anonymous reviewers at *Contexts* magazine, where sections of this book previously appeared.

Many people shared their time and expertise with me. Arlene Lev, Margaret Nichols, Jack Pula, Marilyn Volker, and Katherine Rachlin helped me to better understand the therapeutic process as it plays out in the lives of transgender individuals. I am very grateful to each of them for their patience and generosity, though they do not necessarily agree with all of the conclusions I drew from our conversations. Likewise, Michael Brownstein, Charles Garramone, Sherman Leis, Russell Sassani, and Paul Weiss spoke with me about gender surgery and their experiences serving transgender men, and they were generous with their time. Jamison Green shared his personal and political history with me, as did Macauley DeVun, Chris Donovan, Kristin Pula, and Carson Terry. Ben Singer answered some of my questions about transgender health activism, and Henry Rubin helped me better understand the history of social research on transgender. Esther Newton and Deborah Edel talked with me at length about the history of butch lesbian subcultures and loaned me some documentary materials.

In Florida, guests and staffers at New Beginnings, including Daemon, Pete, Sally, Len, Rose, Tristan, James, and others, shared their stories with me. Leland Koble graciously offered his time and insights into Florida's transgender community, as did Bishop S. F. Makalani-MaHee. Sadly, Bishop passed away unexpectedly as this book was nearing completion.

Raine Dozier, Sal Johnston, Ken Plummer, Elizabeth Reis, and stef shuster read the entire manuscript and gave me valuable feedback that helped make this a much better book. Their incisive comments are proof that intellectual work is a collective enterprise, even if it is not always acknowledged as such. I would also like to express gratitude for the work of many pioneering transgender scholars and authors, some of whom are listed in the bibliography. And big thanks to Ted Conover for helping me hone my storytelling skills.

Miriam Altshuler, my agent, found a wonderful home for this project. My editor, Maria Goldverg, offered feedback on multiple drafts and ably guided the manuscript to publication. Her sage advice was invaluable. Copyeditor Helen Maggie Carr navigated the complexities of gendered language with finesse and good humor.

Finally, Cynthia Chris talked through many of the ideas in this book, read a draft, walked our aging beagle, and cooked more than her share of meals. For that and much more, I am truly madly deeply grateful.

Notes on Methods of Research

This book explores one corner of the rapidly changing transmasculine world, focusing on a group of individuals who underwent chest masculinization on the same day, with the same surgeon. I spoke with Ben, Parker, Nadia, and Lucas regularly for more than a year after we first met, either by phone or Skype, and interviewed friends and family members who accompanied them to surgery. Six months after his surgery, I also visited Ben at his home in Maine, and I interviewed several of his close friends and reinterviewed his parents. To ensure that I represented them as accurately as possible, Ben, Parker, Lucas, and Nadia read drafts of all or parts of the book, and I modified some aspects of my account in response. Other interviewees also checked quotes if they wished.

While many transgender men see top surgery as a key aspect of the process of transitioning, some individuals who identify as transgender do not undergo top surgery because they cannot afford to do so, or because they simply choose not to undertake it. The surgical experience is at times central to what it means to be transgender or gender nonconforming, but at other times it may play little or no role. Focusing on one group of individuals who underwent body modifications means that I under-sample transgender men who cannot (because of financial and other constraints) or choose not to (because of identifications or preferences) masculinize their chests. By recruiting interviewees from among those who are undergoing a medical procedure, I surely under-sample trans-identified individuals who do not choose surgical interventions, such as those who use testosterone only, or those who do not undergo body modifications at all.

Because the surgeon I focus on does not accept insurance and is particularly celebrated, my book represents a more homogeneous group of transgender people than the transgender population as a whole. While there was somewhat greater racial/ethnic diversity among the patient population the second day I visited the surgeon's office, since I had decided in advance to focus on those having surgery the same day as Ben, I did not interview them. I've tried my best to compensate for this shortcoming by including additional voices in the book.

Readers may wonder why I include in a book about transgender men one key respondent who does not identify as such. I do so because she is "masculine of center" in terms of her identity and self-presentation, and therefore grapples with some (though not all) of the same challenges transgender males confront. By flouting gender norms, she pushes up against expectations that one clearly identifies with one gender or the other—while readily admitting that she does not endure the kind of oppression that many trans people face. Moreover, since the boundaries separating butch lesbians and trans men have historically been highly permeable, I believe that we can deepen our knowledge of one group by understanding the other, rather than by reifying these categories.

To help me better understand the role that health professionals play in managing the process of transition, I also interviewed ten surgeons, psychiatrists, and therapists who work with the transgender population. I conducted these interviews in their professional offices. I also attended three transgender health conferences, where experts and activists offered workshops on varied aspects of trans health, and several meetings of gender specialists in the fields of psychiatry, psychology, social work, endocrinology, and surgery at the New York State Psychiatric Institute. Finally, I interviewed fifteen individuals who possess insider knowledge of the transgender world: social scientists who had conducted studies of transgender life, some of whom are transgender; transgender activists; and others who have observed the evolution of the trans community from afar. In all, I conducted in-depth interviews with approximately fifty individuals, and these interviews were transcribed.

Writing about a group one is not a member of, especially when it is a vulnerable one, can be a risky endeavor. There is a danger of exoticizing one's subjects and making them the object of curiosity, appropriating their knowledge and experience for one's own ends, or speaking for, or on behalf of them. I've tried my best to avoid these pitfalls by being conscious of how I portray people, by getting their feedback on those portrayals whenever possible, and by employing what one might call critical empathy—placing myself in others' shoes, while understanding that the job of the sociologist is to observe as an outsider, more or less. While I enjoy privileges that trans folks do not have access to, as someone who has at times grappled with not being a "good enough" female, some aspects of transgender experience were very familiar to me. The quest for understanding across differences seems to be in very short supply these days. To the extent that it is possible, I hope that this book furthers that goal.

Glossary of Terms

cisgender

People whose gender identity corresponds with their sex assignment at birth. (Some critics suggest that this term leaves out gender-nonconforming people who do not identify as transgender.)

gender

The cultural meanings, norms, and expectations attached to sex differences, which include components such as gender role, gender presentation, and gender identity, as well as other forms of social organization. Due to efforts of transgender activists, the term now incorporates biologically based differences as well as cultural codes and expectations and encompasses a critique of the gender binary.

gender dysphoria

Gender nonconformity that causes suffering; the diagnostic label required for gender-variant people to undergo surgery. While many medical experts believe this comes from within, it is also a product of social stigma.

gender identity

One's personal experience of gender. For most (but not all) individuals, this tends to be fairly consistent over time and defined in relation to male or female categories. Gender identity can correlate with assigned sex at birth, or it can diverge from it.

gender presentation (or expression)

Includes gendered attire, but also bodily gestures, posture, manner of speech, and style of interaction, as well as secondary sex characteristics (such as facial hair).

genderqueer

Identities that signal a critical stance toward the gender binary, as well as a gender presentation that lies outside the categories of male and female. Also referred to as non-binary.

gender role

Types of behaviors that are generally considered acceptable, appropriate, or desirable for people based on their actual or perceived gender identity.

gender variance

Nonconformity to gendered expectations. Gender-variant people feel that the binary gender model, or the gender assignment they were given at birth, does not adequately describe them. Gender-variant people existed before the categories transsexual or transgender were in circulation. Today some (but not all) gender-variant people identify as transgender.

intersex

People who are born with (or develop naturally in puberty) genitals, reproductive organs, and/or chromosomal patterns that do not fit standard definitions of male or female; sometimes known as hermaphrodites. Some intersex people identify as transgender.

non-binary

Term used to describe people whose gender is not exclusively male or female, including those who identify as a gender other than male or female, as no gender, or as more than one gender.

sex

Categories that describe biological differences between males and females. Includes sexed body and sex assignment. More recent interpretations suggest that such differences are not simply biological but also cultural. Sex categories, like gender, tend to be defined in binary ways, though the existence of intersex people complicates this.

sex assignment

Categorization of an individual as male or female (or at times, intersex) at birth, which is typically determined on the basis of the appearance of the genitals.

sexed body

Physical characteristics such as genitals, presence or absence of breast tissue, facial and body hair, fat distribution, height, bone size, and other characteristics.

sexuality

The cultural way we live our bodies and pleasures. Includes sexual identity, or how one classifies oneself in relation to sexual categories, such as homosexual, heterosexual, bisexual, pansexual, or asexual, among others.

stealth

The strategy of refraining from openly disclosing one's transgender status to others. Assumes that individuals should have the choice to disclose only if they wish to. Going stealth is somewhat different from "passing," which for a transgender person means living successfully in the gender of choice and being accepted as a member of that gender.

top surgery

Chest masculinization surgery, which involves removing tissue from the breast and reshaping it to accord with social understandings of what masculine chests look like.

transgender

When this term emerged in the 1990s, it set itself apart from the older term *transsexual*. Resisting medical pathologization, it was conceived as a broad "umbrella" term that describes people who are gender-nonconforming, including transsexuals, cross-dressers, people who do drag, and butch lesbians. It encompasses a broad range of gender-variant identifications, presentations, and trajectories, and it includes many individuals who live as their chosen gender rather than the gender to which they were assigned at birth. Some of these individuals undergo medical transitions that involve surgery and cross-gender hormones.

transitioning

The process in which a person begins to live according to their gender identity, rather than the gender they were thought to be at birth. This process aligns the body with one's gender identity, sometimes (but not always) through medical procedures such as surgery and/or the use of cross-sex hormones. Such surgery, which used to be termed "sex reassignment surgery," is now called gender or sex "confirmation surgery." Many transgender people (particularly female-to-male individuals) choose not to undergo genital surgery; some undergo no surgery at all.

trans men, or transgender men

Individuals who were assigned female at birth who now identify as transgender or as on the "transmasculine" spectrum. Some seek to "pass" as male; others identity as transgender men, disclosing their female body history to others in varied contexts. In the past, they were often called FTMs, a term that assumes that individuals are undergoing gender transitions.

transphobia

Negative attitudes, including hatred, disgust, and fear, evoked by or directed toward trans people.

Note: Since transgender is such a fast-moving field of inquiry and activism, these definitions are very much in flux. For updates, see: http://www.hrc.org/resources/glossary-of-terms and https://trans genderlawcenter.org/.

Sources Consulted

Abelson, Miriam. "Negotiating Vulnerability and Fear: Rethinking the Relationship Between Violence and Contemporary Masculinity." In *Exploring Masculinities*, edited by C. J. Pascoe and Tristan Bridges. New York: Oxford University Press, 2016.

American Society of Plastic Surgeons. "New Statistics Reflect the Changing Face of Plastic Surgery." February 25, 2016. https://www.plasticsurgery.org/news/press-releases/new-statistics-reflect-the-changing-face-of-plastic-surgery.

Anderson, Victoria. "Lil' Kim and the Unbearable Whiteness of Being." The Conversation, April, 28, 2016. http://theconversation.com/lil-kim-and-the-unbearable-whiteness-of-being-58459.

Banet-Weiser, Sarah. *Authentic™: The Politics of Ambivalence in a Brand Culture*. Critical Cultural Communication. New York: New York University Press, 2012.

Bauer, Robin. "Transgressive and Transformative Gendered Sexual Practices and White Privileges: The Case of the Dyke/Trans BDSM Communities." *Women's Studies Quarterly* 36, nos. 3 and 4 (Fall/Winter 2008): 233–53.

Bauman, Zygmunt. *Liquid Modernity*. Cambridge, UK: Polity Press with Blackwell Publishers, 2000.

Beemyn, Genny, and Susan Rankin. *The Lives of Transgender People*. New York: Columbia University Press, 2011.

Benjamin, Harry. *The Transsexual Phenomenon*. New York: Julian Press, 1966.

Bettcher, Talia Mae. "Evil Deceivers and Make-Believers: On Transphobic Violence and the Politics of Illusion." *Hypatia* 22, no. 3 (2007): 43–65.

Bordo, Susan. *Unbearable Weight: Feminism, Western Culture, and the Body*. Berkeley: University of California Press, 1995.

Bornstein, Kate. *Gender Outlaw: On Men, Women, and the Rest of Us*. New York: Vintage Books, 1995.

boyd, danah. *It's Complicated: The Social Lives of Networked Teens.* New Haven, CT: Yale University Press, 2014.

Boylan, Jennifer Finney. *She's Not There: A Life in Two Genders.* New York: Broadway Books, 2003.

———. "We Want Cake, Too." *The New York Times,* August 11, 2011. http://www.nytimes.com/2011/08/12/opinion/we-want-cake-too.html.

Brown, Chip. "The Many Ways Society Makes a Man." *National Geographic,* January 2017. http://www.nationalgeographic.com/magazine/2017/01/how-rites-of-passage-shape-masculinity-gender/.

Brownstein, Carrie. *Hunger Makes Me a Modern Girl: A Memoir.* New York: Riverhead Books, 2015.

Brubaker, Rogers. *Trans: Gender and Race in an Age of Unsettled Identities.* Princeton, NJ: Princeton University Press, 2016.

Butler, Judith. *The Psychic Life of Power: Theories in Subjection.* Stanford, CA: Stanford University Press, 1997.

———. *Undoing Gender.* New York: Routledge, 2004.

Califia, Patrick. *Sex Changes: Transgender Politics.* 2nd ed. Jersey City, NJ: Cleis Press, 2003.

Chapkis, Wendy. *Beauty Secrets: Women and the Politics of Appearance.* Boston: South End Press, 1999.

Chodorow, Nancy. "Gender as a Personal and Cultural Construction." *Signs* 20, no. 3 (Spring 1995): 516–44.

Clare, Eli. *Exile and Pride: Disability, Queerness, and Liberation.* 2nd ed. Boston: South End Press, 2009.

Compton, Julie. "Gender Non-Conforming Professionals Look for Jobs that Fit." *NBC Out,* July 25, 2016. http://www.nbcnews.com/feature/nbc-out/gender-nonconforming-professionals-look-jobs-fit-n616066.

Connell, Catherine. "Doing, Undoing, or Redoing Gender? Learning from the Workplace Experiences of Transpeople." *Gender and Society* 24, no. 1 (February 2010): 31–55.

Connell, R. W. "Teaching the Boys: New Research on Masculinity, and Gender Strategies for Schools." *Teachers College Record* 98, no. 2 (Winter 1996): 206–35.

Cooley, Charles Horton. *Human Nature and the Social Order.* Social Science Classics Series. New York: Scribner's, 1902.

Coontz, Stephanie. *Marriage, a History: How Love Conquered Marriage.* New York: Viking Penguin, 2005.

Cromwell, Jason. *Transmen and FTMs: Identities, Bodies, Genders and Sexualities.* Champaign: University of Illinois Press, 1999.

Currah, Paisley. "Expectant Bodies: The Pregnant Man." In *Gendered Bodies: Feminist Perspectives,* 2nd ed., edited by Judith Lorber and Lisa Jean Moore. New York: Oxford University Press, 2010.

Currah, Paisley, and Tara Mulqueen. "Securitizing Gender: Identity, Biometrics, and Transgender Bodies at the Airport." CUNY Academic Works, City University of New York, New York, 2011. http://academicworks.cuny.edu /gc_pubs/306.

Davis, Kathy. *Reshaping the Female Body: The Dilemma of Cosmetic Surgery.* New York: Routledge, 1995.

van Deven, Mandy. "Bending Gender, Breaking Binaries." Interview with Kate Bornstein and S. Bear Bergman about *Gender Outlaws. Herizons Women's News + Feminist Views* 24, no. 3 (Winter 2011): 16–19. http://www.herizons .ca/node/448.

Devor, Aaron. *FTM: Female-to-Male Transsexuals in Society.* Bloomington: Indiana University Press, 1997.

Devor, Aaron H., and Nicholas Matte. "One Inc. and Reed Erickson: The Uneasy Collaboration of Gay and Trans Activism, 1964–2003." *GLQ* 10, no. 2 (2004): 179–209.

Dozier, Raine. "Beards, Breasts, and Bodies: Doing Sex in a Gendered World." *Gender and Society* 19, no. 3 (2005): 297–316.

Edmonds, Alexander. "Beauty, Health and Risk in Brazilian Plastic Surgery." *Medische Antropologie* 21, no. 1 (2009), 21–38.

Erickson-Schroth, Laura, ed. *Trans Bodies, Trans Selves: A Resource for the Transgender Community.* New York: Oxford University Press, 2014.

Fausto-Sterling, Anne. *Sex/Gender: Biology in a Social World.* The Routledge Series Integrating Science and Culture. New York: Routledge, 2012.

———. *Sexing the Body: Gender Politics and the Construction of Sexuality.* New York: Basic Books, 2000.

Feinberg, Leslie. *Stone Butch Blues.* New York: Firebrand Press, 1993.

Flores, Andrew R., Jody L. Herman, Gary L. Gates, and Taylor N. T. Brown. "How Many Adults Identify as Transgender in the United States?" Los Angeles: The Williams Institute, UCLA School of Law, 2016. http:/williams institute.law.ucla.edu/wp-content/uploads/How-Many-Adults-Identify-as -Transgender-in-the-United-States.pdf.

Gilman, Sander. *Making the Body Beautiful: A Cultural History of Aesthetic Surgery.* Princeton, NJ: Princeton University Press, 1999.

Goetsch, Diana. "New Minority: A Zombie Narrative." *Life in Transition* (blog). *The American Scholar,* March 30, 2016. https://theamericanscholar.org/new -minority/#.V1rbU2Y7pPY.

Goffman, Erving. *Stigma: Notes on the Management of Spoiled Identity.* New York: Simon and Schuster, 1963.

Goldstein, Zil Garner, and Matthew Oransky. "A Parent's Guide to Supporting Transgender Youth." *Huffington Post,* May 12, 2017. http://www.huffington post.com/entry/a-parents-guide-to-supporting-transgender-youth_us_5915 beaae4b02d6199b2ee3f.

Grant, Adam. "Unless You're Oprah, 'Be Yourself' Is Terrible Advice." *New York Times*, June 4, 2016. https://www.nytimes.com/2016/06/05/opinion/sunday /unless-youre-oprah-be-yourself-is-terrible-advice.html?_r=0.

Green, Jamison. *Becoming a Visible Man*. Nashville, TN: Vanderbilt University Press, 2004.

———. "Introduction to Media Spotlight Series." In *Trans Bodies, Trans Selves*, edited by Laura Erickson-Schroth. New York: Oxford University Press, 2014.

Greenberg, Gary. *The Book of Woe: The DSM and the Unmaking of Psychiatry*. New York: Blue Rider Press, 2013.

Haas, Ann P., Philip L. Rogers, and Jody L. Herman. *Suicide Attempts Among Transgender and Gender Non-Conforming Adults: Findings of the National Transgender Discrimination Survey*. American Foundation for Suicide Prevention and Williams Institute, January 2014.

Halberstam, J. Jack. *Female Masculinity*. Durham, NC: Duke University Press, 1998.

Hall, Radclyffe. *The Well of Loneliness*. Garden City, NY: Sun Dial Press, 1928.

Hall, Stuart. *The Fateful Triangle: Race, Ethnicity, Nation*. Edited by K. Mercer. Cambridge, MA: Harvard University Press, 2017.

Harris, Malcolm. *Kids These Days: Human Capital and the Making of Millennials*. New York: Little, Brown and Company, 2017, e-book.

Holliday, Ruth, David Bell, Meredith Jones, and Olive Cheung. "Clinical Trials: Cosmetic Surgery Tourism." *Discover Society*, no. 9, June 3, 2014. http://dis coversociety.org/2014/06/03/clinical-trails-cosmetic-surgery-tourism/

Jacques, Juliet. *Trans: A Memoir*. New York: Verso Books, 2015.

James, S. E., J. L. Herman, S. Rankin, M. Keisling, L. Mottet, and M. Anafi. *The Report of the 2015 U.S. Transgender Survey*. Washington, DC: National Center for Transgender Equality, 2016. http://www.transequality.org/sites /default/files/docs/USTS-Full-Report-FINAL.PDF.

Jordan-Young, Rebecca. *Brain Storm: The Flaws in the Science of Sex Differences*. Cambridge, MA: Harvard University Press, 2010.

Kennedy, Pagan. *The First Man-Made Man: The Story of Two Sex Changes, One Love Affair, and a Twentieth-Century Medical Revolution*. New York: Bloomsbury, 2007.

Kessler, Suzanne. *Lessons from the Intersexed*. New Brunswick, NJ: Rutgers University Press, 1998.

Kimmel, Michael. *Guyland: The Perilous World Where Boys Become Men*. New York: HarperCollins, 2008.

Klein, Fritz. *The Bisexual Option*. New York: Harrington Park Press, 1978.

Krieger, Nick. *Nina Here Nor There: My Journey Beyond Gender*. New York: Beacon Press, 2011.

Laqueur, Thomas. *Making Sex: Body and Gender from the Greeks to Freud*. 8th ed. Cambridge, MA: Harvard University Press, 1994.

Lev, Arlene Istar. "Gender Dysphoria: Two Steps Forward, One Step Back." *Clinical Social Work Journal* 41, no. 3 (2013): 288–96. Published online on July 18, 2013. http://choicesconsulting.com/wp-content/uploads/2013/08/Gender-Dysphoria-Two-Steps-Forward-One-Step-Back-FINAL.pdf.

_____. *Transgender Emergence: Therapeutic Guidelines for Working with Gender-Variant People and Their Families.* Binghamton, NY: Haworth Clinical Practice Press, 2004.

Mac, Amos. "Masculinity Means." *Matter Magazine,* Medium.com, September 15, 2015. https://medium.com/matter/masculinity-means-7c11e2d976b4#.no6fhj9au.

Manion, Jen. "Transbutch." *Transgender Studies Quarterly* 1, nos. 1 and 2 (2014): 230–32.

Martínez–San Miguel, Yolanda, and Sarah Tobias, eds. *Trans Studies: The Challenge to Hetero/Homo Normativities.* New Brunswick, NJ: Rutgers University Press, 2016.

McBee, Thomas Page. *Man Alive: A True Story of Violence, Forgiveness and Becoming a Man.* Nashville, TN: Vanderbilt University Press, 2004.

Menon, Alka. "Reconstructing Race and Gender in American Cosmetic Surgery." *Ethnic and Racial Studies* 40, no. 4 (2017): 597–616.

Meyerowitz, Joanne. *How Sex Changed: A History of Transsexuality in the United States.* Cambridge, MA: Harvard University Press, 2004.

Middlebrook, Diane Wood. *Suits Me: The Double Life of Billy Tipton.* Boston: Houghton Mifflin, 1998.

Mock, Janet. *Redefining Realness: My Path to Womanhood, Identity, Love and So Much More.* New York: Atria Paperback, 2014.

O'Brien, Jodi. "Seeing Agnes: Notes on a Transgender Biocultural Ethnomethodology," *Symbolic Interaction* 39, no. 2 (2016), 306–29.

Pascoe, C. J., and Tristan Bridges, eds. *Exploring Masculinities: Identity, Inequality, Continuity and Change.* New York: Oxford University Press, 2016.

Plemons, Eric. "Description of Sex Difference as Prescription for Sex Change: On the Origins of Facial Feminization Surgery." *Social Studies of Science* 44, no. 5 (2014): 657–79.

_____. "Envisioning the Body in Relation: Finding Sex, Changing Sex." In *The Body Reader: Essential Social and Cultural Readings,* edited by Lisa Jean Moore and Mary Kosut. New York: New York University Press, 2010.

Plummer, Ken. *Cosmopolitan Sexualities: Hope and the Humanist Imagination.* Cambridge, UK: Polity Press, 2015.

Preciado, Paul B. *Testo Junkie: Sex, Drugs, and Biopolitics in the Pharmacopornographic Era.* New York: Feminist Press, 2013.

Psihopaidas, Demetrios. "Intimate Standards: Medical Knowledge and Self-Making in Digital Transgender Groups." *Sexualities* 20, no. 4 (June 2017): 412–27.

Reed, Bernard, Stephenne Rhodes, Pietà Schofield, and Kevan Wylie, "Gender Variance in the UK: Prevalence, Incidence, Growth and Geographic Distribution," Gender Identity Research and Education Society, June 2009.

Reis, Elizabeth. *Bodies in Doubt: An American History of Intersex.* Baltimore, MD: Johns Hopkins University Press, 2009.

Reisner, S. L., J. M. Hughto, E. E. Dunham, K. J. Heflin, J. B. Begenyi, J. Coffey-Esquivel, and S. Cahill. "Legal Protections in Public Accommodations Settings: A Critical Public Health Issue for Transgender and Gender Nonconforming People." *Milbank Quarterly* 93, no. 3 (September 2015): 484–515.

Rosenberg, Rosalind. *Jane Crow: The Life of Pauli Murray.* New York: Oxford University Press, 2017.

Rottnek, Matthew. *Sissies and Tomboys: Gender Nonconformity and Homosexual Childhood.* New York: New York University Press, 1999.

Rubin, Gayle. "Thinking Sex: Notes for a Radical Theory of the Politics of Sexuality." In *Pleasure and Danger: Exploring Female Sexuality,* edited by Carol Vance. New York: Routledge, 1984.

Rubin, Henry. *Self-Made Men: Identity and Embodiment Among Transsexual Men.* Nashville, TN: Vanderbilt University Press, 2003.

Scalzi, John. "Straight White Male: The Lowest Difficulty Setting There Is." May 15, 2012. http://whatever.scalzi.com/2012/05/15/straight-white-male-the-lowest-difficulty-setting-there-is/.

Schilt, Kristen. *Just One of the Guys? Transgender Men and the Persistence of Gender Inequality.* Chicago: University of Chicago Press, 2011.

Schwartz, Barry. "The Tyranny of Choice." *Scientific American,* April 2004, 71–75. https://www.swarthmore.edu/SocSci/bschwar1/Sci.Amer.pdf.

Serano, Julia. "Before and After: Class and Body Transformation." In *Gendered Bodies: Feminist Perspectives,* 2nd ed., edited by Judith Lorber and Lisa Jean Moore. New York: Oxford University Press, 2010.

shuster, stef. "Uncertain Expertise and the Limitations of Clinical Guidelines in Transgender Healthcare." *Journal of Health and Social Behavior* 57, no. 3 (September 2016): 319–32.

Solomon, Andrew. *Far from the Tree: Parents, Children, and the Search for Identity.* New York: Simon and Shuster, 2012.

Spade, Dean. *Normal Life: Administrative Violence, Critical Trans Politics, and the Limits of Law.* Durham, NC: Duke University Press, 2015.

Stein, Arlene. *Sex and Sensibility: Stories of a Lesbian Generation.* Berkeley: University of California Press, 1997.

Stein, Joel. "Nip. Tuck. Or Else." *Time,* June 18, 2015. http://time.com/3926042/nip-tuck-or-else/.

Sterling, Drake Cameron. *Top Surgery Unbound: An Insider's Guide to Chest Masculinization Surgery.* Sausalito, CA: Sterling OmniMedia, 2016.

Stokes, Mike. "Expanding Coverage Offers Lifeline to Transgender Individuals

Seeking SRS." *Plastic Surgery News,* March 2015. http://www.uplasticsurgery
.com/wp-content/uploads/2015/03/3-15-PSN-SRS-article.pdf.

Stryker, Susan. *Transgender History.* Berkeley, CA: Seal Press, 2008.

Summers, A. K. *Pregnant Butch: Nine Long Months Spent in Drag.* Berkeley, CA: Soft Skull Press, 2014.

Talusan, Meredith. "Unerased: Counting Transgender Lives," Mic. December 8, 2016. https://mic.com/unerased.

Taylor, Charles. *Sources of the Self: The Making of the Modern Identity.* Cambridge, MA: Harvard University Press, 1992.

Tobin, Harper Jean, Raffi Freedman-Gurspan, and Lisa Mottet. "Counting Trans People in Federal Surveys." In *A Blueprint for Equality: Federal Agenda for Transgender People.* Washington, DC: National Center for Transgender Equality, 2015.

Valentine, David. *Imagining Transgender: An Ethnography of a Category.* Durham, NC: Duke University Press, 2007.

Viloria, Hida. *Born Both: An Intersex Life.* New York: Hachette Books, 2017.

Warner, Michael. "Introduction: Fear of a Queer Planet." *Social Text,* no. 29 (1991): 3–17.

Westbrook, Laurel, and Kristen Schilt. "Penis Panics: Biological Maleness, Social Masculinity, and the Matrix of Perceived Sexual Threat." In *Exploring Masculinities: Identity, Inequality, Continuity, and Change,* edited by C. J. Pascoe and Tristan Bridges. New York: Oxford University Press, 2015.

World Professional Association for Transgender Health. *Standards of Care for the Health of Transsexual, Transgender, and Gender Nonconforming People,* 7th version. World Professional Association for Transgender Health, 2017. http://www.wpath.org/site_page.cfm?pk_association_webpage_menu=1351 &pk_association_webpage=3926.

Zeisler, Andi. *We Were Feminists Once: From Riot Grrrl to Covergirl, the Buying and Selling of a Political Movement.* New York: Public Affairs, 2016.

Zerubavel, Eviatar. *The Fine Line: Making Distinctions in Everyday Life.* Chicago: University of Chicago Press, 1993.

Zimmerman, Bonnie, ed. *Lesbian History and Cultures: An Introduction, Volume 1.* New York: Garland Publishing, 2000.

Notes

Introduction

1. I use the female pronoun here to illustrate how, during this early moment in the transition process, Ben's parents have not yet become accustomed to using his chosen male pronouns.

2. Jordan-Young, *Brain Storm*, 1. On the sex-gender distinction, see John Money and Anke Ehrhardt, *Man and Woman, Boy and Girl: Gender Identity from Conception to Maturity*, The Master Work Series (Baltimore, MD: Johns Hopkins University Press, 1972), 4.

3. Cited in Betty Friedan's obituary, *The Telegraph* (UK), February 6, 2006. http://www.telegraph.co.uk/news/obituaries/1509730/Betty-Friedan.html.

4. Fausto-Sterling, *Sexing the Body*; Kessler, *Lessons from the Intersexed*; Reis, *Bodies in Doubt*.

5. Quoted by Meyerowitz, *How Sex Changed*, 26.

6. Plummer, *Cosmopolitan Sexualities*, 129–30.

7. Middlebrook, *Suits Me*.

8. Kennedy, *The First Man-Made Man*. On the history of transmasculinity, see also Devor, *FTM*.

9. Benjamin, *The Transsexual Phenomenon*; Meyerowitz, *How Sex Changed*.

10. Benjamin, *The Transsexual Phenomenon*, 147.

11. Green, "Introduction to Media Spotlight Series" in Erickson-Schroth, ed., *Trans Bodies, Trans Selves*, xx.

12. Rosenberg, *Jane Crow*, Loc 2550 of 13828, e-book.

13. At least among those who seek out therapy, according to the experts I spoke with.

14. Samantha Allen, "How Obama Became the Trans-Rights President," *The Daily Beast*, May 13, 2016. https://www.thedailybeast.com/articles/2016/05/13/how-obama-became-the-trans-rights-president.html.

ONE | Pre-Op

1. Sterling, *Top Surgery Unbound*. However, some medical providers operate along a more informed consent model and will perform top surgery without a letter from a mental health professional, particularly if the patient is older. See https://www.ghc.org/html/public/services/transgender. Expanding medical coverage is also influencing the evolution of such protocols. The number of large corporations offering employee insurance plans that pay for care specific to the needs of transgender employees has recently grown. In New York City, for example, in 2016, several doctors performed chest masculinization and accepted insurance, and getting insurance reimbursement for hormones was relatively easy. See Stokes, "Expanding Coverage Offers Lifeline to Transgender Individuals."

2. Solomon, *Far from the Tree*, 2.

3. Because I am trying to document a family's changing recognition of their child's gender transition, I am faithful to the original language, even if it uses inappropriate pronouns at times.

4. Sterling, Preface, *Top Surgery Unbound*. Loc 5 to 34 of 879, e-book.

5. Schilt, *Just One of the Guys?*, 50.

6. Connell, "Doing, Undoing, or Redoing Gender?" Thanks to Raine Dozier for pointing this out to me.

7. For transgender women, surgical facial feminization may play an analogous role to top surgery for transgender men, according to Plemons, "Description of Sex Difference as Prescription for Sex Change."

8. Kessler, *Lessons from the Intersexed*, 90.

9. See Brubaker, *Trans: Gender and Race in an Age of Unsettled Identities*.

10. Harris, *Kids These Days*, 11, e-book.

11. James et al., *The Report of the 2015 U.S. Transgender Survey*; Spade, *Normal Life*. As I write, a black transgender woman has been murdered in Chicago, the twentieth trans woman of color reported killed in 2016 alone. See Meredith Talusan, "Unerased: Counting Transgender Lives."

TWO | Gender Trouble

1. J. Jack Halberstam, "An Introduction to Female Masculinity: Masculinity Without Men," in Pascoe and Bridges, eds., *Exploring Masculinities*, 353.

2. Fausto-Sterling, *Sexing the Body*, 8.

3. Valentine, *Imagining Transgender*.

4. Devor and Matte, "One Inc. and Reed Erickson," 202.

5. Polycystic ovarian syndrome (PCOS) is relatively common, affecting between 5 and 10 percent of those who were assigned female at birth. Some

studies suggest that trans men have higher rates of PCOS. To say PCOS is correlated with transgender does not suggest that it "causes" someone to be transgender. Most women with PCOS simply deal with the symptoms. But there may be a connection between elevated levels of testosterone and feelings of dysphoria or stress related to gender nonconformity. See Laura Erickson-Schroth, Miqqi Alicia Gilbert, and T. Evan Smith, "Sex and Gender Development," in Erickson-Schroth, ed., *Trans Bodies, Trans Selves,* 97–98.

6. For a wide-ranging rebuttal to born-this-way arguments vis-à-vis homosexuality, see Suzanna Danuta Walters, *The Tolerance Trap: How God, Genes, and Good Intentions Are Sabotaging Gay Equality* (New York: New York University Press, 2014).

7. While this doubles a prior estimate, it probably still undercounts the trans population. See Tobin et al., "Counting Trans People in Federal Surveys." See also Flores et al., "How Many Adults Identify as Transgender in the United States?" Meyerowitz in *How Sex Changed* reported at least 25,000 Americans had undergone sex-reassignment surgery (2004). Reed and colleagues reported a doubling of the numbers of people accessing care at gender clinics in the United Kingdom every five or six years, in Reed et al., "Gender Variance in the UK."

8. Goetsch, "New Minority."

9. Katy Steinmetz, "Laverne Cox Talks to *TIME* About the Transgender Movement," *Time,* May 29, 2014.

THREE | One Life to Live

1. According to the American Society of Plastic Surgeons, laser hair removal was the fourth most popular minimally invasive cosmetic procedure in 2015. Unchanged from 2014, it was up 52 percent from 2000. See ASPS, "New Statistics Reflect the Changing Face of Plastic Surgery." https://www.plasticsurgery.org /news/press-releases/new-statistics-reflect-the-changing-face-of-plastic-sur gery. On pubic hair preferences, see Mona Chalabi, "The Pubic Hair Preferences of the American Woman," FiveThirtyEight, April 11, 2014. http://fivethirtyeight .com/datalab/au-naturel-or-barely-there-the-data-on-pubic-hair-preferences/.

2. Psihopaidas, "Intimate Standards," 413.

3. Ibid.

4. Greenberg, *The Book of Woe,* 15.

5. Lev, "Gender Dysphoria: Two Steps Forward, One Step Back," 288–96.

6. World Professional Association for Transgender Health, *Standards of Care for the Health of Transsexual, Transgender, and Gender Nonconforming People,* 7th version, 5.

7. Green, *Becoming a Visible Man.* On body dysmorphia, see Nicole Schnackenberg, *False Bodies, True Selves: Moving Beyond Appearance-Focused*

Identity Struggles and Returning to the True Self (London: Karnac, 2016). In the early 1990s, sociologist Kathy Davis, interviewing women undergoing cosmetic surgery in the Netherlands, similarly found that they tended to hate a particular part of their body and felt it doesn't belong to the rest of them (Davis, *Reshaping the Female Body*).

8. On the tension between medical expertise and culturally situated gender identities as it plays out in transgender medicine, see shuster, "Uncertain Expertise and the Limitations of Clinical Guidelines in Transgender Healthcare."

9. Bordo, *Unbearable Weight*.

10. Brubaker, *Trans: Gender and Race in an Age of Unsettled Identities*, 18.

11. Cooley, *Human Nature and the Social Order*.

12. Laqueur, *Making Sex*.

13. Coontz, *Marriage, a History*.

14. Grant, "Unless You're Oprah, 'Be Yourself' Is Terrible Advice."

15. Bettcher, "Evil Deceivers and Make-Believers."

FOUR | Transitioning

1. James et al., *The Report of the 2015 U.S. Transgender Survey*.

2. Fred McConnell, "There's No Such Thing as a Sex Change," *The Guardian*, August 12, 2014. https://www.theguardian.com/world/video/2014/aug/12/transgender-kellie-maloney-lgbt-sex-change.

3. WPATH, *Standards of Care*, version 7.

4. "Hormones: A Guide for FTMs," Vancouver Coastal Health, Transcend Transgender Support and Education Society, and Canadian Rainbow Health Coalition, February 2006.

5. James et al., *The Report of the 2015 U.S. Transgender Survey*.

6. For data on children's transgender feelings, see James et al., *The Report of the 2015 U.S. Transgender Survey*. On transgender children and families, see Amy Ellis Nutt, *Becoming Nicole: The Transformation of an American Family* (New York: Random House, 2016); Tey Meadow, *Trans Kids: Being Gendered in the Twenty-First Century* (Berkeley: University of California Press, 2018).

7. Goldstein and Oransky, "A Parent's Guide to Supporting Transgender Youth."

8. Ibid.

9. boyd, *It's Complicated*, 9.

10. Ibid., 58.

11. Westbrook and Schilt, "Penis Panics," in Pascoe and Bridges, eds., *Exploring Masculinities*, 385, 387.

12. Abelson, "Negotiating Vulnerability and Fear."

13. Banet-Weiser, *Authentic™: The Politics of Ambivalence in a Brand Culture*.

14. Data was collected in May 2014.

15. On the history of activism of transgender people of color, see Stryker, *Transgender History*; Marlon Bailey, *Butch Queens Up in Pumps: Gender, Performance, and Ballroom Culture in Detroit*, Triangulations: Lesbian/Gay/Queer Theater/Drama/Performance (Ann Arbor: University of Michigan Press, 2013).

FIVE | Designing Men

1. American Society of Plastic Surgeons, "New Statistics Reflect the Changing Face of Plastic Surgery."

2. Benjamin, *The Transsexual Phenomenon*, viii.

3. Brownstein, *Hunger Makes Me a Modern Girl* (audiobook).

4. Arcade Fire, "Modern Man," *The Suburbs*, 2010.

5. Fausto-Sterling, *Sex/Gender*.

6. Currah, "Expectant Bodies: The Pregnant Man," in Lorber and Moore, eds., *Gendered Bodies: Feminist Perspectives*. At the same time, however, intersex activists have enjoyed growing success in calling for the suspension of "corrective" surgery on children's ambiguous genitals.

7. Fausto-Sterling, *Sexing the Body*, 59. See also Trystan T. Cotten, "Surgery," *TSQ Keywords* 1, nos. 1 and 2 (2014): 205.

8. Denise Grady, "Penis Transplants Being Planned to Help Wounded Troops," *New York Times*, December 6, 2015. https://www.nytimes.com/2015/12/07/health/penis-transplants-being-planned-to-heal-troops-hidden-wounds.html.

9. Davis, *Reshaping the Female Body*, 118.

10. See Chapkis, *Beauty Secrets: Women and the Politics of Appearance*.

11. Edmonds, "Beauty, Health and Risk in Brazilian Plastic Surgery," 25; Joel Stein, "Nip. Tuck. Or Else," 45.

12. Davis, *Reshaping the Female Body*, 20.

13. Stein, "Nip. Tuck. Or Else," 42.

14. Ibid.

15. Gilman, *Making the Body Beautiful*, ch. 1.

16. Ibid; Anderson, "Lil' Kim and the Unbearable Whiteness of Being."

17. Zeisler, *We Were Feminists Once*, 228–29. One can now find ethnic-specific beauty standards in cosmetic surgery, according to recent research by Alka Menon, which may complicate established notions of racial difference. See Menon, "Reconstructing Race and Gender in American Cosmetic Surgery."

18. Preciado, *Testo Junkie*, 77.

19. Serano, "Before and After: Class and Body Transformation," in Lorber and Moore, eds., *Gendered Bodies: Feminist Perspectives*, 124.

20. Davis, *Reshaping the Female Body*, 21.

21. Holliday et al., "Clinical Trials: Cosmetic Surgery Tourism."

22. Dr. Garramone's website: http://drgarramone.com/.
23. Ibid.

SIX | What Kind of Man Am I?

1. Brown, "The Many Ways Society Makes a Man."
2. Connell, "Teaching the Boys," 210.
3. See Pascoe and Bridges, eds., *Exploring Masculinities.*
4. Mac, "Masculinity Means."
5. https://www.lambdalegal.org/know-your-rights/article/trans-work place-faq.
6. Schilt, *Just One of the Guys?*, 111.
7. James et al., *The Report of the 2015 U.S. Transgender Survey*; Spade, *Normal Life.* On transgender men's efforts to manage violence from other men, see Abelson, "Negotiating Vulnerability and Fear," in Pascoe and Bridges, eds., *Exploring Masculinities.*
8. Scalzi, "Straight White Male: The Lowest Difficulty Setting There Is."
9. James et al., "Executive Summary," in *The Report of the 2015 U.S. Transgender Survey,* 10.
10. Kimmel, *Guyland,* 4.
11. More than half of the trans men Kristen Schilt interviewed had been lesbians earlier in their lives, and few reported ever being harassed, or being subjected to violence for it. When they transitioned, however, some expressed fears of being seen as gay men, and the negative reactions that might elicit. Schilt, *Just One of the Guys?*, 58.
12. Toi Scott, "Living on the Outside: Black Woman? Black Man? Neither? or Both?" in Erickson-Schroth, ed., *Trans Bodies, Trans Selves,* 33.
13. Dozier, "Beards, Breasts, and Bodies."
14. Butler, "Melancholy Gender/Refused Identification," in *The Psychic Life of Power,* 139, 184, 146.

SEVEN | Last Butch Standing

1. Informal gathering places catering to lesbians, such as speakeasies, could be found in American cities in the 1920s. In New York City's Harlem, black lesbians met in cabarets and clubs, and in apartment speakeasies, called "buffet/party flats." See "Bars," in Zimmerman, ed. *Lesbian History and Cultures.*
2. See Alice Echols, *Daring to Be Bad: Radical Feminism in America, 1967–1975,* American Culture (Minneapolis: University of Minnesota, 1989). See also Stein, *Sex and Sensibility.*
3. *San Francisco Bay Area Women's Yellow Pages,* 1981–82.

4. Stryker, *Transgender History,* 114–20.

5. Benjamin, *The Transsexual Phenomenon.*

6. Boylan, "We Want Cake, Too."

7. Rubin, *Self-Made Men.*

8. Hall, *The Well of Loneliness,* 204.

9. On the relationship between the concept of inversion and homosexuality, see Fausto-Sterling, *Sexing the Body,* 17; Valentine, *Imagining Transgender.*

10. Zerubavel, *The Fine Line: Making Distinctions in Everyday Life.*

11. Currah and Mulqueen, "Securitizing Gender: Identity, Biometrics, and Transgender Bodies at the Airport."

12. WPATH, *Standards of Care,* version 7. http://www.wpath.org/site_page .cfm?pk_association_webpage_menu=1351&pk_association_webpage=3926.

13. David Colman, "A Night Out With: James Collard; the Corner of Straight and Gay," *New York Times,* July 19, 1998. http://www.nytimes.com/1998 /07/19/style/a-night-out-with-james-collard-the-corner-of-straight-and-gay .html.

14. Casey E. Cohen, Anjani Chandra, and Isaedmarie Febo-Vazquez, "Sexual Behavior, Sexual Attraction, and Sexual Orientation Among Adults Aged 18–44 in the United States: Data from the 2011–2013 National Survey of Family Growth," *National Health Statistics Reports,* no. 88, January 7, 2016.

15. Summers, *Pregnant Butch.*

16. James et al., *The Report of the 2015 U.S. Transgender Survey.*

17. Manion, "Transbutch."

EIGHT | Waiting for the Big Reveal

1. Goffman, *Stigma.*

2. Benjamin, *The Transsexual Phenomenon,* 123.

3. American Civil Liberties Union, "Know Your Rights: Transgender People and the Law," https://www.aclu.org/know-your-rights/transgender-people -and-law.

4. Haeyoun Park and Iaryna Mykhyalyshyn "L.G.B.T. People are More Likely to be Targets of Hate Crimes Than Any Other Groups," *New York Times,* June 16, 2016. https://www.nytimes.com/interactive/2016/06/16/us/hate-crimes -against-lgbt.html?_r=0.

5. Rubin, "Thinking Sex."

6. Warner, "Introduction: Fear of a Queer Planet."

7. Butler, *Undoing Gender,* 95.

8. Haas et al., *Suicide Attempts Among Transgender and Gender Non-Conforming Adults.*

9. Abelson, "Negotiating Vulnerability and Fear," in Pascoe and Bridges, eds., *Exploring Masculinities,* 395.

10. Bauer, "Transgressive and Transformative Gendered Sexual Practices and White Privileges," 238.

NINE | Turn and Face the Strange

1. Reisner et al., "Legal Protections in Public Accommodations Settings," 484–515.

2. On the partners of trans men, see Carla A. Pfeffer, "Bodies in Relation—Bodies in Transition: Lesbian Partners of Trans Men and Body Image," *Journal of Lesbian Studies* 12, no. 4 (2008): 325–45.

3. Schilt, *Just One of the Guys?*, 13, 70.

4. James et al., *The Report of the 2015 U.S. Transgender Survey.*

5. Bauer, "Transgressive and Transformative Gendered Sexual Practices and White Privileges," 238.

TEN | I Am Enough

1. Julia Serano, "Detransition, Desistance, and Disinformation: A Guide for Understanding Transgender Children Debates," medium.com, August 2, 2016. https://medium.com/@juliaserano/detransition-desistance-and-disinformation-a-guide-for-understanding-transgender-children-993b7342946e.

2. Leo Caldwell, personal website: http://www.leocaldwell.com/.

3. Amber Randall, "New School 'Gender Unicorn' Sparks Parental Outrage," *The Daily Caller,* August 10, 2016. http://dailycaller.com/2016/08/10/new-school-gender-unicorn-sparks-parental-outrage/#ixzz4UFUPqblH.

4. Brubaker, *Trans: Gender and Race in an Age of Unsettled Identities,* 99.

5. Thanks to Sonja Pei-Fen Dale at Sophia University in Tokyo, who shared her research on x-gender with me.

6. Shepherd Laughlin, "Gen Z Goes Beyond Gender Binaries in New Innovation Group Data," J. Walter Thompson Intelligence, March 11, 2016. https://www.jwtintelligence.com/2016/03/gen-z-goes-beyond-gender-binaries-in-new-innovation-group-data/.

7. Beemyn and Rankin, *The Lives of Transgender People.*

8. Nahema Marchal, "Here Are the 31 Gender Identities New York City Recognizes." Heat Street, May 25, 2016. https://heatst.com/culture-wars/here-are-the-31-gender-identities-new-york-city-recognizes.

9. Chodorow, "Gender as a Personal and Cultural Construction," 521.

10. Lee Naught, "Rar@: Chican@, Mixed-Race, Gender Queer, Invisible," in Erickson-Schroth, ed., *Trans Bodies, Trans Selves,* 25–26. See also Bettcher, "Evil Deceivers and Make-Believers."

11. Tom Vanderbilt, "The Psychology of Genre: Why We Don't Like What

We Struggle to Categorize," *New York Times,* May 28, 2016. https://www.nytimes
.com/2016/05/29/opinion/sunday/the-psychology-of-genre.html.

12. Quoted in Greenberg, *The Book of Woe,* 48.

13. Tom Verde, "Aging Parents with Lots of Stuff, and Children Who Don't
Want It," *New York Times,* August 18, 2017. https://www.nytimes.com/2017/08/18
/your-money/aging-parents-with-lots-of-stuff-and-children-who-dont-want-it
.html?mcubz=3.

Afterword

1. A 2015 survey of twenty-eight thousand transgender and gender-
nonconforming people in the United States found that 29 percent of those
surveyed lived in poverty—twice the proportion of the general population. The
rates were even higher among transgender people of color: 43 percent of Latino
respondents lived in poverty in 2015. See James et al., *The Report of the 2015 U.S.
Transgender Survey;* National Women's Law Center, "Transgender People are
Facing Incredibly High Rates of Poverty," *The Latest,* December 9, 2016.

2. Spade, *Normal Life,* 11. See also Martínez–San Miguel and Tobias, *Trans
Studies.*

3. Jeffrey Weeks, "The Remaking of Erotic and Intimate Life, La recon-
figuración de la vida erótica e íntima," *Política y Sociedad* 46, nos. 1 and 2
(2009): 13–25. http://revistas.ucm.es/index.php/POSO/article/viewFile/POSO
0909130013A/21833.

4. "Anti-LGBT Groups Celebrate Trump's Ban on Transgender Citizens
Serving in the US Military," Hatewatch Stuff, Southern Poverty Law Center,
July 26, 2017. https://www.splcenter.org/hatewatch/2017/07/26/anti-lgbt-groups
-celebrate-trumps-ban-transgender-citizens-serving-us-military.

5. To some extent, it is true of race as well. Twentieth-century redefini-
tions of race reveal how identities and attitudes can be transformed through the
medium of language. See Hall, *The Fateful Triangle.* However, the concept of
transracialism is far more controversial than transgender, for reasons discussed
by Rogers Brubaker in *Trans,* and others.

Index

Page numbers beginning with 303 refer to endnotes.

A Note About the Author

ARLENE STEIN is a professor of sociology at Rutgers University, where she directs the Institute for Research on Women. She received the Simon and Gagnon Award for career contributions to the study of sexualities, and the Ruth Benedict Prize for her book *The Stranger Next Door*. She has written for *The Nation*, *Jacobin*, *The New Inquiry*, *Haaretz*, and elsewhere. She lives in New Jersey.

A Note on the Type

This book was set in Minion, a typeface produced by the Adobe Corporation specifically for the Macintosh personal computer and released in 1990. Designed by Robert Slimbach, Minion combines the classic characteristics of old-style faces with the full complement of weights required for modern typesetting.

Composed by North Market Street Graphics, Lancaster, Pennsylvania

Printed and bound by Berryville Graphics, Berryville, Virginia

Designed by Cassandra J. Pappas